American History and Baseball

Liberty, Freedom, and the National Pastime

Charles DeMotte

Second Edition

cognella®
SAN DIEGO

Bassim Hamadeh, CEO and Publisher
Carrie Montoya, Manager, Revisions and Author Care
Kaela Martin, Project Editor
Abbey Hastings, Associate Production Editor
Jess Estrella, Senior Graphic Designer
Alexa Lucido, Licensing Manager
Natalie Piccotti, Director of Marketing
Kassie Graves, Vice President of Editorial
Jamie Giganti, Director of Academic Publishing

cognella® | ACADEMIC PUBLISHING

3970 Sorrento Valley Blvd., Ste. 500, San Diego, CA 92121

Brief Table of Contents

Table of Contents

Introduction

The highly distinguished and long-lived cultural historian Jacques Barzun wrote "whoever wants to know the heart and mind of America had better learn baseball." Similarly, author Mark Twain, in a speech delivered in 1889, saw baseball as "the very symbol, the outward and visible expression of the drive, and push, and rush and struggle of the raging, tearing, booming nineteenth century." Barzun and Twain were not alone in observing that baseball is intertwined with America, reflecting its energy, passions, heroism, and tragedy. It therefore offers a convenient segue into a study of America from the Civil War to the present.

A close study of American society reveals a nation of contradictions. Its history has spawned a host of myths that have distorted and simplified a complexity of social forces and aggregations of events. Practical and materialistic on one hand, the country also holds to high ideals that are frequently referenced and often unrealized. Ideals are not static but are constantly changing over the course of time. Moreover, ideals are contested and are thereby open to interpretation. To get an understanding of the principles that have guided the republic, it is important to start with clear definitions.

American society is the record of how American citizens (and sometimes noncitizens) have responded to certain ideas and ideals and the array of forces that structure the world in which we live, move, and have our being. Foremost among the dominant ideas guiding the course of American history have been those of freedom, liberty, equality, and democracy. Each of these terms will underscore the topics considered in the following chapters.

The understanding of the above terms and their influence on American history involves clear thinking, which is also critical thinking. Take the ideal of democracy, for instance. **Democracy** can be *defined as control of an organization or group by the majority of its members,* or as government by the people. But who are the people? The obvious answer would be citizens of the United States, but for a large part of this country's history many citizens were disenfranchised. Although the 13th amendment to the U.S. Constitution gave the vote to African Americans, the laws and rules of segregation prevented many Blacks from casting their ballot and denied them the fundamental rights of citizenship. By the same token, women were denied the right to vote until the passage of the 19th amendment in 1920 and likewise were considered dependents and not fully citizens. Today, there have been efforts by legislators in certain states to deprive lawful citizens of the right to vote and thus deny their participation in the electoral process.

If democracy means that the people rule, then is our form of government democratic? We tend to think of democracy as representative government but technically this is not the case. In fact, democracy is a purely localized concept. In defending the U.S. Constitution to the residents of New York in the *Federalist Papers*, James Madison pointed to the difference between a democracy and a republic. Both pertain to the delegation of governmental power in a society predicated on liberty. In terms of democracy, government is small, participatory, and direct, whereas a republic encompasses a greater number of citizens and is more impersonal and indirect. Madison supported the latter concept at the expense of the former. Since a republic was designed to represent and negotiate between factions or interests and not so much the people, constitutionally speaking the United States is not a democracy. In fact, the nation has evolved as a republic, as have many other countries around the world including those that are more authoritarian.

Even if we accept the notion that democracy in principle, if not in fact, involves the popular control of government, does this mean that the majority of people enjoy political power? Not necessarily. Mary Elizabeth Lease, who was a spokesperson for an agrarian protest movement known as populism, which came to prominence in the 1880s and 1890s, noted that the country is no longer a government of the people, by the people, and for the people, but a government of Wall Street, by Wall Street, and for Wall Street. The implication as stated is that those who run the country are the bankers, business leaders and powerful elites who control political affairs for their own interest. So, is the United States to any degree democratic?

The answer is complex and involves considerable qualification. Democracy in fact is indicative of a "bottom up" society and flourishes in the many groups, organizations, and parties where the people participate directly. While the the country has a strong democratic component, it is other things as well. Constitutionally, the United States is a republic, as specified by James Madison. It is also an oligarchy (government by the few) and likewise a plutocracy (rule by the wealthy) as indicated by the comments of Mary Elizabeth Lease. Moreover, as will be discussed in later chapters, the United States is also an imperialist power controlling directly or indirectly territories beyond its borders. In other words, American democracy is merely a label that only partially explains what the country is all about.

The perspective of this book, therefore, is to shy away from the use of clichés and platitudes, the products of lazy thinking, and to go beyond obvious and simplistic meanings of words such as freedom, liberty, equality, and, of course, democracy, so as to clearly differentiate between the real and the unreal in seeking to better understand the contours and dynamics of American history and society.

CHAPTER 1

Liberty and Freedom

HISTORICAL BACKGROUND

It would be hard to think of any two words that better define the American experience than liberty and freedom. At the same time, it would be difficult to think of words that have been so used and misused. While individuals may have a vague sense of what they mean by liberty and freedom, it is important to recognize that these words have been understood differently at different times. According to English Common Law, liberty meant freedom from personal restraint, unless by due process of law. The political philosopher James Harrington wrote in 1675 that property is the foundation of liberty. The French philosopher Baron de Montesquieu noted that liberty is not the power to do what one likes but rather doing what one ought to do. Thomas Jefferson wrote that freedom is the equilibrium between liberty and order. President Theodore Roosevelt noted that the permanence of liberty and democracy depends upon the majority of people being steadfast in morality. Today, one might think of liberty and freedom in terms of promoting social justice, defending the rights of minorities, experiencing liberation from oppression, maintaining one's own independence, having limited government, or enhancing national security. Thus, how the words liberty and freedom are employed can tell us much about the way Americans think and interact from one period to the next. A question to bear in mind is whether the United States is primarily a nation of liberty or freedom?

LINGUISTIC ROOT ORIGINS OF LIBERTY

Whereas we tend to use the terms liberty and freedom interchangeably, and indeed they frequently overlap, in fact these two words have distinctive meanings. The historian David Hackett Fischer has sought to investigate liberty and freedom not as political ideas but as ethnographic concepts, enabling one to explore the customs, habits, and folkways of a given society. Both liberty and freedom, he argues, have different linguistic origins. Liberty is derived from the languages of southern Europe, notably the Greek (*eleutheria*) and Latin (*libertas*). Essentially, **liberty** refers to *release, separation, personal freedom, and protection from the power of the state.* Since the Mediterranean world consisted of political and social hierarchies founded upon slave societies, liberty was seen as a set of privileges that could be bestowed or taken away. Interestingly, the exercise of one's liberty existed in concert with arbitrary rule within the Roman Empire. From its root definition, liberty gave rise to the words *liberal*, *libertine*, and *liberate*, all of which pertain to the condition of being made free. In the American context, liberty was taken to mean independence and individual freedom, protected by laws from the imposition of tyranny. Prior to the American Revolution, liberty symbolized the assertion by colonists of their rights as citizens through expressing their grievances against the British king and parliament. It was this thought that guided Thomas Jefferson in writing the Declaration of Independence. Jefferson argued that in dissolving the bonds of allegiance to Great Britain and declaring the American colonies to be separate and independent nation states, the principle of liberty could be ensured. So fearful were the American colonists that government could easily become tyrannical, and thus deprive citizens of their liberty, they wrote into newly formed state constitutions restrictions on executive power, thus giving greater authority to representative legislative bodies.

Since liberty centered around the idea of personal freedom, it correlated to other spheres of life. Drawing upon Protestant Christianity, liberty implied freedom of conscience, suggesting that a church or state would not be allowed to dictate or interfere with the personal beliefs or convictions of the individual. The forgiveness of sin within the Christian tradition can be seen as an act of liberty since one is freed from the limiting force of one's transgressions. The pluralistic idea of religious liberty fostered diversity, which was the basis for separation between church and state. Hence, the state would, therefore, develop as a secular institution whereas religion would be a private matter.

Furthermore, in the economic sphere liberty provided the basis for free enterprise, whereby individuals could purchase, utilize, and dispose of their property without outside interference. This conception of liberty furnished the platform for free market capitalism that proved to be the impetus for westward expansion and economic development. So central was property to the well-being and prosperity of those relatively few landholders in 18th-century America, that the role of government, in the eyes of the country's ruling elite, was essentially constituted to protect property.

LINGUISTIC ROOT ORIGINS OF FREEDOM

Unlike the geographical origins of liberty, the word *freedom* was rooted in the German, Scandinavian, and Dutch cultures of northern Europe. The German word (*frei*) and the Norse (*fri*) are clear derivations of freedom. So is the word *friend*, which has an interesting connotation. Contrary to southern Europe, societies to the north were organized into **tribes,** which are *a social division in a traditional society consisting of families or communities linked by social, economic, religious, or blood ties, with a common culture and dialect, typically having a recognized leader.* Consequently, the concept of **freedom** evolved as *a set of inalienable rights that gave specific entitlements to the tribe, kinship group, or inclusive society.* The term *inalienable* means enjoying the benefits of freedom by virtue of birth. In other words, freedom pertains to belonging to a community of free people and thus sharing in the inherited rights of that community. Primarily, among these rights is the rule of law. Whereas in the Roman world laws were handed down from on high, freedom in the Germanic and Scandinavian worlds was a bottom-up process derived from the customs and folkways of the group. Moreover, the law applied to everyone. Hence, no one was considered above or below the law and were to be treated equally.

Whereas liberty involves using one's personal freedom responsibly while avoiding excess, freedom requires one to provide service, give support, and render respect for the good of the community. The requirement to pay taxes, sit on juries, and (when there was a draft) serve in the military are all duties imposed by freedom. At the same time, freedom involves equality among members of a community or society. In a speech before President Rutherford B. Hayes and other government leaders in 1877, Chief Joseph of the Nez Perce tribe stated that if the white man wanted to live in peace with the Indian, everyone had to be treated alike, enjoy the same laws, have equal rights, and a be given a chance to live and grow as a people. Consequently, Chief Joseph was using the language of freedom pertaining to what Native Americans considered to be their inalienable rights. This points to a clear distinction between liberty and freedom. Liberty, denoting separation and individualism, means that while the individual has autonomy and personal freedom, each person is responsible for his or her own fate. On the other hand, freedom implies connection, whereby the well-being of each member of the group is the responsibility of every other member. Apart from having a common meaning, liberty and freedom point in opposite directions indicating a conflict in values, which underlies the American experience.

TABLE 1.1. Liberty vs. Freedom

	LIBERTY	FREEDOM
Distinctive Characteristics	separation, release from restraint	kinship, common identity
Political Structure	hierarchical	democratic
Economic Structure	unrestricted free enterprise	regulated for the well-being of the community
Social Obligations	to use one's personal freedom responsibly	to serve and support the community, respect the rights of others
Basis of Authority	privilege, status	custom, the rule of law
Basic Values	independence, security	equality, entitlements, rights

LIBERTY AND FREEDOM IN COLONIAL AMERICA

Whereas we tend to think of the United States as a unified country, it was, from its inception, a number of diverse societies with different cultural streams, which characterized liberty in different ways. In Puritan New England there developed the idea of collective liberty related to an ordered **theocracy**, or *a form of government in which God or a deity is recognized as the supreme civil ruler. His laws being interpreted by the ecclesiastical authorities*. The General Court, representing civil authority, passed sweeping regulations that were enforced by the magistrates, charged with dealing with various infractions. At the same time, exemptions from the laws were granted. Certain privileges were allocated to some groups but denied to others. The Puritans' obsession with social control was ironically understood as liberty, which was seen as the protection against sin and deviant practices.

Whereas New England was ordered along the lines of tightly knit religious communities, Cavalier society in colonial Virginia was highly stratified with a small royalist elite at the top with graded ranks among the middling classes, reaching down to indentured servants and slaves. Within this social hierarchy, most people were dependents and therefore denied privileges—such as low taxes and loose social constraints—that were afforded to affluent white male landowners. Liberty was thus associated with the protection of property and the rights enjoyed by those near the top of the pyramid.

Among the Quakers who settled in the Delaware Valley (including Pennsylvania and parts of New Jersey), liberty was equated with pluralism, or toleration of diverse social groups. Those who settled in this region were people described as the "middling sort," and consequently there was no rigid hierarchy. The Quakers believed in the perpetuation of ancient rights and liberties, as contained in the unwritten English constitution, and favored a balanced and egalitarian society, so defined as freedom predicated on the rule of law.

Those settlers in the Backcountry, or the borderlands on the frontier, were a mixture of Scots, Irish, and those immigrants from the north of England. Among them was a strong attitude of cultural conservatism, which played out as exclusiveness. For those living on the borderlands, liberty was cross-fertilized with freedom, meaning identity with one's family and kinship group and a willingness to defend themselves, their families, and their territory against all outside influences. Overall, these various folkways and patterns of thought and behavior persisted after the formation of the American republic, underscoring the peculiar cultural diversity of our national life.

MEANINGS AND TENSIONS

Far from being unifying principles, liberty and freedom have contested meanings that have underscored significant cleavages in American society. According to a Black minister commenting on the system of slavery at the end of the Civil War, "Freedom lived in the black heart before freedom was born. If masters devised an elaborate ideology defending slavery as a benign, paternalist system that served the best interests of white and black alike, slaves developed their own worldview, centered on their desire for liberation." This passage presents contrasted perceptions of freedom. For freedmen (former slaves), freedom was the natural longing of humankind that was part of the Black man's birthright opposed to the injustices and indignities that slavery imposed on them. Conversely, those who supported slavery believed that the system gave slave owners the freedom to exercise authority over their slaves, much as a father would have over his children and other dependents. Thus, both slave and slave owner had opposing perceptions of freedom.

Consequently, the meaning of liberty and freedom rests in the "eye of the beholder" and can be used in any of a number of ways. A Texas congressman, Dick Armey, wrote in 1995 that whatever cause one seeks to advocate, it must always be sold in the language of freedom. Even those who wish to deny people their liberty will promulgate freedom to advance their own interests What is indicated here is that liberty and freedom are applied so randomly and recklessly that they serve to trigger emotional responses rather than coherent comprehension. Aside from their proper definitions (given earlier), liberty and freedom cannot be clearly understood apart from the circumstances in which they are used. Therefore, the historical context of these words is of upmost importance.

BASEBALL

BASEBALL AS AN EXPRESSION OF LIBERTY AND FREEDOM

What makes baseball the national pastime (among other things) is the embodiment of fundamental American ideals. "Americans identify the game with the country," wrote A. Bartlett Giamatti, former commissioner of Major League Baseball, "because baseball simulates and stimulates the condition of freedom. What he meant by freedom is the communal rights of a free people. As a game of individual skill and expression, baseball encompasses the principles of liberty. Liberty implies order that is contained in the rules of the game, enforced by umpires. Others have spoken of baseball as being emblematic of the striving for greater equality, or a level playing field, where every player has the opportunity to succeed or fail according to the player's effort and ability. As a localized game that can be adapted to any environment—and that welcomes wide participation—baseball is the most democratic of team sports. In essence, baseball, as a metaphor for the American way of life, is symbolic, for better or worse, of national identity.

What makes baseball relevant to the study of American history is that it parallels the themes and trends of the wider society. The spirit of entrepreneurship gave rise in the late 19th century to large trusts and corporations, controlled by captains of industry, a number of whom were crooks. There was a similar development in baseball whereby professional teams were owned by moguls who amassed great fortunes in industries, such as the production of beer and liquor, and ran their teams without any regulation as private fiefs. Race relations was another dominant theme, and during the long period of racial segregation in the United States, African Americans developed their own brand of baseball that in many ways mirrored the White organized game.

Baseball also relates to the American experience through the use of metaphors. The purpose of the game is for the hitting team to round the bases and score a run by reaching home plate. As with baseball, home has a special meaning in our society. Home is where we grew up, return to, and which provides a place of comfort and safety. One's home is also communal, as in the case of a person's hometown or community where one feels "at home." The French writer Alexis de Tocqueville, who was an observer of early American society, opined that liberty and freedom were "habits of the heart," by which he meant the beliefs and traditions of a free people. Part of this tradition has been and continues to be baseball.

SUMMARY

The two concepts of liberty and freedom are threads that will be woven through the entire book. The word *liberty* derived from the Greek and Latin languages, and refers to separation, independence, and protection from the power of the state. *Freedom*, routed in the northern European languages, has to do with inalienable rights, equality among citizens, obligations to the community, and entitlements. While both words are used virtually interchangeably in the English language, it is important to recognize their distinctive meanings and the way these words are used and by which groups or individuals.

From its beginning, American society consisted of a number of different cultural streams, with different traditions and folkways that had their own distinctive meaning of liberty and freedom.

Baseball, which arose in the mid-19th century as the national game, reflected the values of the broader society with its emphasis on ordered liberty.

STUDY QUESTIONS

1. Contained in the Declaration of Independence is the phrase, "We hold these truths to be self-evident that all men are created equal, that they are endowed by their creator with certain inalienable rights..." Based upon the definitions of liberty and freedom, is this phrase more a statement of liberty or freedom? Why?

2. Discuss the different ways that the Puritans in New England, the Cavaliers in Virginia, the Quakers in the Mid-Atlantic states, and the settlers in the Back-country used and understood the concept of liberty.

3. A. Bartlett Giamatti wrote that to know baseball was to aspire to a condition of freedom, individually and as a people, for baseball, above all other games, is unique to the American experience. What does he mean by this statement?

CHAPTER 2

Myths and Origins

HISTORICAL BACKGROUND

This chapter looks at early American society and baseball as a prelude to an investigation of both topics in the post-Civil War period. Origins can be viewed from both a mythical and a historical perspective. **Myth** *refers to a fictitious narrative that comprises a composite idealization of the past.* **History** *is a methodical narrative of events, or the record of human responses to forces and events within a society.* The distinction between these two terms is important to keep in mind. A question: Why is myth usually more compelling and long-lasting than the historical narrative of what actually happened?

AMERICA AS A COLONIAL SETTLER SOCIETY

Fundamental to understanding the development of American history is that it was from the beginning a settler society. By definition, a **settler society** is *a theoretical term in history that describes a common link between modern, predominantly European, attempts to permanently settle in other areas of the world, particularly those regions that are largely unsettled.* Thus, colonial development must be seen in secular terms as the result of the diaspora of peoples from the British Isles, beginning in the 17th century. These immigrants brought with them the folkways, ideas, and values of their culture, along with familiar institutional structures, which they implanted into American soil. To secure and survive in their new homeland, more immigrants were needed, which accounts for the fact that the non-Indian population of the North American colonies rose dramatically from about 260,000 in 1700 to approximately 1.5 million in 1760. With vast territories of land available, liberty became associated with property ownership. The joining of England and Scotland by the Act of Union in 1701 solidified the British Empire, which hastened the process of immigration.

From the perspective of the British government 3,000 miles away, the settlers—regardless of race, class, or ethnicity—were subjects of the crown and were likewise treated as such. Inevitably, the high-handed attitude of colonial governors and other officials, who were servants of the king, coupled with various restrictions such as the Navigation Acts of 1651, 1660, and 1696 (which sought to limit foreign and colonial competition and maintain the supremacy of British shipping), led to opposition and unrest. After the British and their Indian allies routed the French and their Indian allies in the Seven Years' War, ending in 1763, the need to secure the frontier led to the Proclamation of 1763, effectively closing the door to further settlement west of the Appalachian Mountains. Coupled with this imposition, the British Parliament passed a Currency Act in 1764 prohibiting the colonials from printing paper money, thus restricting their ability to transact business. Especially hated was the Quartering Act that required the colonials to provide housing and supplies for British troops. The British government in 1766 further claimed the right to legislate for the colonists in all cases.

To pay for a more expanded empire, the British imposed taxes on the colonists. With the Stamp Act crisis (1765), Parliament asserted the right to tax the colonists. This same justification stood behind the tea duty, which was deeply resented, primarily by the mercantile classes in New England and the mid-Atlantic colonies. The celebrated Boston Tea Party, whereby colonials dressed as Indians dumped cases of tea from British ships into Boston Harbor, led a frustrated and indignant British Parliament to pass the Coercive Acts (1774). These acts effectively curbed and destroyed colonial institutions of self-government. The shifting political ideas concerning individual liberties and the need to temper the absolute power of monarchs fostered a set of republican ideals, which bore the seeds that would eventually flower into a call for independence.

THE MYTH OF AMERICAN EXCEPTIONALISM

As people flowed into the English American colonies, the idea emerged of the New World as a pure, virginal, and uncorrupted land, in contrast with the corruption, poverty, and brutality of the world they left behind. This perception gave rise to a view of **American exceptionalism,** which posited that *America has had a peculiar and unique destiny, placing it outside the evolution of history up to that point.* To those of a religious bent, the notion of American uniqueness suggested that God had bestowed favor upon the land and was guiding the course of its affairs. Writing in 1980, religious fundamentalist leader Jerry Falwell expressed his belief that God led in the development of the U.S. Constitution, which resulted in the country enjoying more than two centuries of unparalleled freedom. Exceptionalism was also used to explain the spread of a settler society and to justify the subjugation of native peoples. Later, it would underscore the process of imperialism whereby the United States expanded its interests and control to territories beyond its borders. During the Second World War, the newspaper magnate

Henry Luce remarked that if the 20th century was to obtain a significant degree of health, nobility, and vigor, it must be to a significant degree an American century. This was yet another expression of the myth of American exceptionalism. Though untrue, this myth has been widely accepted to a greater or lesser degree up to the present time.

THE INSTITUTION OF SLAVERY

Slavery is as old as human society. Over the centuries, it adapted to changing social, economic, and historical conditions. With European colonization of the New World, the law of supply and demand required a multitude of bodies to work in the fields and on large plantations that arose to accommodate the production of indigenous products. From the start of colonization in the Americas, Africans, who were seen as more fit for strenuous labor than native Indians, were imported to meet the need for cheap labor. During the 17th and 18th centuries, slightly fewer than five million slaves were transported, largely to Dutch, British, and French colonies in the Caribbean and to Portuguese Brazil, where they worked on plantations producing cash crops such as tobacco and sugar, and to a lesser extent, rice and grain.

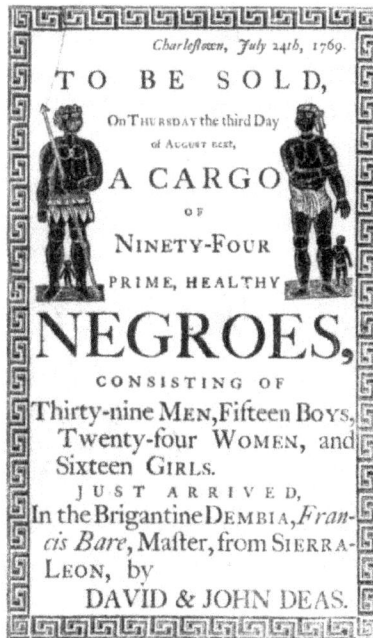

FIGURE 2.1 A 1769 broadside advertising the sale of slaves from Africa.

The so-called Middle Passage, where thousands of slaves were packed much as sardines into slave ships for transport to the Americas, was one of the most horrific stories of the age. Mortality rates during this journey exceeded 10% of the total number of persons enslaved. As more men of means poured into the southern colonies of North America, the demand for slaves increased. By the 1730s, when the Carolinas were divided into North and South Carolina, two-thirds of the populations in these regions were Black slaves. To a far lesser extent, slavery existed in the North, but the institution never had the same economic importance as it did in the South.

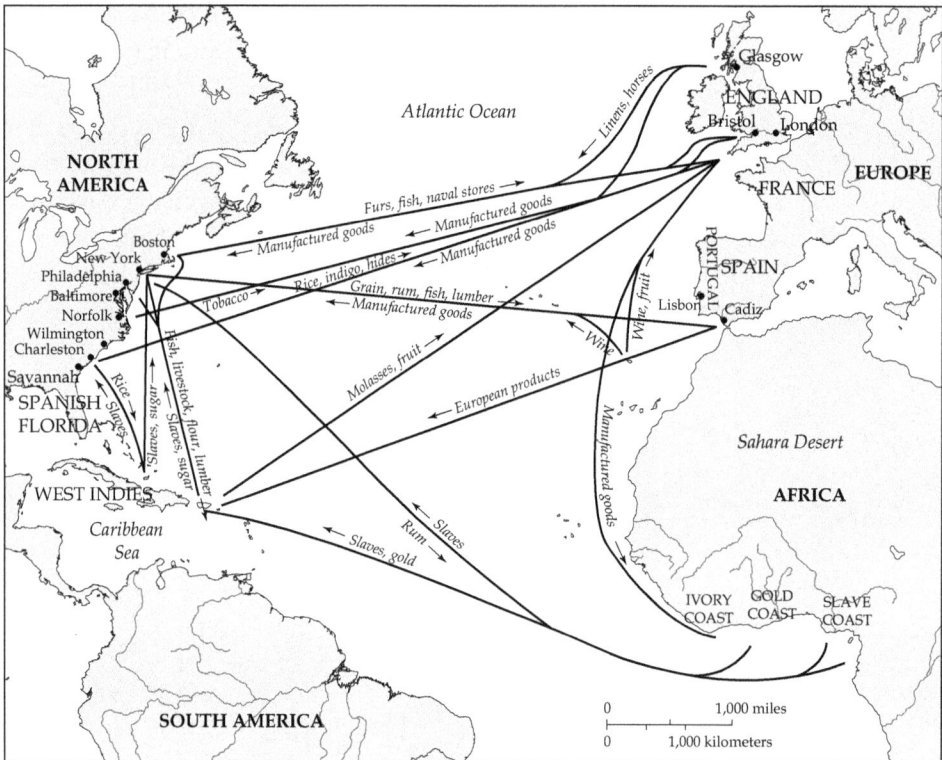

MAP 2.1 The Destination by Percentage of Slaves Transported to the New World, 1640–1770

From the late 17th century, the southern states began to pass laws that restricted the lives of slaves and solidified the institution of slavery into a caste system. A 1662 act in Virginia defined slavery as lifelong and inheritable through the line of slave mothers to their children. Slave codes also stripped slaves of any civil or political rights, such as testifying against Whites in court, requiring them to carry passes, and prohibiting Blacks from gathering into groups. As property, slaves could be bought and sold at will, which negated family life. This would have long and tragic consequences. Worries over the threat of violence and possible slave rebellions only served to make the restrictions on African Americans more extensive and punitive.

FORMATION OF THE AMERICAN REPUBLIC

When American settlers revolted against the mother country in what became the American Revolution (1776–1781), the justification was not primarily the litany of perceived abuses by the British government, but the fear that liberty and the fundamental inheritable rights of all Englishmen were being taken away. What caused the revolutionaries the most anxiety was arbitrary and absolute government.

MAP 2.2 British North America After the Treaty of Paris, 1763

When the Revolution did come, the colonies were relatively equally divided between those (particularly the merchant classes) who favored a split from the mother country, and those who wished to remain loyal to the crown and/or pursue less draconian measures. With the Declaration of Independence, American settlers cast their lot in favor of republican citizenship, as opposed to remaining British subjects. The outcome of the war, resulting in the British surrender at Yorktown in Pennsylvania, had as much to do with British geopolitical concerns and a desire to cut losses on what had been a long, drawn-out, and expensive campaign as with colonial tactical and guerrilla military assaults.

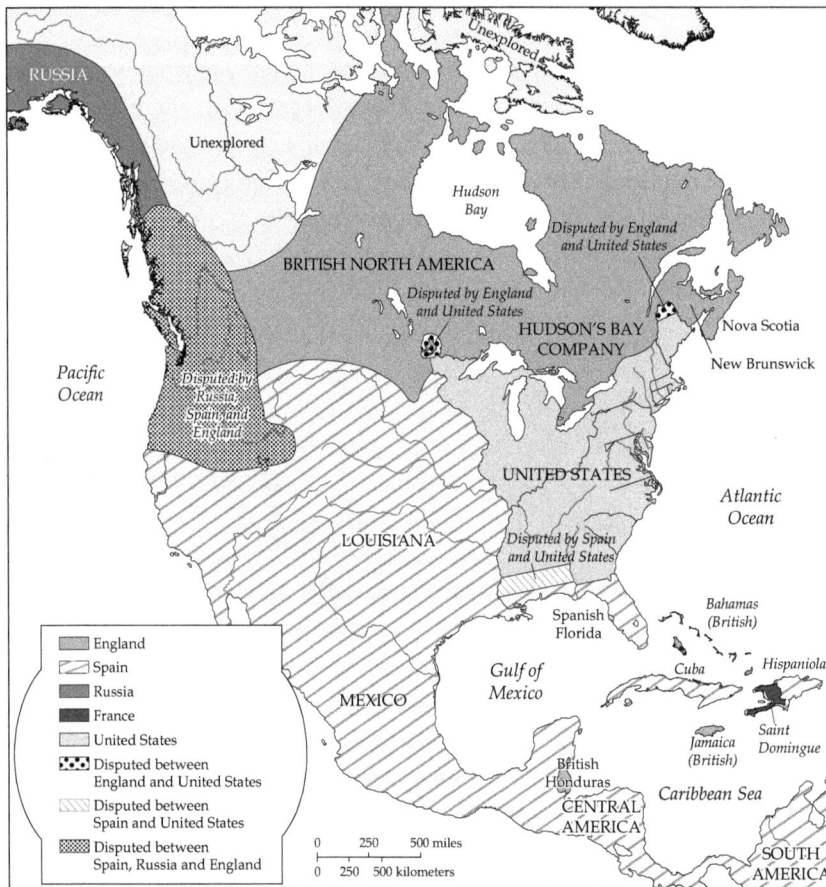

MAP 2.3 North America After the Revolutionary War, 1783

The period after the war (1783–1789) proved to be crisis years for the new republic. Large areas of the country were occupied by Britain and Spain in defiance of the peace agreement (Treaty of Paris, 1783) and in the face of a weakened federal government. The new country was financially broke and lacked the power to tax. Threats to civil government, such as Shays' Rebellion in Massachusetts, were also problematic. Clearly, the Articles of Confederation, created by the Second Continental Congress, failed to provide sufficient power at the national level to govern effectively.

THE CONSTITUTION

When the colonial elites met in Philadelphia during the summer of 1787 to draw up a new system of national government, there was no lack of foresight as to the country's future course. The problem was that these men of vision did not have the same vision. John Adams, who would become the second president, sought a free republic based on a balanced constitution. Alexander Hamilton, the first secretary of the treasury, wanted a government ruled by elite property owners. Thomas Jefferson looked to a government of independent and self-governing groups of citizens, while James Madison, who followed Jefferson as president, wanted a diverse and pluralistic republic. George Washington, commander in chief of the American forces during the war, a property owner and a freemason, who would become the country's first president, desired a republic of virtue run by men of courage, integrity, and honor.

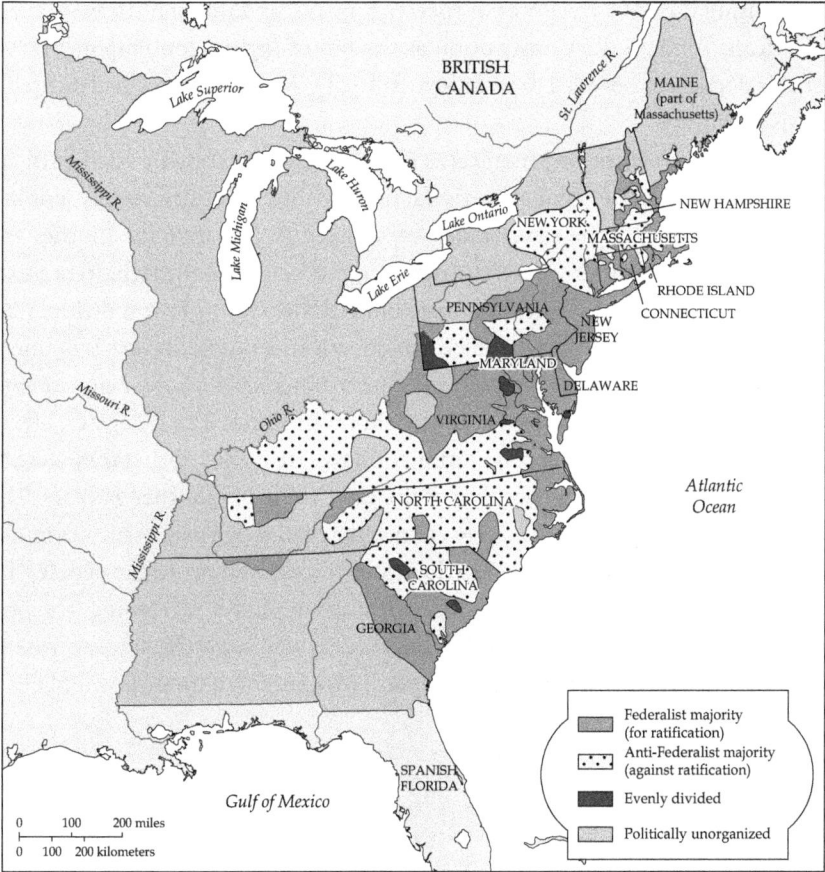

MAP 2.4 Regional Divisions Over the Constitution

The question was how to create a republic where there was no sufficient precedent to guide it? Inevitably, the result would be a unique form of government following no fixed pattern. There was a consensus that the new national state needed to curb the power of the executive (president) so as to prevent the emergence of absolute power. Thus, the Constitution would impose a system of checks and balances so that none of the three branches (legislative, executive, and judicial) would have too much power and authority. The framers of the Constitution gave numerous responsibilities for governing to Congress, which represented individual states and the relatively small group of people who were citizens. Since the United States, unlike earlier republican models, would be a large country, the Constitutional Convention sought to preserve, along with the national government, a federal system of state governments that would create and maintain jurisdiction over counties, and have primary concern for the welfare of the people. Almost as an afterthought, a Bill of Rights was added to the Constitution, which restated the fundamental rights and protections of Englishmen, going back to the Magna Carta, and restricting the power of government to pass laws limiting the basic freedoms of speech, religion, and the right to assemble. While most Americans think of the Constitution as the Bill of Rights, contemporaries who put together this document believed that the structure of government they had created would be the basis for liberty.

In the end, the Constitution emerged as an ambiguous document filled with compromises so as to appeal to the various diverse factions within American society. For instance, under Article 1, section 9, the slave trade was allowed to continue for another 20 years, which appealed to the southern states. Congress also proclaimed the right to regulate commerce, impose taxes, and establish tariffs, and limited the power of the individual states to do so. The problem of slavery proved to be a major sticking point. **Slavery** is defined as *the state of a person who is a chattel or property of another.* Since slaves were included in the U.S. census, it would give inordinate power to the southern states. The delegates, after much haggling, decided upon partial representation for slaves, recognizing that they were human property. They also extended the legality of the slave trade for another 25 years. The 10th amendment, which stated that "the powers not delegated by the Constitution, nor prohibited by it to the states, are reserved to the states respectively, or to the people," became a bone of contention during the early decades of the republic, producing irreconcilable sectional differences as to whether ultimate power rested with the states or the federal government as the representative of the people. This conflict of interest would eventually result in the American Civil War.

BASEBALL

THE MYTHICAL ORIGINS OF BASEBALL

As with the wider scope of American history, the origins of baseball are deeply rooted in mythology. The most persistent and blatantly bogus myth surrounded Abner Doubleday. According to the myth, he authored the rules and structure of the game in 1839 while residing in Cooperstown, New York. The origin of this myth appears to have come from A. G. Spalding, a noteworthy person in the history of baseball. Following the surge of patriotism in the years after the nation's first centennial celebration in 1876, Spalding wished to prove that baseball was purely an American game. His ulterior motive was to combat the argument that baseball had descended from the English game of rounders. On his own initiative, he appointed a national board of baseball commissioners (Mills Commission) to collect evidence and come to a definitive decision as to the origins of baseball.

Writing to the commission in July 1907, Spalding directed its attention to a letter, written by a man named Abner Graves, who recollected having been in Cooperstown in 1839 and witnessed Doubleday laying out the shape of the baseball diamond while he explained the game and gave it a name. On the basis of this single piece of evidence, the commission ruled that baseball was purely an American sport. The problem was that Doubleday was an army cadet at West Point at the time of this alleged event, and there is no evidence that he ever saw or played baseball, much less invented the game. The most logical explanation would be that Spalding, in his zeal to prove the American origins of baseball, promoted his old friend and distinguished Civil War hero as the game's founder. The fact that the National Baseball Hall of Fame is in Cooperstown, and the word "Doubleday" is used to name ballparks, teams, and businesses, indicates how this myth has been perpetuated.

Another more plausible myth concerns Alexander Joy Cartwright, a New York bank clerk, who, along with his Knickerbocker club, played a form of town ball known as the "New York Game," and set out the rules of modern baseball in 1845. The team reportedly played its first game at the Elysian Fields of Hoboken, New Jersey. Cartwright soon headed west, joining the California gold rush, and eventually ended up in Hawaii. The extent to which he promoted baseball during his travels is a subject for debate. The truth is that the distinctive sport of baseball had been played simultaneously at a number of venues prior to this time. This suggests that baseball underwent an evolutionary development from earlier forms of bat-and-ball games, and the dates of its alleged founding are just milestones in the history of the sport.

TRADITION OF BAT-AND-BALL GAMES

The moral of the story is that we must be on guard against assertions of a single origin and oft-repeated explanations. In fact, baseball owes its beginnings to a variety of prototype sports that were introduced to the American colonies from England. David Brock, in his book, *Baseball Before We Knew It*, points to a number of curiously named games that preceded baseball—the pastime of stool-ball, for instance, dating back to the Middle Ages, was widely played in Britain by both sexes. The sport consisted of throwing a ball, hitting the ball, and running circular bases.

Another version of the same idea was trap-ball, also dating back to medieval times. While this form of ball did not involve running the bases, it did introduce the concept of boundaries, whereby a hit ball was determined to be fair or foul. Although trap-ball was popular in England, it was never transported to the colonies.

One forerunner of baseball that may have crossed the Atlantic was any of a variety of cat-ball, or old cat, which were informal games involving the basic baseball skills of base running, fielding, throwing, and batting a ball. There are literary references from the 18th century to playing base-ball in England that appeared in novels and children's books. One might assume, however, that baseball was a cover term for all kinds of bat-and-ball games.

Alongside cat-ball and related games was that of rounders, which included some of the characteristics of baseball. Englishman Henry Chadwick, who came to the United States and became a strong promoter of baseball, saw a connection between those sports and American versions of baseball. While in England, he played both rounders and the national game of cricket. Ironically, rounders and cricket (especially the latter) were popular for a while in the United States and enjoyed parallel popularity with baseball before fading into the background.

By the end of the 18th century (1700s), the kinds of bat-and-ball games transported to the New World under the heading of baseball morphed into what came to be called town ball. It appears that town ball sprang up all over the Northeast from Pennsylvania to Massachusetts, though the form it took had regional characteristics. There is evidence that the old game of baseball flourished in western Massachusetts before the ratification of the American Constitution.

Two kinds of town ball emerged as predominant. The Massachusetts game consisted of four stakes 60 feet apart marking each base, with a thrower (pitcher) standing in the middle of the square and a striker (batter) positioned halfway between the first and last stake. When the ball (made of soft material) was hit, the striker would head for the first stake. When a base runner touched the last stake, a tally (run) was recorded. A striker could be called out if he hit the ball in the air and it was caught, or if he was soaked—hit by a thrown ball while running between the stakes. Curiously, the runner could run all around the field to avoid getting soaked.

FIGURE 2.2 Woodcut of boys playing trap-ball (1810), a version of the English game of "old cat." This is considered to be one of the early forerunners of baseball.

The New York brand of town ball resembled modern baseball, with a diamond-shaped field consisting of three bases and a home plate. The batter, after hitting the pitched ball, would move around the bases and would score a run by touching the home base, where he began. A batter would be called out if the hit ball was thrown to a base ahead of the runner, or if the batted ball was caught in the air. Although more like the contemporary game, the New York style of baseball remained a crude form of what it would become. The rules of baseball evolved over a number of decades and, technically speaking, is still not a finished product.

For whatever reason, primarily because of its dynamic growth in popularity, the New York game soon outstripped and supplanted Massachusetts baseball. This did not happen immediately, however. The Massachusetts game was still very popular in the 1850s, though a decade later, after the Civil War, it experienced a decline. Coincidentally, the New York game made very little headway in New England until after 1857 when the game took off. One of the pioneer New York City teams, the Brooklyn Excelsiors, organized a 10-day road trip to upstate New York cities in 1860 and played teams in places such as Albany, Troy, Rochester, and Buffalo. Such tours helped to solidify New York-style baseball into what would become the national pastime.

EARLY BASEBALL

As the sport evolved, by the mid-19th century, baseball became the pastime of the respectable middle class, though the game was quickly picked up by those lower on the social scale. The gentlemanly spirit of baseball was often seen in the detached or dismissive attitudes that players felt toward the game. Quoting the aforementioned Henry Chadwick, historian Warren Goldstein writes that baseball during the late 1850s and early 1860s was defended as "healthful recreation," an "invigorating exercise and manly pastime." Such attitudes were reflected in a game between the Lightfoot Baseball Club of Oxford, in Chenango County, New York, and a nearby Harpersville team, which led to a 37–37 draw. Rather than play extra innings, the visiting team made excuses, such as continuing the game would prevent them from getting home at a decent hour, and so departed. For early practitioners, the outcome of the game was secondary to an opportunity to demonstrate manly skill, enjoy the fresh air, and associate with worthy opponents.

FIGURE 2.3 Schoolboys playing a primitive form of baseball on the Boston Commons, 1834.

Town teams playing organized baseball, or an approximation of it, were prevalent on the eve of the Civil War. In upstate New York, teams sprang up in various neighborhoods. Baseball in Rochester during the early years was hampered by the lack of appropriate fields, so players, much to the annoyance of many townsmen, would transform public squares and quiet neighborhoods into ball diamonds.

FIGURE 2.4 Currier & Ives print of an 1866 baseball game indicating its widespread popularity as America's national sport.

The "manly" sport of baseball often had a social aspect. Many teams were drawn from fraternal clubs, and the conclusion of games would often be followed by a banquet, whereby the adversaries on the field would meet in a spirit of camaraderie at the dinner table. Early baseball rules, aside from laying down the particular regulations on how the game was to be played, also had codes of responsible behavior and good sportsmanship. Individual club rules mandated that players could be fined for deporting themselves in an ungentlemanly manner. Since self-control and civility were widely held virtues at this time, many thought that baseball should reinforce these values. Even after baseball developed a standardized format, teams often modified the rules and adapted them to their situation. This soon changed when baseball became more formalized as it spread across the country.

SUMMARY

As a nation settled by immigrants, largely from the British Isles, colonial America developed as a settler society with its own institutions and as the amalgamation of diverse folkways and cultural traditions. The reality of a settler society was shrouded in the myth of American exceptionalism that posited that the country had a unique history and destiny apart from other nations.

From its colonial origins, Americans incorporated the institution of slavery, primarily in the southern states, that would cast a dark shadow over the political, social, economic, and moral evolution of the country.

From declaring its independence from Great Britain, the United States sought to form a new government, predicated on liberty that would be based on checks and balances and the separation of powers. Added to the Constitution was a Bill of Rights that encompassed the principles of both liberty and freedom.

A. G. Spaulding promoted a mythology that baseball was created by a man named Abner Doubleday and was, thus, a purely American game. In fact, baseball evolved from a number of English bat-and-ball games, so it was not an American creation but an evolutionary development.

STUDY QUESTIONS

1. To what extent is the United States Constitution an expression of liberty and freedom (as defined in the Introduction)?
2. Discuss the various arguments that underscored the creation of the U.S. Constitution. Do you believe the Constitution was a patchwork of diverse interests, some of which would prove to be irreconcilable?
3. In what way is baseball's "Cooperstown myth" a form of American exceptionalism?

Credits

Fig. 2.1: Source: http://commons.wikimedia.org/wiki/File:Slave_Auction_Ad.jpg.

Fig. 2.2: "Trap Ball," Library of Congress, 1810.

Fig. 2.3: "Playing Ball," Library of Congress, 1834.

Fig. 2.4: Currier & Ives, "Baseball Game at the Elysian Fields," http://www.loc.gov/pictures/resource/cph.3a04558/, 1866.

CHAPTER 3

Rebellion, Reconstruction, and Expansion

HISTORICAL BACKGROUND

This chapter gives an overview of the period of the 1860s and 1870s when the country endured a Civil War (1861–1865), a period of Reconstruction (1865–1877), and the invasion of White settlers into the uncharted lands west of the Mississippi. These were transformative forces that have shaped the course of America ever since. We might ask, in what ways did the Civil War, Reconstruction, and the move of settlers on to the frontier affect the course of liberty and freedom?

With respect to baseball, as the informal and loosely constructed game became more standardized, the amateur and gentlemanly game evolved into a professional and competitive sport. Baseball cut across race and gender lines but the prevalence of rigid attitudes toward racial segregation and the "proper" role of women marginalized both groups.

THE COMING OF CIVIL WAR: A NATION DIVIDED

The Civil War (1861–1865) was the defining moment in American history because it was the culmination of unresolved conflicts and contradictions embedded in the U.S. Constitution and American society, which had been festering since the birth of the republic. Foremost was the issue of states' rights. If the United States was a union of states, the question arose: What would be the role and power of the states with respect to the federal government? The issue was highlighted by the nullification crisis in 1828, triggered by the objection of South Carolina over a tax on textiles passed by Congress. The argument was that if the Union was a sovereign compact among the people in the states, any disagreement between the federal government and the states over the constitutionality of a federal law meant that the states could determine whether such a law was constitutional.

This line of thinking, which gained strength in the South, was reinforced by the issue of slavery. The perpetuation of the institution of slavery from colonial times led to the creation of two societies. The introduction into the South of cotton production, which was heavily labor intensive, carried with it the demand for greater numbers of slaves. Whereas the northern states were becoming more industrialized during the first half of the 19th century, the southern states, particularly in the Deep South, were becoming economically more dependent on agriculture and the plantation system, dominated by the cultivation of cotton. The inevitable result of this two-societies model was a number of crises that paved the road leading to war.

As people pushed west into the open territories of the Great Plains, the question arose as to whether the new states that emerged would be slave or free states. The Missouri Compromise of 1820 established the principle that creation of a slave state (Missouri) would be offset by creation of a free state (Maine). Later, the Wilmot Proviso, introduced into Congress by David Wilmot of Pennsylvania, provided that slavery would not be allowed in the land seized from Mexico during the Mexican War (1845–1848). The firestorm that ensued resulted in a compromise by which people in each territory would decide for themselves whether or not to allow slavery. The Compromise of 1850 admitted California as a free state and allowed settlers in New Mexico territory to decide the issue for themselves. This compromise was a further attempt to avert a constitutional crisis. The Kansas–Nebraska Act (1854), which created a latitudinal demarcation between slave and free regions, overrode the Missouri Compromise and led to vigilante violence in the new territories.

The other factor leading to war was the growing intolerance of slavery, particularly in the northern states, which turned the debate into a moral and ideological struggle. The abolitionists, who had emerged out of the Puritan religious tradition, led the fight against slavery, making the cleavage between the two sides unbridgeable. Plantation owners and apologists for the institution of slavery defended their culture and way of life with equal ferocity.

When civil war broke out in 1861, few realized it would last another half decade. On paper, the outcome of the war seemed a no-brainer. The Union had nearly three times the population, 11 times the number of industrial workers, more than twice as many miles of railroad, and produced well over 90% of the weapons of war compared with the Confederate South. What the Union lacked were competent generals, at least during the early years of the war, which gave the Confederacy some advantage in battles against their better-equipped and overmanned adversaries. After the battles of Gettysburg (July 1–3, 1863) and the Confederate surrender at Vicksburg (July 1863), the Union forces took the upper hand. The advantage in human and material resources paid off, leaving the South—where the war was mostly fought—bankrupt and devastated. No small credit went to President Abraham Lincoln, whose shrewdness, wisdom, and indomitable will overcame the faction, timidity, and desire to seek accommodation with the Confederates within his own party, and focused on winning the war.

PUTTING THE COUNTRY BACK TOGETHER—RECONSTRUCTION

With the conclusion of the Civil War following the assassination of President Lincoln, the problem facing the nation was how to restore "a more perfect union." There were two essential problems that had to be addressed: The first was how and under what terms would the southern states be restored to the Union; and second, what would be the legal position and rights of the newly freed slaves?

Pertaining to the first problem, the question revolved around whether the president or Congress would dictate the terms of Reconstruction, and whether it would be a conciliatory or a harsh peace. Vice President Andrew Johnson, who became the chief executive after Lincoln's assassination, favored a quick resolution and imposed minimal conditions on the return of the southern states to the Union. Congress, dominated by the Radical Republicans—a number of whom had been abolitionists—wanted to punish the South and force it to accept a social and political revolution that would give parity to freed slaves (freedmen), which was anathema to Whites. After a barely failed attempt to impeach Johnson over his alleged violation of the Tenure of Office Act, the Radical Republicans passed the Reconstruction Act of 1867, which treated the unreconstructed southern states as conquered territories under military authority and promoted the enfranchisement of Blacks and Whites who supported the congressional agenda. Violence against those two groups, and the decline in sympathy for such radical measures among political leaders and citizens in the North, led to a resurgence of southern White political dominance from 1870, which became firmly entrenched with the withdrawal of military troops after the election of 1877.

FIGURE 3.1 Thaddeus Stevens, leader of the Radical Republicans in the House of Representatives during Reconstruction.

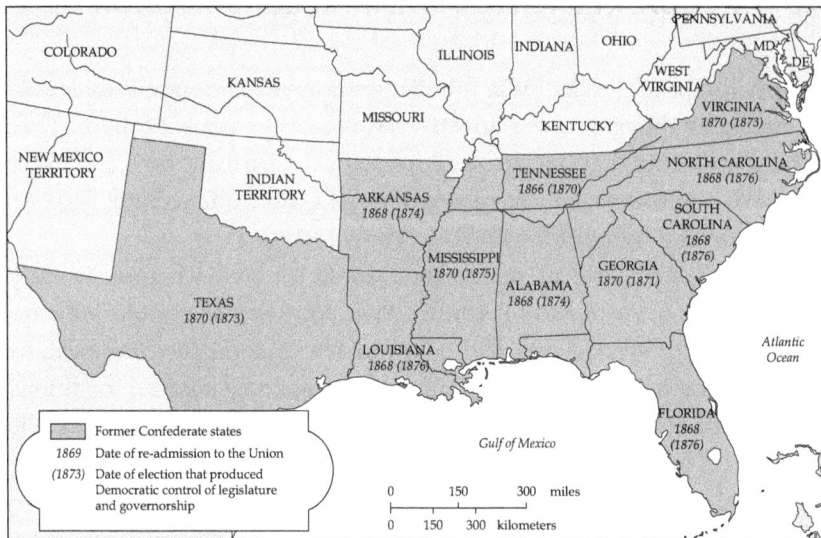

MAP 3.1 Progress of Returning Southern States to the Union, 1867–1877

With respect to the second problem, the status of freedmen was determined by three constitutional amendments: The thirteenth amendment, adopted in 1865, effectively abolished slavery; the fourteenth amendment (1868) contained a number of provisions, but set forth the principle of equal protection under the law; while the fifteenth amendment (1870) extended to all citizens the right to vote. Each of these amendments gave Congress the power to enforce the various provisions through appropriate legislation.

FIGURE 3.2 Lithograph of President Lincoln extending emancipation freeing the slaves, which was seen as benefitting both Whites and Blacks.

WHAT DID FREEDOM MEAN TO EX-SLAVES?

President Lincoln in his *Emancipation Proclamation*, published September 23, 1863, stated that all slaves in states rebelling against the United States "shall be, then, hence forward and forever free." But, practically speaking, what was meant by *free*? With the end of slavery, Blacks were no longer someone's property, but what rights and freedoms did they have? When asked what he understood as slavery and freedom, Garrison Frazier a Baptist minister who had acquired his freedom, defined post–Civil War slavery as being forced to work for someone else without their consent. His meaning of the term slavery was somewhat different from chattel slavery. By freedom, Frazier meant being taken from under the yoke of bondage and placed in a position where one could reap the fruits of his or her own labor. In other words, having access to ownership of land, which was a fundamental right in a settler society. There were other freedoms affecting personal circumstances such as the right to marry and set up an independent household, the right to enjoy leisure time, the right to an education, and freedom of movement, which encompassed the broader definitions of liberty and freedom.

At the federal level, Congress proposed a Civil Rights Act (1866), which declared African Americans and all persons born in the United States to be citizens, and defined the rights of all citizens regardless of race. President Andrew Johnson, who was overtly hostile to Blacks, vetoed this bill, much to the anger and indignation of the Republicans in Congress. The Republican-dominated Congress also implemented the short-lived Freedmen's Bureau, which was set up to provide rudimentary education and basic social services to former slaves. With strong opposition from the Klu Klux Klan and other southern terrorist groups, Congress discontinued funding for the Freedman's Bureau in 1872. Shortly thereafter, Congress passed the Civil Rights Act of 1875 in response to hostilities imposed on Blacks in the South by the so-called Redeemers (southern Democrats opposed to Reconstruction). The bill provided for equal access to public facilities and the right of African Americans to serve on juries. This law was largely ignored, and the Supreme Court soon declared it unconstitutional. After a decade of much promise, the position of the majority of African Americans, though no longer slaves, was only marginally better. As the former Confederate states one by one passed restrictive legislation, the lives of southern Blacks remained one of subordination and subjugation.

FIGURE 3.3 An engraving from *Harper's Weekly* in 1867 showing a Black man casting his vote in one of the first biracial elections in the history of the southern states.

WESTWARD EXPANSION AND THE EXPRESSION OF LIBERTY

During the Civil War, Congress passed three pieces of legislation that would have a major influence on the further development of the country. The Homestead Act (1862) provided 160 acres of free land to any settler who would live on the land for five years and was willing to improve the homestead. Persons with the financial means could buy additional land for $1.25 an acre. This was a godsend to speculators, who gobbled up large amounts of property and then sold it for a profit.

That same year, the Morrill Land College Act became law. This law set aside funds derived from the sale of public land to establish colleges that would provide agricultural, technical, and mechanical education, and would train teachers. A number of public land grant colleges, and later state universities, owed their origin to this act.

The third major piece of legislation passed by Congress in 1862 was the Pacific Railway Act, which created two corporations for the building of the Transcontinental Railroad across the country. Work began almost immediately and was completed six years later, on May 10, 1869. Large gangs of workers were employed on building the railroad, including a sizable number of imported Chinese and Irish immigrants. Clearly, the railroad facilitated western expansion and further perpetuated the notion of a settler society that equated land owing with individual liberty.

While the opening of the West to White settlers was ballyhooed as the fulfillment of America's **manifest destiny**, or *the 19th-century doctrine or belief that the expansion of the United States throughout the American continents was both justified and inevitable,* it conveniently overlooked the fact that the western territories were occupied by indigenous native peoples, who roamed the plains following the huge buffalo herds that numbered in the millions. Early explorers and the trickle of settlers who moved on or through the territories west of the Mississippi River decades before the Civil War often had compatible relations with the natives, who would share food and supplies and act as guides. As the number of western settlers expanded from a trickle into a flood from the 1850s, these invasions began to compromise and threaten the lifestyle of Native Americans. Further fuel was added to the fire after the Civil War, when many soldiers headed to the frontier to pacify the territories. Many of these soldiers had an uncomplicated view of indigenous natives that could be summed up in the statement, "The only good Indian is a dead Indian."

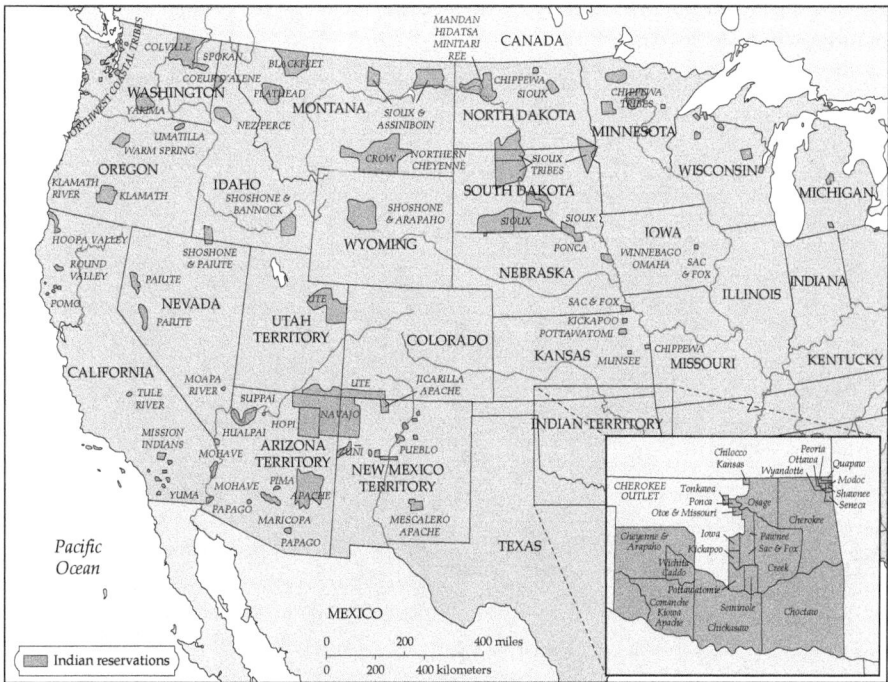

MAP 3.2 Indian Reservations, ca. 1890

The Plains Wars of the 1860s and 1870s comprise one of the more grim periods of American history. There were many tribes such as the Apache and the Comanche in the Southwest; the Potawatomi, the Pawnee, the Sioux, and the Arapaho in the central and northern Plains; and the Nez Percé, the Walla Walla, and the Blackfeet in the Northwest, among many others.

Treaties were made and broken, massacres of tribal groups (women and children included) occurred, and the slaughter of millions of buffalo, as a means of depriving the natives of their ability to survive, went unabated. In the end, greater firepower, coupled with overwhelming numbers of settlers continuously encroaching on Indian land, claiming territory, and building towns, forced most of the natives onto reservations. Although lasting only a few decades, the Indian Wars represented one of the largest land grabs in history. The passage of the **Dawes Act** in 1887, which was *a federal law intended to turn Native Americans into farmers and landowners by providing cooperating families with 160 acres of reservation land for farming or 320 acres for grazing.* This act essentially struck at the heart of Native American culture which was nomadic and traditional beliefs.

Sociologists characterize the relations between a majority and a minority culture in terms of **pluralism**, or *the maintenance of unique cultural identities and values;* **assimilation,** or *the process in which a minority group or culture comes to resemble a dominant group or assume the values, behaviors, and beliefs of that group;* **segregation,** or *the enforced separation of different racial groups in a country, community*; and **genocide**, meaning *the deliberate killing of a large group of people, especially those of a particular ethnic group or nation.* The contact between Native Americans and the dominant European-based settler society was marked by all four of these relationship types.

FIGURE 3.4 A Norwegian immigrant family in front of their sod house in Nebraska, in 1866.

Between 1870 and 1890, a network of railroads allowed for easy access to the West. Two groups emerged: ranchers, who claimed huge territories for the grazing and herding of cattle; and settlers, who used their acreage for the cultivation of crops. These incompatible forms of agriculture coupled with the range wars of the 1860s and 1870s, which generated the myth of the American cowboy as a symbol of the independent hero at war against any kind of restraint. The formation of cattle kingdoms and the annual long drives of herds to cattle markets led to skirmishes with ranchers. Settlers responded by cordoning off large tracts of land for cultivation through the introduction of barbed wire. Contrary to sentimental myths of heroic pioneers, farming in the West was not only harsh, but predatory, where the strong, the well connected, and the well-heeled ground down those with less power and means, who sought to eke out a living in an unforgiving environment.

BASEBALL

While the hub of baseball on the eve of the Civil War remained in the Northeast, the game quickly spread across the country. Larger cities in the Midwest, including Chicago, Cleveland, Detroit, and Milwaukee, picked up the sport, as did smaller towns such as Oberlin, Ohio, and Davenport, Iowa. As settlers moved into uncharted territories in the West, they carried baseball with them. On the Pacific Coast, the game was played in the emerging cities of San Francisco, Sacramento, and Stockton. Modern forms of baseball penetrated slowly into the South, and while plantation owners displayed little enthusiasm for the game, citizens in seaport towns took it up with keen enthusiasm. Some forms of baseball were played even by slaves.

The rapid spread of baseball required some degree of oversight. The game's first governing body, the National Association of Base Ball Players, was formed in 1858. The NABBP was instrumental in imposing standardized rules predicated on the New York game. By 1867, the National Association had grown to include more than 300 clubs. Meanwhile, the forces of change were moving swiftly and would soon override the ability of the National Association to control the course of baseball.

With the onset of the Civil War, the rhythms and routines of people's lives became disrupted. Baseball was no exception. At the same time, the game was woven into soldiers' lives. Military authorities permitted—and even encouraged—sport during down moments, on holidays, and in winter camps, so as to relieve boredom and to take the minds of soldiers off the dangers and the possibility of death that awaited them. War diaries, memoirs, and regimental histories provided ample evidence of recreation during wartime. Beyond the combative sports such as boxing and wrestling, baseball was commonly featured at army outposts. There is some evidence that baseball was played in prison camps, but with a couple of exceptions, such accounts are sketchy.

FIGURE 3.5 Currier & Ives 1860 political cartoon showing President-elect Abraham Lincoln with his defeated opponents on a baseball field. Lincoln with his foot on home plate indicates his victory.

While it may be assumed that most military baseball was played by teams drawn from militias in the Northeast (particularly in the metropolitan New York area), the diaspora of baseball by the 1860s was such that games were played in regionally diverse regiments on both sides of the conflict. Teams continued to enjoy different styles of baseball; for instance, New Englanders played the Massachusetts game when they competed among themselves. Confederate teams often played variations of town ball, along with modern versions of the game, in their camps.

On the home front, call-ups depleted many teams, and some were forced to disband during the war. Member clubs in the National Association of Base Ball Players sank from 59 in 1860 to 34 by 1865. The ability of numerous men, especially in Northeast cities, to evade military service kept the game alive. While the early years of the war (1861–1862) were particularly disruptive, by 1863, with the economy in the North on a war footing, the fortunes of baseball began to pick up. Whereas human and material resources in the South were being bled dry as the war progressed, there were numerous cities and communities in the North where the war hardly intruded on normal life.

THE TWILIGHT OF AMATEUR BASEBALL

At the start of the Civil War, organized baseball was dominated by the leading teams in the National Association, which included the New York Mutuals, Brooklyn Eckfords, the Atlantics of Brooklyn, and a host of other clubs from the New York, New Jersey, and Pennsylvania regions. By 1870, prominent members of the National Association included the Forest City club in Rockford, Illinois, the Olympics in Washington, DC, and teams from Indianapolis and Cleveland, to name a few. Baseball mushroomed until it could be found in every little town and hamlet. In upstate New York, baseball soon appeared in Newburgh and the small Hudson Valley communities. The sport generated a hotbed of interest in Ulster County along the Hudson River, and according to one local historian, no other county of its size in the state took to the game so fervently. By the mid-1870s, other New York State towns such as Monticello, Port Jervis, Binghamton, Ithaca, Oswego, Norwich, and Oneonta fielded teams.

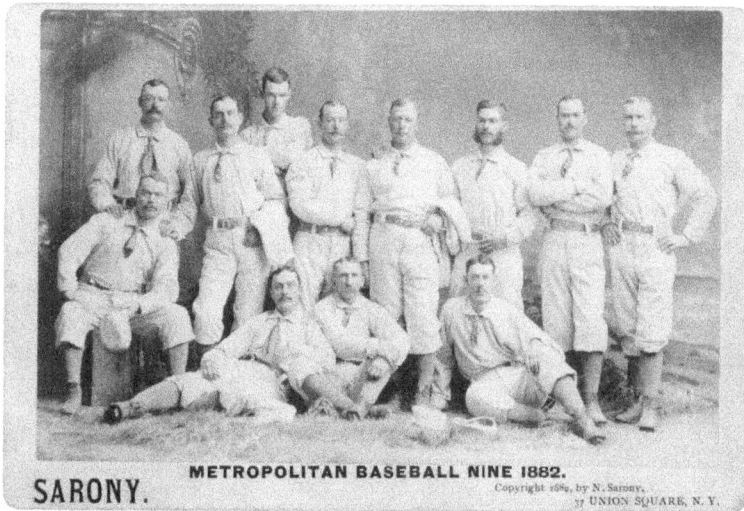

METROPOLITAN BASEBALL NINE 1882.

SARONY.

FIGURE 3.6 The New York Metropolitan team, 1882.

Beginning in the 1860s, male promoters organized professional women's teams as a novelty. One account advertised an exhibition of baseball and other sports "participated in by twenty handsome young ladies to the accompaniment of a brass band in uniform." In 1867, an all-Black women's team called the Dolly Vardens was formed in Philadelphia. The first of the White women's professional teams to gain widespread publicity were the Blonds and the Brunettes in 1875. More famous was a team known as "the Bloomer Girls," who barnstormed around the country, playing both men's and women's teams in the larger towns. Press reports indicated they played excellent baseball. There were other women's barnstorming teams throughout the 1870s and 1880s that played men's teams in what was portrayed as the "battle of the sexes."

Colleges formed teams and played local clubs. Two years after Cornell University was founded, it fielded a rather successful baseball team. Long before strict rules governed college sports, teams would often include nonstudents who possessed admirable baseball skills. Upper-class girls attending some of the early women's colleges such as Mount Holyoke, Smith, Vassar, Radcliffe, and Barnard were encouraged to play baseball on the assumption that a healthy mind required a healthy body. Men's and women's preparatory schools also fielded baseball teams. Women were playing baseball at Vassar College in 1866, only seven years after the first intercollegiate game was played between Amherst and Williams colleges. A year later there is evidence of girls playing baseball at Miss Porter's boarding school at Farmington, Connecticut. Exaggerated notions of women's frailty and femininity eventually led schools and colleges to curtail or eliminate women's baseball.

Reports claimed that this capital sport was all the rage among informal teams and organized clubs. Pickup games involving young men and boys took place in parks and open spaces in large metropolitan cities such as Philadelphia and New York. There were accounts of games between carrier boys of different newspapers. The printers took up the game, and rival offices organized teams to play one another. Teams of lawyers challenged those of doctors, and in Rochester, New York, even the shoeblacks were looking to arrange a match. Games between married men and bachelors, older men versus younger men, etc., took place, as did games between church groups.

Local clubs barnstormed around the country and engaged teams of local players. Teams of African American players thrived in the 1860s. In October 1867, two organized Black baseball clubs, the Excelsiors of Philadelphia and the Uniques of Brooklyn, played a game described as the "championship of colored clubs," won by the Excelsiors. Games between Blacks and Whites, however, were soon phased out as the country succumbed to the rising tide of segregation. At its 1870 meeting, the National Association of Base Ball Players modified the rules for the admission of new clubs so as to bar teams that included "gentlemen of color."

Challenges to baseball's amateur status were soon forthcoming. The initial step toward professionalism commenced with gate money, or "passing the hat," among patrons, with the receipts shared by players and team officials. It was then only a short step to charging admission. On July 20, 1858, a contest between the New York and Brooklyn All-Stars at a race course in Queens resulted for the first time in a fee of 50 cents charged to patrons. A further stride toward professionalizing the game came through the introduction of a free-agent market. Clubs sought to strengthen their teams by acquiring players from other organizations. The three top players on the Excelsiors, for instance, joined the rival Atlantics in 1862. One of these players was Jim Creighton, a multiskilled ballplayer who also distinguished himself at cricket. After jumping to the Atlantics, Creighton's career was cut short after a mighty swing of the bat caused an internal rupture and hemorrhaging, leading to his untimely death shortly thereafter. Soon, New York players were in demand by clubs in other parts of the country.

While technically only amateur teams were allowed in the National Association, the press began referring to association clubs as "professionals." The governing board overlooked the pervasive practice of charging money for games, since many clubs engaged in unofficial gate-money practices. The board made some effort to bar professional players from participating in matches and, in 1866, threatened the expulsion of any club that paid its players, and also any rival club that played against them. This threat, however, proved to be hollow. Essentially, the National Association's attempt to preserve amateur baseball was "a voice crying in the wilderness." By 1868, it was clear that the National Association had insufficient power, and judging from the many internal conflicts, a lack of authority to act as the governing body for baseball.

The question of what constitutes professionalism underscored the emergence of commercialized baseball. Many so-called amateur clubs were forced to raise money to meet expenses, and no doubt a number of them charged admission. As competition between leagues and clubs became more formalized, the next logical step was to use some of the receipts to pay players, particularly the better players, and to entice players from other teams through the promise of monetary rewards. Complaints appeared in the press as to the prevalence of "gate-money teams," whose members claimed to be amateurs while practically transforming themselves into professionals. The line between amateur and professional, obvious at first glance, was anything but, which would prove challenging, especially with regard to Sunday baseball, which was outlawed in a number of states.

THE COMING OF PROFESSIONALISM

Nevertheless, the pace of professional baseball advanced quickly from the late 1860s. In 1869, the New York Mutuals became the first baseball team to pay its players, closely followed by the Cincinnati Red Stockings. The Red Stockings went on to an undefeated season in 1869, led by one of the outstanding figures of the game, a former cricket player named Harry Wright. The success of the Red Stockings proved that the public would happily pay to watch top-flight players in action, which only professional baseball could provide.

After a few glorious years at the top of the baseball world, the Cincinnati club declined and soon folded. Wright was invited to put together a team in Boston and immediately stocked the team with the best players he could find. Among those players was the previously cited Albert Goodwill Spalding, who came from a prosperous Illinois farm family. As a teenager, he demonstrated a remarkable ability to play baseball and was soon a star player on the local Rockford team. Pitching there in 1868, 1869, and 1870, Spalding acquired a national reputation and was enticed by Wright to sign a contract with Boston for $1,500 a year. Spalding would later become baseball's most noteworthy promoter and executive. He furthermore made a fortune as a baseball equipment manufacturer.

FIGURE 3.7 *Harper's Weekly* photo of a game played between the Boston Red Stockings and the Philadelphia Athletics at the Lords Cricket Ground in London, England, in 1874. Many Englishmen were dismissive of the "American sport."

Professionalism led to the demise of the National Association of Base Ball Players. It was replaced in 1871 by the National Association of Professional Base Ball Players, which took over the constitution of the previous organization and arranged for match tours between professional clubs. The professional association remained in the hands of the players, who often made decisions based on what was good for the players or their respective teams. Serious financial problems soon arose. The professional association was saddled with an abundance of clubs and heavy expenses. The league contained a few stalwarts such as the New York Mutuals, the Boston Red Stockings, the Philadelphia Athletics, and the Chicago White Stockings. For the most part, however, there was a vast turnover of teams. Good ballplayers do not necessarily make good businessmen, and since professional play required a more sophisticated level of organization, the National Association of Professional Base Ball Players was soon doomed.

By the 1870s, the trend toward professional baseball was irreversible. In the decades after the Civil War, the United States embarked on an era of industrial expansion, which saw the rise of a multitude of inventions, entrepreneurship, territorial expansion, and the amassing and losing of fortunes. Baseball mirrored this process. While play-for-pay baseball caused financial instability and reflected a survival-of-the-fittest mentality, it did promote stiff competition and better playing skills. The line between amateur and professional was still rather fine, and for many amateur clubs, it was a feather in their cap to play well-known professional teams. This intercourse between amateur and professional baseball would continue for the remainder of the century.

FIGURE 3.8 Photo-etching of a game involving the Boston Beaneaters in 1888 at the South End grounds in Boston.

SUMMARY

Slavery and the issue of state's rights were the primary factors igniting the Civil War. After the war, the 13th, 14th, and 15th amendments to the U.S. Constitution offered the promise of providing full citizenship for African Americans along with two aborted civil rights bills. These efforts, however, were ignored or compromised.

The Reconstruction period (1865–1877) coincided with the opening of the West for settlement. This led to the protracted Indian Wars that forced Indians onto reservations, undermining their culture and means of livelihood. Essentially, this was a clash between two irreconcilable cultures.

Baseball during and after the Civil War was played strictly on an amateur basis and quickly spread across the country. The pressure of competition and the desire by fans to see a higher class of baseball led to an opening of the door to professional baseball.

STUDY QUESTIONS

1. What did freedom mean for former slaves after the Civil War?
2. What were some of the factors that facilitated the expansion of a settler society in the West in the post-Civil War period?
3. In what ways did baseball reflect the bottom-up approach that was a predominant feature of American society?

Credits

Fig. 3.1: Source: http://loc.gov/pictures/resource/cwpbh.00460/.

Fig. 3.2: Source: https://www.whitehousehistory.org/photos/photo-15.

Fig. 3.3: A.R. Waud, "The First Vote," *Harper's Weekly*, 1867.

Fig. 3.4: "Norwegian Immigrant Family in Nebraska," National Park Service, 1886.

Fig. 3.5: Currier & Ives, "The National Game," http://www.loc.gov/pictures/collection/app/item/2003674584/, 1860.

Fig. 3.6: Napoleon Sarony, "Metropolitan Baseball Nine," http://commons.wikimedia.org/wiki/File:NY_Metropolitans.jpg, 1882.

Fig. 3.7: "Baseball in England," *Harper's Weekly*, 1874.

Fig. 3.8: "Boston National League Team," Boston Public Library, 1888.

CHAPTER 4

American Capitalism and the Rise of Organized Baseball

HISTORICAL BACKGROUND

The rise of industrial America after the Civil War led to the emergence of capitalism as a dominant force. In many ways capitalism was a logical offshoot of the settler idea of personal freedom, or liberty that gave one the ability to accumulate wealth with few if any restrictions. The predatory nature of capitalism often meant that the luxury of the few was bought at the expense of the many. In a number of cases, however, the system of free enterprise gave aspiring persons a means of upward social mobility. The capitalist system was supported by powerful ideologies that still persist. Baseball, as a part of this system, exemplified its dynamism and corruptive aspects, expressed in what can be called the capitalist paradox. Given that we have defined freedom and inherent rights of a people, and liberty as personal freedom, to what extent did the rise of industrial capitalism pose a contradiction between these two concepts?

THE RISE OF AMERICAN CAPITALISM

American society has been dominated by two fundamental institutions: a republican form of representative government (known as American democracy) and the economic institution of capitalism. Modern capitalism was the product of new ways of thinking about money and the creation of goods and services that were articulated by Adam Smith in his influential book, *The Wealth of Nations* (1776), based on the idea that wealth comes from individuals, not the state. Consequently, capitalism, as stated earlier, was seen as an expression of liberty. As the country developed its infrastructure and incipient industries, American capitalism evolved on a modest scale. It was during the period after the Civil War that industrial capitalism took off—with both dramatic and disastrous results.

What is Capitalism?

Capitalism is defined as a system of ownership, by which investment and control of the means of production, distribution, and exchange are in the hands of private individuals or corporations. The basis of capitalism is therefore competition between companies and individuals over resources. Since capitalism relies on continued growth and expansion, there is a contradiction to this system. The **capitalist contradiction** *means that resources through growth and expansion inevitably fall into the hands of fewer and fewer people (more particularly, trusts, corporations, or conglomerates), which snuffs out competition.* At the same time, capitalism embodies a paradox. **The capitalist paradox** *encourages both creativity and corruption.* Creativity, because competition promotes entrepreneurship and new ideas, while at the same time, it generates corruption by fanning the flames of greed, acquisitiveness, and materialism. Nineteenth-century American capitalism demonstrated both these characteristics.

FIGURE 4.1 Cartoon from *Puck* magazine, January 23, 1889, showing the domination of oversized capitalists who dominated and controlled the U.S. Senate.

AMERICA'S GILDED AGE (1865–1900)

The gilded age *was an era of rapid economic growth, especially in the North and West. As American wages grew much higher than those in Europe, especially for skilled workers, the period saw an influx of millions of European immigrants. It was also a time of great ostentation and the existence of extremes of wealth and poverty.* While some millionaires began in poverty and rose to great fortunes, most did not. A study of 303 textile, railroad, and steel executives of the 1870s showed that 90% came from the middle and upper classes. Rags-to-riches stories were largely myths. For the most part, the rich were able to benefit from their connections to other persons of means and to those possessing political power. With the backing of the government and the courts, large corporations formed **trusts** (*an illegal combination of companies in which stock is controlled by a board of trustees*) and **monopolies** (*control of an entire market by a single industry or corporation*) that often worked against the public interest. National and state laws protected private property. Changes in the structure of corporate law at the state level enabled trusts and corporations under the 14th amendment to seek equal protection under the law and be treated as persons. Limited liability laws meant that owners of corporations could not be sued or held liable for the debts and transgressions of a corporation. The issuing of stock allowed corporations to raise capital and expand their operations

Increasingly, America was run by captains of industry. J. P. Morgan, founder of the House of Morgan, made a fortune and used his wealth to bring some degree of rationality to the economy. He controlled banks, railroads, and insurance companies, and often dictated economic policies to the government. John D. Rockefeller bought his first oil refinery in 1862, and by 1870 had set up the Standard Oil Company of Ohio. To enhance his fortune and to drive out competitors, Rockefeller engaged in cost-cutting measures, the acquisition of new technologies, and the hiring of able managers. The negotiation of secret deals with railroads to ship his oil at discount prices enabled Rockefeller to drive his competitors out of business. Another entrepreneur, the Scottish-born Andrew Carnegie, came to the United States and built a million-dollar steel plant. By 1880, his mills were producing 10,000 tons of steel a month; by 1900, he was making $40 million a year. When he sold his steel interest to Morgan, it was for $492 million.

The railroads were also beneficiaries of unregulated capitalism. In 1865, scores of smaller railroads operated in the Northeast and the Midwest. By 1900, this haphazard system had developed into a massive, consolidated, and integrated network of 193,000 miles, dominated by seven large corporations. Four of the rail systems were controlled partially or completely by the House of Morgan. The railroads were viewed, particularly by farmers, as an enemy as they charged high prices and controlled critical access to markets. Where railroad companies laid tracks often determined whether a town or region prospered or declined.

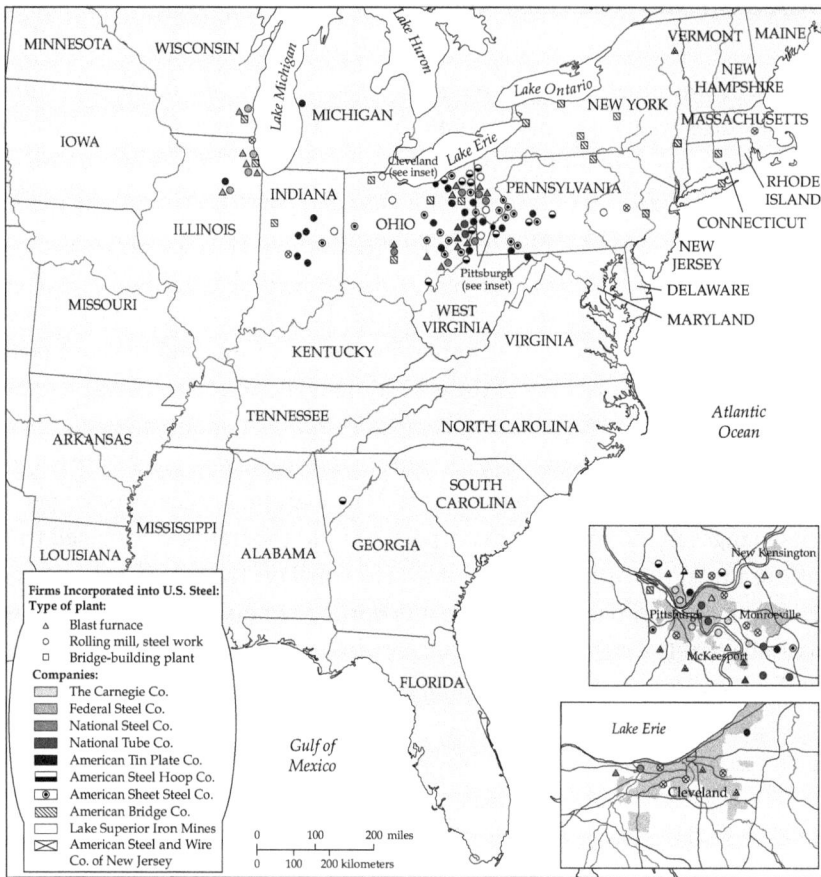

MAP 4.1 U.S. Steel: A Vertically Integrated Corporation

The map legend reads:

Firms Incorporated into U.S. Steel:
Type of plant:
△ Blast furnace
○ Rolling mill, steel work
□ Bridge-building plant
Companies:
The Carnegie Co.
Federal Steel Co.
National Steel Co.
National Tube Co.
American Tin Plate Co.
American Steel Hoop Co.
American Sheet Steel Co.
American Bridge Co.
Lake Superior Iron Mines
American Steel and Wire Co. of New Jersey

Business trusts and monopolies were structured along the lines of vertical and horizontal integration. Through **vertical integration**, *a single firm controlled all aspects of production and distribution.* Such an example was the meatpacking industry. Since meat is perishable and needed to be transported over long distances, the invention of the refrigerator car enabled Gustavus Swift to build his meatpacking empire in Chicago though the control of meat transport and production from a single source. Andrew Carnegie likewise owned the mines and employed the men who extracted the ore that was converted to steel in his factories. **Horizontal integration** *involved larger companies driving out competitors who produced the same product, thus reducing competition and controlling prices.* The prime example of horizontal integration was Rockefeller's Standard Oil Company. Captains of industry largely benefited from the frequent boom-and-bust cycles that forced out small and weaker companies during hard times, enabling trusts and corporations to consolidate their gains during periods of prosperity.

FIGURE 4.2 *Puck* magazine cartoon showing the Standard Oil Company as an octopus grabbing other industries, including the U.S. government.

The gravitation from competition among small firms to the emergence of large trusts in many industries was further facilitated by two important developments during the late 19th century. One was the creation of a mass-market economy, whereby a wide variety of goods was made available in large retail outlets at relatively cheap prices. The second was the growth of bureaucracies, as businesses became more complex and performed more specialized functions.

THE PROCESS OF INDUSTRIALIZATION

Historian Edward E. Baptist has convincingly argued that through slavery the United States gained control of the world market for cotton, which provided the raw material of the Industrial Revolution. Hence, America's wealth as an industrial nation was built on the backs of slaves. Industrialization in the United States occurred rapidly over several decades after the Civil War. Agriculture, which employed half of the total labor force in 1870, possessed only 31% of the labor force by 1910. At the same time, agriculture was becoming mechanized, thanks to the McCormick reaper and harvester. Between the Civil War and 1900, steam power replaced human muscle, iron replaced wood, and steel replaced iron. There were machines that could drive steel tools, oil to lubricate machines, and light homes, streets, and factories. People and goods were transported by rail. The invention of the Pullman car enabled people to sleep on trains and refrigerated box cars allowed for the transportation of meat and other perishables. The telephone, the type-writer, and the adding machine speeded up business operations. In 1860, 20 million tons of coal were mined in the United States; by 1900, it was 270 million tons. More coal meant more steel. More steel enabled industries to greatly expand the variety of produced goods. By 1900, there were over 369,000 more factories than there had been in 1860.

Immigration supported the new industrial system. From the 1880s, a wave of immigrants arrived in the United States. Earlier immigrants had largely come from the British Isles and Germany (about a million Irish came after the potato famine of the 1840s). The new immigrants came mostly from southern and eastern Europe, and unlike the predominantly Protestant, White native population, they were largely Catholics and Jews. On a much smaller scale, people from Latin America and Asia (China and Japan, mostly) were part of the great influx. Between 1860 and 1914, New York City grew from a population of 850,000 to 4 million; Chicago, from 110,000 to 2 million; and Philadelphia, from 650,000 to 1.5 million.

It could hardly be said that the new immigrants were welcomed with open arms. Racial and cultural differences resulted in widespread prejudice and discrimination, not only by the native population against the foreigner, but also between immigrant groups themselves, since rivalries and long-standing hatreds that existed in the old country were transported to the new world.

Many immigrants were unskilled and illiterate, and thus were easily exploited. Competition was fierce, and those who were lucky enough to find work were employed in harsh and unregulated factories and sweatshops, while others worked as casual laborers. More than a few turned to crime and prostitution to survive. The precariousness of life meant that many immigrants (those from Italy in particular) relied on family connections to find work and become established in their new country. If the new immigrants to America were looking for a better life, many were in for a cruel shock. Perhaps as many as one third of all immigrants returned to their home country after a few years.

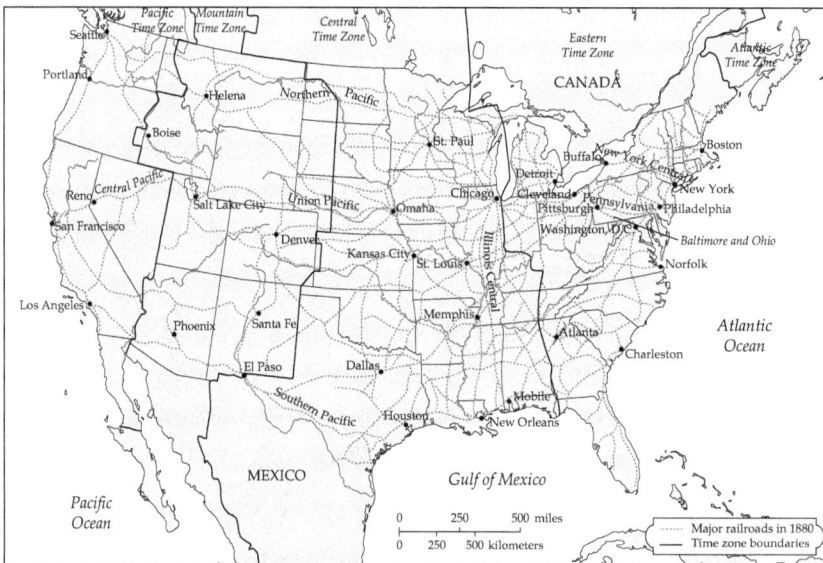

MAP 4.2 National Railway System, 1880

LABOR AND THE UNIONS

The social world of 19th-century industrial society was defined by class. **Social class** refers to *a division of a society based on social and economic status.* Half of all Americans were working class, in all their many grades. Farmers and farm laborers constituted about a third of the population. A smaller percentage of people were designated middle class, consisting mostly of clerks, shopkeepers, office workers, owners of small businesses, and a small but growing professional class. At the top of the social hierarchy was a powerful upper class that controlled the lion's share of wealth and resources and lived ostentatious lives of great opulence.

FIGURE 4.3 Parade of labor unions taken from Frank Leslie's *Illustrated Newspaper*, September 1, 1884. The large placard compares Black slavery to wage slavery.

It was the workers at the bottom of the social hierarchy who were the most vulnerable and subject to wage cuts and layoffs, especially during hard times. Many factory workers were young and female. In 1880, there were 1,118,000 children under the age of 16 (one out of six) at work in the United States. Female immigrants dominated the textile industries. A large number of women became domestic servants in the employ of respectable middle-class households and the mansions of the rich. Many poor women were reduced to prostitution to survive. Since women and children were easily controlled and could be paid less, they fit more easily into a predatory system that extracted profit by grinding down its workers. Men, of course, dominated heavy industries that relied on the brute strength of its workers.

Low pay and the deplorable conditions of many unskilled workers led to the rise of labor organizations. The Knights of Labor (KOL), founded in 1869, was the first successful broad-based union in the United States. It opened its doors to all workers, regardless of race, gender, or level of skill. The KOL, led by superb organizers such as Terence Powderly, created a number of local unions, which allowed it to grow. The KOL counted 10,000 members in 1879; by 1886, the number of members had climbed to 700,000. A police crackdown on so-called radical groups followed the 1886 Haymarket Riot in Chicago, when a peaceful demonstration became violent, resulting in a backlash against organized labor and other radical groups that turned into a witch hunt. The KOL was soon replaced by the American Federation of Labor (AFL), which sought to unionize skilled craft workers and had a far less ambitious agenda. The Socialist Labor Party gained a limited following and emerged out of largely German communities in cities such as Chicago and Milwaukee.

Overall, America experienced the most violent labor struggles of any country in the Western world. In the same year as the Haymarket Riot, there was a battle between strikers and police in East St. Louis, Illinois, leading to the death of seven workers and the calling in of the National Guard. Simultaneously, there were many demonstrations in cities such as Detroit, New York, and Chicago. From 1881 to 1885, strikes averaged 500 a year, involving perhaps 150,000 workers each year. In 1886 alone, there were 1,400 strikes involving 500,000 workers. And in 1892, strikes occurred all over the country, which included a general strike in New Orleans; a coal miners' strike in Tennessee; a railroad switchmen's strike in Buffalo; a strike among copper miners in Idaho; and a strike at the Carnegie Steel Company plant in Homestead, Pennsylvania. Two years later, a strike at the Pullman Car Company in Chicago left 13 dead and 53 seriously wounded. The list goes on.

FIGURE 4.4 Jacob Riis photo of Baxter Street, 1890, in one of New York City's slums.

The class war between capitalists and workers also gave rise to competing ideologies. Social Darwinism was an adaptation of Charles Darwin's natural selection, based on his observations of plants and animals in their various habitats. Alfred Russell Wallace's theory regarding struggle of the fittest was also applied to survival in the social world. The view of **social Darwinism** taken by William Graham Sumner and other theorists *was that laissez-faire capitalism reflected the competition for scarce resources, whereby those who were most able and fit rose to the top, leaving behind those who were less able.* This highly individualistic theory, which was interpreted by some as liberty, naturally supported the interests of the men who had accumulated vast fortunes and could point to the fact that their fortunes were justified and well deserved based on their competitive advantage.

Men such as Henry George, Edward Bellamy, and George E. McNeill saw the gap between rich and poor in a different light. To them, the problem was how to close the economic gap and so make society more equal. George proposed a tax on land as a means of achieving this end. Bellamy, in his novel *Looking Backward*, visualized the creation of a national organization of labor, in which the nation would become the sole employer; the people, by virtue of their citizenship, would become employees within a single, democratically run, corporation. Labor leaders and progressive religious thinkers also put forward ideas to reduce the inequities brought about by an unregulated capitalist system. McNeill argued that the extremes of wealth and poverty threatened the existence of government. Therefore, it was the job of state legislatures to intervene in disputes between capital and labor so as to enlarge the boundaries of labor's opportunity. This McNeill interpreted as freedom.

Gender Segregation

The rise of industrial America was also a period of heightened separation and segregation, and not only in racial terms. Ethnic groups lived in distinct neighborhoods, replete with their own churches, schools, social clubs, and other institutions. Men and women also lived in separate spheres. Millions of males after the Civil War flocked to fraternal orders and were initiated into Freemason lodges, the Knights of Pythias, the Odd Fellows, the Improved Order of Red Men, the Grange, and numerous other societies. Many Catholic men joined the Knights of Columbus. Middle-class women had their own societies, but their lives often centered around managing households, or in the case of farm women, performing a host of chores. The working and lower classes had a more vulnerable existence. Rarely did couples work at the same venue and their times together were, in many cases, infrequent. Bars and taverns attracted mostly men in large numbers, especially in large towns and cities. A surprising number of men and women remained single due in part to gender imbalance, social duties, and the strict norms that worked against informal liaisons and relationships. There was also a significant amount of bigamy and desertion by which men (usually) would abandon home life and look for adventure or work elsewhere, thus establishing a new identity and conjugal lifestyle. Hence, the comfortable image of domestic life and conjugal bliss, portrayed in novels and by sentimental propagandists, was more often than not a myth. The harsh and brutal conditions that defined the lives of the multitudes had a centrifugal effect on family life and generally stifled the better human qualities.

BASEBALL

WILLIAM HULBERT AND CREATION OF THE NATIONAL LEAGUE

Professional baseball achieved some stability when the National League was formed in 1876. The new league took the place of the National Association of Professional Base Ball Players, which suffered from the lack of sound business practices. The driving force behind the formation of the National League was William Hulbert. Similar to Spalding and Harry Wright, Hulbert was smitten with the entrepreneurial spirit of the age, which favored upstart businesses and organizational skills.

Hulbert was determined to improve the infrastructure of professional baseball. National League teams would be formed on the basis of managed clubs organized around a clear set of principles. Each club would honor the contracts of other clubs and reject any black-listed player who was suspended by any team for whatever reason. There would be franchise exclusivity, thereby allowing one team per city. Cities that were granted clubs had to be of a size that would ensure a suitable market. Penalties were imposed for gambling, game fixing, drunkenness, and disreputable behavior so as to maintain high standards. A set admission of 50 cents would be charged, and the mechanism for the honest accounting of receipts would be instituted.

The league commenced with eight teams, situated in Boston, Chicago, Cincinnati, Hartford, Louisville, New York, Philadelphia, and St. Louis. There was a constant shuffling of teams, as certain clubs were dropped from the league to be replaced by others. At various times, the cities of Buffalo, Indianapolis, Providence, Cleveland, Milwaukee, Toronto, Detroit, Worcester, and Baltimore were represented in the National League. Train travel and problems of scheduling restricted the location of clubs to the Northeast and Midwest.

From the league's inception, there were disputes between member clubs over admission charges, which the league had set at 50 cents. Buffalo delayed joining the league over this issue, while Syracuse, which spent one disappointing year in the National League, balked repeatedly at the standard charge before agreeing to increase its admission to the required level. Initially, Sunday baseball was banned, in keeping with the moral sentiments of the period. Such a policy would later be put to the test by competition from rival leagues.

FIGURE 4.5 A baseball game played at a resort in the White Mountains, New Hampshire.

The National League clubs, in assessing the 1878 season, issued a report stating that efforts to present a distinctly national game in the best possible manner and under the most stringent regulations had been met. They thought that baseball was appreciated and approved by lovers of this "pure and manly sport," and that the moral tone of the game had been elevated. The experience of the league clubs in 1878, however, showed that the business depression that had gripped the country affected receipts to such an extent that these losses might affect salaries for the coming year.

At a meeting of the National League in Buffalo the following year (1879), the owners were again satisfied with the performance on the field and the enthusiasm of the general public. Some concern was expressed in the pages of one newspaper over "evil influences" that surrounded such contests, particularly gambling, and what was referred to as control by unprincipled managers. Financially, the 1879 season was better than 1878, but the expenses of many clubs exceeded their receipts due entirely to salaries. To remedy this so-called evil, clubs decided on the use of mandatory uniform player contracts that restricted the money paid to players until it was earned. In other words, no advances would be given. Gambling on games was a constant problem, and while the National League owners sought to limit this practice, it remained a persistent issue.

ALCOHOLISM, GAMBLING, AND VIOLENCE IN PROFESSIONAL BASEBALL

The most enduring and insidious affliction to befall professional baseball, and to some degree amateur ball, was its long-standing association with gambling. Reports of gambling emerged as early as the 1860s—and the problem never went away. "One of the greatest drawbacks to the progress of healthy sports and pastimes and their popularity with the best classes of society," noted the *New York Clipper*, was the tendency of the professional class of the sporting fraternity "to enter into fraudulent collusion with knaves to wager bets." Gambling was situational and rampant at many ballparks, hotel lobbies, betting shops, restaurant bars, and other places where the sporting crowd tended to congregate.

Game fixing had a close association with gambling. The first reported case of a game that was thrown occurred in a match played on September 28, 1865, in Hoboken, New Jersey, between two New York teams. Players on the New York Mutuals were said to have received $100 to lose a game to their archrival, the Brooklyn Eckfords. Two months later, club officials charged William Wansley as the person who organized the fix and handled the negotiations. Wansley was later expelled from the team. Although the frequency of throwing games cannot be determined precisely, it was well known that professional players on some teams, especially the Mutuals (controlled by the infamously corrupt William March "Boss" Tweed, leader of New York's Tammany Hall political machine), were more than willing to take money from gamblers in exchange for sloppy play on the field.

Despite the National League's moral posturing in the 1880s, the vigilance against gambling and its consequent evils appeared to collapse into humbug in the 1890s, when owners, players, and managers made little effort to mask their gambling activities. Monte Ward of the New York Giants, for instance, was supposedly said to have won 20 shares of stock from a club director in 1892 as a result of betting on where the team would place in the standings that year.

The professionalization of baseball coincided with an array of abuses that would continue to mar the game for decades to come. During the late 19th and early 20th centuries, alcohol flowed through baseball, both on and off the field. Club owners often conducted their business in bars, making the tavern their home away from home. Nearly every team in Harry Wright's National Association of Professional Base Ball Players found their games marred by drunkenness and riot, stemming from the sale of liquor at games. It was unusual for teams not to have at least one player who was an alcoholic. The problem continued—regardless of fines, the threat of suspension, or blacklisting. Players sometimes hid whiskey bottles in a corner of the dugout or in the outfield so they could take sips during the game.

Pete Browning, who played centerfield for Louisville of the American Association in the 1880s, was usually drunk on and off the field, and although he had a career batting average of .341, he claimed that he couldn't hit the ball until he hit the bottle. In some cases, liquor was passed from the stands to the field. With lots of time on their hands, the bar or tavern became the off-field resort for many players. Given the pervasiveness of alcoholic consumption and the culture of drinking that permeated urban society, teams often had little choice but to tolerate its drunkards and hope their antics would not embarrass the club or compromise the game. While clubs frequently criticized their players for drunkenness, they did little or nothing to confront the problem.

Baseball also had to contend with violence. Mistreatment of the arbiters of the game by partisan fans was particularly noteworthy. The abuse of umpires was as old as organized baseball itself. Umpire baiting during the 1879 season was almost as disgraceful as in the previous season, cried the *New York Clipper*. It was bad enough that umpires were verbally harangued by the "betting crowd" and physically attacked by players, but they also had to endure humiliation from the press over alleged bad decisions. The umpire's physical safety was threatened by extreme partisanship, and it appeared that no legislation on the part of professional baseball could protect an umpire from such abuses. The irony was all the more galling because it was generally agreed in baseball circles that "good umpiring is essential to the life of baseball."

For those concerned with what was perceived to be the overall erosion of authority in society, umpire abuse was a reinforcing symbol. The context for such abuse was a climate of rowdiness, marred by violence and dirty tactics among players, fights among fans, and even fisticuffs between fans and players. The ganging up of both fans and players on umpires was yet further proof to the respectable classes in urban and rural regions alike that professional baseball was a sport of ruffians, and drew to itself obnoxious and dangerous elements.

WOMEN AND BASEBALL

From the very early days of baseball in America, women were involved. Initially, they were spectators. The Brooklyn *Daily Eagle* of August 4, 1859, reported on a game between two local teams that "was witnessed by a large number of people, most of whom were ladies." In the 1860s, Evette Griffore, a player on the Detroit River Belles Ladies Vintage Base Ball Club, stated that "baseball outside of school was a highly rough, physical sport for men, and it frequently got violent and unruly at a match. Team owners thought it would calm the men down to a more gentlemanly form of play if women were permitted to attend." She went on to say that a community baseball game became one spot where a woman could be with men, sans chaperones. "For once they had the freedom to be in a public space, hollering and drinking beer in public with the men in the crowd."

Women had played baseball at both the amateur and professional levels. The *Daily Kansas Tribune* in Lawrence reported in July 1867 that a women's baseball team had been created in Niles, Michigan. Teams were subsequently formed in Coldwater, Michigan, Plymouth, Indiana, and in other American towns. Most notable were various clubs known as the "Bloomer Girls" that barnstormed around the country, playing against not only other women's clubs, but men's teams as well. Some of the teams included both men and women, with the men appropriately attired in wigs. There were also teams of African American women. In 1867, a team known as the Dolly Vardens barnstormed the country and provided theatrical enjoyment by playing the game in red calico dresses.

CHALLENGES TO THE SUPREMACY OF THE NATIONAL LEAGUE

The National League's change in heart was due unquestionably to the emergence of a rival league that did not hold to the National League's so-called "high standards." The American Association, formed in 1882, structured its constitution after the National League's, but allowed for some degree of revenue sharing. It parted company from the Nationals in that the new league allowed Sunday baseball, charged a cheaper admission fee of 25 cents, and sold liquor at ballpark grounds. The latter point was not surprising, considering that large amounts of brewery money had been invested in the league. At the same time, on pain of expulsion, clubs were forbidden to allow betting on their grounds, and the league came down hard on teams that sanctioned "dishonest play" or permitted drunkenness. As so many other professional baseball associations, the "Beer and Whiskey League" (as the American Association was called) had a short life. It was gone after 1891.

One of two other brief challenges to the National League came from the Union Association, formed in 1884. The league included clubs from Baltimore, Boston, Chicago, Cincinnati, Philadelphia, St. Louis, Washington, and Altoona, Pennsylvania. The association signed players who were under contract with other major league clubs, which unsurprisingly became the object of much litigation. The association lasted only a year. Franchise shifts, bankruptcies, and the threat of blacklisting by National League owners caused some players to change their minds about jumping to the Union Association.

The other challenge came in response to the parsimonious policies of the owners, when the players banded together to form their own league in 1890. The plan of the so-called Players' League called for pooling gate receipts, from which operating expenses and players' salaries would be paid. Share-and-share-alike socialism has rarely profited within the bounds of American capitalism, and the Players' League was no exception. Similar to the Union Association, it disbanded after one season when league clubs lost their financial backing. In 1891, the National League asserted its monopoly by incorporating the defunct

American Association, expanding to 12 teams. Over the next decade, the league became a byword for factionalism, monopoly, and dishonest practices.

CREATION OF THE RESERVE CLAUSE

The previously cited league meeting in Buffalo was further significant, in that the owners introduced a reserve clause that would become one of the hallmarks of professional baseball. The **reserve clause** *was part of a player contract that stated the rights to players were retained by the team upon the contract's expiration. Players under these contracts were not free to enter into another contract with another team.* The idea, originally formulated in 1879, was to hold salaries down by reserving the five best players on each club, thus guaranteeing them a job, but making them ineligible to sign contracts with other teams. By the mid-1880s, the policy was expanded by club owners to include all players. Since all contracts were uniform, except for salary designations, the reserve clause would apply to every club. Players could be retained by a team, even though they had not been paid a salary or were unable to play. Such was the case of Charles Foley, who missed the entire 1883 season and received no pay during his illness. Nevertheless, the Buffalo team, which held his contract, refused to sign him or release him from the reserved list. Opposition to the reserve clause generated a growing movement to cap players' salaries, led by Albert Spalding, John Montgomery Ward, and eight other players in 1885 who formed the first players' union in baseball—the Brotherhood of Professional Base Ball Players. The Brotherhood offered a better on-field product, but it could not compete with the more established leagues and finally folded in 1891.

NEO-SLAVERY

The reserve clause had certain loose parallels with the practice of slavery that existed in the southern states prior to the Civil War. In both cases, the owner could dispose of his property (slaves) as he so wished. In terms of their careers, professional ballplayers were no longer free agents, having little or no room to negotiate their contracts, and were thus beholden to their employers; however, ballplayers had choices over whether to play or pursue some other field of employment. With Black slavery, there was no choice or escape, and of course Blacks, unlike ballplayers, were treated with unthinkable brutality. Within the industrial sphere, unrestricted capitalism, in theory, sanctioned the supposed freedom of a worker to choose where he or she could work, but in practice it required the worker to accept whatever employment was available under nonnegotiable conditions. **Wage slavery** *was thus seen as compulsion by industrialists, forcing factory operatives to work at starvation wages in an environment where they could be fired for the* *slightest infraction.* Similarly, women of this period endured a quasi-form of slavery. Elizabeth Cady Stanton, in her article "Home Life," argued that women who were locked into indissoluble marriages, often under the control of domineering husbands, could be characterized as "slaves" to the institution of marriage. It is important to note that neither ballplayers, factory workers, or women were really slaves in the usual sense of the word. More accurately, they were treated as dependents to the institutions of which they were apart.

FIGURE 4.6 The Eymard Seminarian team after its victory over Don Bosco in 1900.

SUMMARY

Late 19th-century America marked an important departure from a country that was primarily an agricultural nation to one marked by the growth of corporations, trusts, and heavy industry. What fueled this economic transformation was the expansion of capitalism that invested wealth, much of it generated through slavery, into industrial production. Large industries developed vertically, whereby one corporation would control the entire process of production and distribution, and horizontally whereby an industry would successfully drive out competition by hook or by crook.

This period also marked the expansion of towns and cities due to immigration and migration from the countryside. The new working class, which was the largest social class by far, was exploited by the capitalist system. The workers banded together to form unions, first the Knights of Labor and later the American Federation of Labor. The United States experienced a great degree of industrial strife and violence that pitted the working class against their bosses and their lackeys.

Organized baseball evolved in the 1870s as a professional sport through creation of the National League that placed franchises in a number of major cities. At the same time, power was transferred from the players to the owners, who introduced a reserve clause that bound a player to a team for the duration of his playing career. The game was marred by drunkenness, gambling, and violence that mirrored such activities in the wider society.

STUDY QUESTIONS

1. To what extent did vertical integration and horizontal integration characterize the capitalist contradiction?
2. Compare and contrast the ideological views of William Graham Sumner, Henry George, Edward Bellamy, and George McNeill with respect to the problem of social inequality in America.
3. Baseball has been characterized as a "clean sport." Discuss some of the problems experienced by professional baseball clubs in the 19th century that belied that characterization?

Credits

Progressivism and the Age of Reform

HISTORICAL BACKGROUND

The harsh inequities of the industrial system, brought on by unregulated capitalism after the Civil War, led to a reaction known as the progressive movement. Whereas the seeds of reform can be traced to the 1880s, the most notable changes occurred over the first two decades of the 20th century. Reform was widespread, and touched many political, economic, and social spheres of life. Since America was a "bottom-up society," such efforts were largely local initiatives involving charitable and voluntary organizations, and municipal and state governments. At the same time, progressivism can easily be overstated. The tides of history are slow moving and for many people life remained the same, with only moderate alterations. The question is, How progressive was progressivism?

WHAT IS PROGRESSIVISM?

The so-called progressive period dates roughly from 1900 to the end of the First World War; however, there was some overlapping. What constituted progressivism is a very broad question that has no simple answer. Suffice to say, the main objectives of the **progressive** movement were *eliminating problems caused by industrialization, urbanization, immigration, and political corruption.* Essentially, it involved an effort to streamline institutions and correct the imbalances wrought by industrialization.

Standardization

Standardization can be defined as *the process of making something conform to a standard.*

One ongoing characteristic of the progressive era, resulting from an expanding and complex industrial economy, was the trend toward standardizing every aspect of social life. The model of standardization was encapsulated in the idea of scientific management put forth by Frederick Winslow Taylor. Scientific management was all about efficiency and expertise and was best characterized by the assembly line, which broke down the manufacturing process into discrete, measurable units that would incorporate maximum efficiency with the least amount of effort. Henry Ford, who in 1908 established the highly profitable Ford Motor Company, employed scientific management to the utmost in turning out cheap and highly profitable motor cars. Other industries quickly followed suit.

Standardization also galvanized the use of statistics to quantify and measure social life, from population composition to the level of one's intelligence. The social sciences derived a better understanding of the nature of society through statistics. Robert Park developed a model of urban ecology in Chicago through the use of data, through which he was able to map the city based upon economic activity, ethnicity, and moral behavior. Statistics gave rise to complex bureaucracies in all spheres of life, creating new occupations that catered to a rising middle class.

In response to the chaotic and unregulated development of the industrial city, the idea of urban planning emerged, centering on the improved use of space, building codes, and the implementation of public utilities, including municipal sewer systems, clean water conduits, better street lighting, and transportation systems. Furthermore, urban planning led to the creation of parks and open spaces, contributing greatly to the improved quality of life in fast-growing metropolitan areas.

Industrial Reform

During the early decades of the 20th century, a number of social critics called muckrakers set about exposing the abuses, squalor, and corruption of the capitalist industrial system. Given that most Americans at this time lived very parochial and private lives, muckrakers brought to light the darker side of life through photographs, journal articles, and novels. **Muckrakers** refers to *those who delve into and publish scandal and allegations of corruption among political and business leaders.* For many city dwellers, poverty and squalor was hidden from view even to those who lived in close proximity to these districts. In 1912 alone, more than a thousand articles appeared in popular weekly magazines such as *Collier's, McClure's,* and the *Saturday Evening Post.* Among the muckrakers was Lewis Hine, who passed through the slums of New York City photographing homeless children. A series of articles in 1904 by Lincoln Steffens chronicled urban blight and corruption. Ida Tarbell provided an exposé on the illegal and immoral practices of the Standard Oil Company. In Theodore Dreiser's novel, *Sister Carrie,* he tells the story of a young woman from Wisconsin who moves to Chicago and is compromised by the characters she meets. The socialist Upton Sinclair wrote about the unsanitary and dehumanizing conditions in Chicago's meatpacking industry. His novel, *The Jungle,* published in 1906, ultimately led to passage of the Meat Inspection Act. Frank Norris, in his book, *The Octopus,* described the battle between farmers, ranchers, and the powerful railroad interests in California.

FIGURE 5.1 Lewis Hine photo of young "breaker boys" set to work in a Pennsylvania coal mine.

Knowledge of such abuses led to a series of reform efforts. Improvements were often the result of tragic events. A fire in the building housing the Triangle Shirtwaist Company in New York City on March 25, 1911, for instance, resulted in the deaths of 146 garment workers, mostly immigrant girls in their teens. This tragedy came in the wake of a series of unsuccessful strikes against intolerable conditions in factories and sweatshops, reflecting a growing discontent among impoverished workers. The reality of this tragedy galvanized support for legislative action. In the years that followed, New York State became a pioneer in legislation to regulate and enforce rules pertaining to working hours, workers' safety, child labor, and fire regulations. These laws became a model for other states to follow.

The passage of legislation aimed at regulating factories led to an expanded notion of liberty, giving greater freedom to workers. John Mitchell, head of the United Mine Workers of America union, observed that while the Declaration of Independence proclaimed civil and political liberty, it did not establish industrial or economic liberty. A person could not be free, he noted, if they were forced to work long hours under inhuman conditions and lacked the basic necessities for a comfortable life. What Mitchell meant by industrial liberty was really what we have defined as freedom, since the rights he was referring to were collective rights, such as the eight-hour work day—entitlements for the many and not just the few, which went beyond personal freedom.

Social Reform

Grassroots efforts arose to assist the swelling immigrant population in large cities. Thirteen million immigrants came to the United States between 1901 and 1914, mostly from southern and eastern Europe. Insofar as many of these immigrants were poor, illiterate, without connections, and from nations with different languages and customs, their needs were addressed to some extent by settlement houses. These agencies were pioneered by Jane Addams and Florence Kelley, and provided a range of social services, from food and clothing to lessons in hygiene, cooking, child care, language instruction, and even legal services. Settlement houses formed the basis for the social work profession, which not only served basic needs, but instilled middle-class values and provided statistical data that generated other changes and enabled a greater measure of social control.

FIGURE 5.2 Striking textile workers of different nationalities in Lawrence, Massachusetts, opposed by the state militia, 1912.

The reform spirit of the progressive movement also contributed to improvements in local government. Many large municipalities were governed by political machines that doled civil service "jobs for the boys," pocketed vast sums of public money through a variety of illegal practices, turned a blind eye to corruption by the police and other public officials, and generally sought to maintain the status quo. In response, reformers worked for a more open government by establishing primary elections and creating civil service exams to ensure open competition for municipal jobs, thus providing for a meritocracy. Reformers also worked to pass laws against immoral and corrupt practices by public officials. While the push for reform made some headway during the early decades of the 20th century, the grip of the political machines on local government continued over a number of decades and relaxed only gradually.

UNIONS AND INDUSTRIAL ACTION

Class warfare, a pervasive characteristic of industrial life during the late 19th century, accelerated during the progressive era. Within a three-year period, from 1898 to 1901, the number of strikes in the United States rose from 1,839 to 3,012. Industrial unrest correlated with the ebb and flow of the business cycle. When times were hard, and workers faced unemployment or a severe cut in pay, agitation was the most pronounced.

While the skilled craft workers were protected to some degree by the American Federation of Labor (AFL), the vast armies of unskilled workers went unprotected and were easily victimized by their employers. Some of these workers were covered by industry-specific unions, such as the United Mine Workers, who were more willing to speak out against industrial abuses. Radical trade unionists, such as Mother Mary Jones and Bill Haywood, joined in 1905 to create the Industrial Workers of the World (IWW), which advocated confrontational tactics along with anarchist ideals. As the protector of the oppressed, the IWW offered an alternative to the unbridled system of free enterprise. From its inception, the IWW openly challenged factory owners, the police, and public authorities. There followed a whole series of industrial actions, including a strike of the New Orleans dock workers during the Panic (Depression) of 1907, the successful strike of the Lawrence, Massachusetts, woolen mill workers in 1912, and the Paterson, New Jersey, silk weavers' strike in 1913. The Ludlow Massacre on April 20, 1914, in which the governor of Colorado sent in troops against striking miners, killing 13 women and children in their encampment, demonstrated the brutality of the authorities in suppressing labor unrest.

Challenges to the capitalist system also came from the Socialist Party, formed in 1901, which believed in common ownership and democratic management of the means of producing the necessities of life. The Socialists on the state and national levels gradually increased their membership and political clout, largely from the immigrant working class. The Socialist Party reached the high point of popularity in 1912, when its candidate for president, Eugene V. Debs, garnered nearly a million votes. The Socialists had some further electoral success at the state and municipal levels. Often, they were joined in demonstrations and public meetings by the anarchists who were opposed to any form of government that undermined fundamental rights and freedoms. Together they provided a specter of fear for those in power. Although a fringe movement, socialism spoke to fundamental American ideals. Upton Sinclair, in his novel *The Jungle*, defined **socialism** as *the common ownership and democratic management of the means of producing the necessities of life.* What is inferred here is that socialism is more compatible with democracy than is capitalism.

PROGRESSIVISM ON THE NATIONAL LEVEL

During the two decades of the progressive era, three presidents—Theodore Roosevelt (1901-1908), William Howard Taft (1908-1912), and Woodrow Wilson (1912-1920)—occupied the White House. Roosevelt, who became president after the assassination of William McKinley by an anarchist in Buffalo, New York, on September 5, 1901, was a proponent of the active life. Following a career in New York politics, where he was seen as a progressive, Roosevelt brought to the White House a reforming spirit. He joined with those progressives opposing the abusive power of large trusts. Differentiating between what he considered "good and bad trusts," he used the authority of his office under the Sherman Antitrust Act of 1890 to go after the latter, most notably the Standard Oil Company and the Northern Securities Trust.

FIGURE 5.3 Mothers with babies outside Margaret Sanger's birth control clinic in Brooklyn, 1916.

Roosevelt also proved to be a friend to labor. When the miners in northeastern Pennsylvania walked off the job on May 12, 1902, demanding an eight-hour day, a 20% increase in wages, and official recognition of the United Mine Workers, Roosevelt stood by them. A settlement was reached after the president threatened to use troops to take over the mines and create a commission to investigate mining conditions. Ultimately, the strike resulted in a partial victory for these workers.

National responses to progressive demands took a back seat during the Taft administration. The former Ohio governor was more conservative than Roosevelt and was sympathetic to business interests. The Republicans' hold on the presidency was broken after the Progressive Party, formed by Roosevelt, split the Republican vote in 1912, allowing the Democratic candidate, Woodrow Wilson, to become president. Wilson sought to restore balance (competition) to the economy. Under his administration, Congress passed the Clayton Antitrust Act (1914), prohibited interlocking directories, and exempted trade unions from prosecution under the Sherman Antitrust Act. Other progressive legislation, such as the Adamson Act, which established an eight-hour day for railroad workers, the Meat Inspection Act, the Pure Food and Drug Act, and creation of a Federal Trade Commission to investigate questionable business practices, all came to pass during the Wilson presidency.

CONSTITUTIONAL AMENDMENTS

During the progressive period, Congress enacted four constitutional amendments. The 16th amendment gave Congress the power to levy a federal income tax, indicating that the federal government was taking on greater responsibilities, including passage of legislation to protect the public and to promote and regulate interstate commerce. This was brought on by the necessity of dealing with issues confronted by an expanding industrial economy. The same year (1913), Congress passed the 17th amendment, enabling election to the U.S. Senate by popular vote. Previously, senators had been selected by the legislators of each state. This amendment coincided with other measures enacted by state legislatures, particularly in the western states, making government more responsive to the people. Six years later, after the First World War, pressure from anti-alcohol lobbying groups, such as the Anti-Saloon League, brought about prohibition that outlawed the manufacture, sale, or transportation of intoxicating liquors. This amendment, and the Volstead Act that made it a law, had disastrous consequences and was repealed in 1933. The last of the progressive constitutional amendments, the 19th amendment, extended the right to vote to women. Several states, particularly in the West, had allowed women's suffrage in state and local elections but now women throughout the country could vote in every election.

BASEBALL

The period covering the rise of professional baseball through the progressive years and the First World War is known as the Dead Ball era. This term refers not only to a time when a less lively baseball was used, but also to a style of play that relied on speed, aggressiveness, and what is referred to as "small ball," as opposed to a reliance on the long ball, or home run. Typifying this style of play were position players such as Ty Cobb, Honus Wagner, Napoleon Lajoie, and Mike Kelly, along with pitchers such as Christy Mathewson and Cy Young, considered by many to be among the game's greatest stars.

BASEBALL: THE TRUSTS AND A CHALLENGE

By the turn of the century, baseball was big business. Clubs were owned by moguls who, similar to the robber barons of the previous age, ran their teams in the spirit of laissez-faire enterprises. Dating from the 1890s, the National League, which had driven the Players' League and the Union League out of business, consisted of 12 teams, later reduced to eight for financial reasons, allowing the fittest clubs to survive. Throughout the decade, National League owners exercised a near monopoly over their players. Moreover, the owners often controlled shares in other teams and freely exchanged players and franchises to their financial advantage.

Of all the National League magnates, the most notorious was Andrew Freedman, the owner of the New York Giants. Freedman, as the rest of the owners, had other business operations and saw owning a baseball club as a means to promote those interests. Apart from alienating his players and running his franchise into the ground, Freedman proposed an elaborate trust scheme, enabling owners to move franchises at will and to peddle players, much as pawns on a chess board, to maximize profits. The plan, proposed by Freedman in conjunction with Cincinnati Reds owner John T. Brush, would create a cartel, by which the trust would be divided into preferred and common stock. This would provide a dividend of 7% that would go to the National League as a body. Profits from the common stock would be divided among the clubs as such: The Giants would control one third of the share, with 12% each going to club owners closely allied to Freedman and Brush, and the remainder divided among the four other National League owners. Mercifully, such an unfair scheme never came to fruition.

The National League soon received a challenge from an unexpected source. Bancroft (Ban) Johnson, a baseball writer, used his influence and connections to acquire the minor Western League and built it up on the basis of signing the best players possible. He also promised to "clean up the game" that had fallen to the depths of violence and unsportsmanlike behavior during the 1890s. In 1900, he changed the name of the Western League to the American League. Johnson soon found men who were willing to put money into the new league. The new owners then actively began to recruit players from the National League, which they did by paying higher salaries. In addition, the American League installed teams in cities such as Boston, Chicago, St. Louis, Philadelphia, and eventually New York, which were already occupied by National League clubs. Lawsuits inevitably followed, and the war over players and ballparks lasted two years. When the dust settled, both leagues agreed on a compromise. Professional baseball would be governed by a three-man committee comprising the presidents of each league and a jointly appointed third commissioner. Each league agreed to honor the contracts of the other and would coordinate schedules and adopt the same playing rules.

The first World Series between the two leagues was played in 1903 between the American League Boston Pilgrims (later to become the Red Sox) and the National League Pittsburgh Pirates. Bad feelings between the American and National League were still evident the following year, when the New York Giants refused to take on the American League pennant–winning Boston club, contending that as the representative of the premier league, they would not condescend to play a "minor league" team. Nevertheless, a precedent had been established. Of the 13 years from 1905 to 1918, the American League won the World Series nine times, thus establishing a degree of dominance.

FIGURE 5.4 Lewis Hine photo of a baseball team of young glass workers in Indiana, 1908.

The "trust issue" popped up again in March 1912, when U.S. Congressman Thomas Gallagher, a Democrat from Illinois, charged that baseball was a combination in restraint of trade. He introduced a resolution in the House of Representatives calling for creation of a seven-man committee to engage in a thorough review of baseball operations, specifically the National Commission and the various leagues that operated under the National Agreement of 1903. Gallagher was quoted as saying that the baseball trust was "the most audacious and autocratic combination of them all." In the court of public opinion, Gallagher's frontal attack on "the great national pastime" fell like a lead balloon. Newspaper editorials and letters, some from the owners, presented the business side of the question, arguing that players were free agents and well paid for their services. Without the reserve clause, the reasoning went, owners could not afford to pay such high salaries. Garry Herrmann, head of baseball's National Commission, compared the work of the commission to the Supreme Court, with its powers limited to interpreting the rules and settling cases within its jurisdiction. The difference was that the Supreme Court adjudicated cases in light of the Constitution, whereas baseball's governing body was held to no such standard.

BASEBALL AND URBAN COMMUNITIES

It was during the progressive period that Major League Baseball became a fixture in the urban communities increasingly dominated by immigrants. Baseball fields were part of the trend toward creating parks and open spaces within crowded cities. New permanent state-of-the-art stadiums made of steel and concrete instead of wood were built, including Forbes Field in Pittsburgh and Shibe Park in Philadelphia (1909), Comiskey Park in Chicago (1910), Fenway Park in Boston (1912), Ebbets Field in Brooklyn (1913), and Wrigley Field in Chicago (1914). Both Fenway Park and Wrigley Field are still home to major league teams. These new stadiums did not pop up out of the blue. Building codes enacted as part of the municipal reform movement stipulated that ballparks had to conform to more stringent codes, so as to prevent fires and the collapse of grandstands that had seriously injured patrons in the past.

FIGURE 5.5 Fans at the Polo Grounds gathered on October 8, 1908, for a crucial game between the Giants and Chicago Cubs.

These new parks, nestled into city neighborhoods, became focal points of community life for decades. Players were generally seen as part of the community, and many either owned homes in ballpark neighborhoods or lived in nearby boarding houses. Thus, players and fans often interacted with one another. Major and minor league teams reflected the parochial nature of American society prior to the First World War, when one's primary focus was more on their race, ethnicity, neighborhood, town, or county, and less on having a national identity.

MORAL REFORM AND SOCIAL MOBILITY

In keeping with the spirit of the times, baseball was caught up in a wave of moral reform. Many states, particularly those in the Northeast, had stringent blue laws that prohibited activity, particularly commercial activity, on Sundays. These laws were perpetuated by the efforts of Protestant religious groups that sought to uphold the sanctity of the Sabbath. Over time, the laws affecting Sunday baseball were amended—though it was not until 1929 and 1934 that professional games were allowed in Boston and the two major league cities in Pennsylvania, respectively. Generally speaking, the rowdiness and on-field violence that marred professional baseball in the 1890s abated somewhat during the progressive era, in part due to the efforts of Ban Johnson and certain owners. Sports gambling, however, continued to be a problem during this time.

FIGURE 5.6 A 1914 Federal League game at Brooklyn's Washington Park between the Buffalo Bisons and Brooklyn Tip Tops.

While baseball had its issues, it enjoyed great popularity, especially among the working classes. For the players, some of whom were drawn from the industrial masses, baseball was a form of upward mobility. Men such as Stanley Coveleski literally came out of the coal mines in Pennsylvania to play professional baseball in a career that spanned 13 seasons. Jimmy Austin, who was born in Swansea, Wales, came to the United States when he was eight years old. As the oldest of eight children, he became a machinist-apprentice before turning his attention to baseball. Joe Wood emerged from a small town in western Kansas to become one of the dominant pitchers of his time. Others, including Harry Hooper, who was a teammate of Wood in Boston, had a college degree in civil engineering.

THE FEDERAL LEAGUE AND ITS CHALLENGE TO BASEBALL'S MONOPOLY

The dominance by the American and National leagues was briefly interrupted by formation of the Federal League that fielded teams during the 1914 and 1915 seasons, and in cities where big-league clubs already existed. From the start, the Federal League was faced with a number of challenges in its attempt to lure top players by driving up salaries and securing adequate playing fields. The Brooklyn entry into the Federal League hoped to solve the latter problem by leasing the old Washington Park that had been vacated by the National League Dodgers. Unfortunately, new municipal building codes required extensive renovations before it could be used again for baseball.

Stymied by the monopoly exercised by both major leagues, the Chicago entry into the Federal League (ChiFeds) initiated an antitrust suit against organized baseball under the Sherman Antitrust Act. The case came before a federal judge, Kenesaw Mountain Landis (later baseball commissioner), who dragged his feet on the case, hoping for an out-of-court settlement. By the end of 1915, the Federal League magnates had run out of money and were forced to disband.

FIGURE 5.7 Forbes Field, Pittsburgh, 1909.

The antitrust issue emerged again seven years later, in 1922, when the matter was taken up by the U.S. Supreme Court. The case, which proved to be baseball's most important legal decision during the 20th century, involved a claim for compensation by the Baltimore club of the defunct Federal League against Major League Baseball. Baltimore's argument was that organized baseball was controlling a relatively limited supply of talented players, thus establishing a monopoly in defiance of the antitrust laws. Since a number of major and minor league teams played one another in different states, it was reasonable to conclude that they were subject to rulings by the Interstate Commerce Commission. Thus, it would seem that Baltimore had a clear-cut case of antitrust violation.

The Supreme Court, however, saw things differently. Justice Oliver Wendell Holmes presided over the unanimous decision in rejecting the plaintiff's case. While admitting that baseball was a business, the justices took a very narrow interpretation of interstate commerce. Since baseball was not food or some other tangible product, it was put into the category of exhibitions for profit. Personal effort, not related to production, could not be construed as commerce. Not being subject to interstate commerce prohibitions nullified further consideration by the Court for baseball being a trust, which remains so to the present day.

SUMMARY

It could be said that the progressive period in American history was largely an effort to correct the abuses brought on by unregulated capitalism. Reform spread across the board. Cities introduced a number of sanitary and public health measures to make urban life more livable. Factory regulation took aim at limiting working hours, installing safety measures, and controlling the labor of women and children. While progressive legislation was primarily at the state and local levels, the federal government stepped in to pass laws aimed at public safety. The focus on personal freedom (liberty) was gradually shifting toward freedom, or recognition that people had collective economic rights and political rights.

Organized baseball experienced a challenge from a new league, the American League, which together formed into a trust. This trust was challenged by a rival, the Federal League, which was successful for a couple of years until it folded due to a lack of funds. With the demise of the Federal League, one of the teams, the Baltimore club, which was not compensated, took the major leagues to court charging that they were operating as a trust and therefore unlawful. The matter reached the Supreme Court in 1922, which decided against the Baltimore suit and ruled that baseball was entertainment, not a business (which it was), and therefore was not in violation of the Sherman Anti-Trust Law.

STUDY QUESTIONS

1. In what way did progressivism expand the idea of liberty to include a broader range of rights we have defined as freedom?
2. Is it correct to say that socialism is more compatible with democracy than is capitalism? Why or why not?
3. If baseball was a trust, why would the Supreme Court in its 1922 decision think otherwise? Was it right to do so? Why or why not?

Credits

Fig. 5.1: Lewis Hine, "Breaker Boys," http://www.loc.gov/pictures/item/ncl2004000118/PP/, 1908.

Fig. 5.2: "Striking Textile Workers in Lawrence, Massachusetts," 1912.

Fig. 5.3: Planned Parenthood of New York City, "Margaret Sanger's Birth Control Clinic," 1916.

Fig. 5.4: Lewis Hine, "Baseball Team Composed of Young Glass Workers," http://www.loc.gov/pictures/item/ncl2004000115/PP/, 1908.

Fig. 5.5: Bain News Service, " Crowd at Cubs vs. Giants Game in Polo Grounds," http://www.loc.gov/pictures/item/ggb2004002322/, 1908.

Fig. 5.6: Bain News Service, "Federal League Game at Brooklyn's Washington Park," http://www.loc.gov/pictures/item/2008677275/, 1914.

Fig. 5.7: "Forbes Field," http://www.loc.gov/pictures/item/95503573/, 1909.

CHAPTER 6

Imperialism and the First World War

HISTORICAL BACKGROUND

The progressive period overlapped entry of the United States into the First World War in 1917. While progressivism reformed domestic institutions and created a regulatory environment for American capitalism, the world war constituted an important landmark in the evolution of America's role in world affairs. As an expansionist nation, at first internally and then externally, the United States entered the 20th century as an imperialist power, alongside the great colonizing countries (Britain, France, Germany, and Russia) in Europe. Former U.S. Marine Corps Major General Smedley D. Butler observed in reference to the Spanish-American War that "war is a racket." Consider what was meant by this statement and how might it apply to American imperialism and the First World War?

BACKGROUND ON IMPERIALISM

The Spanish-American War (1898–1902) occurred when the spirit of nationalism had reached a high point. The centennial celebrations in 1876 had generated much patriotic enthusiasm that carried over into subsequent decades. Historian Frederick Jackson Turner published an important essay in 1893, "The Significance of the Frontier in American History," in which he argued that, by 1890, the frontier had closed, and the United States was a settled nation from coast to coast. The aggressive desire to acquire more and more property, characteristic of a settler society, played into the idea of manifest destiny, which was a form of internal imperialism. The emergence of a popular press, known as "yellow journalism," began publishing shrill and sensational stories, including not only lurid crimes, but also jingoistic tales of Spain's atrocities against its colonists in Cuba and other regions of Latin America. Many articles, either directly or indirectly, advocated American military intervention. Another factor was race. The White, largely Protestant native population of the

United States, descended from northern European stock, saw the peoples of the world through a racial lens. They, of course, believed themselves to be at the top of the food chain, with "lesser races"—the Latin "race," Asians, indigenous peoples, and Blacks—lower down. The implication was that it was "the White man's burden" to educate and civilize those further down the chain, especially those categorized as "savages" at the bottom.

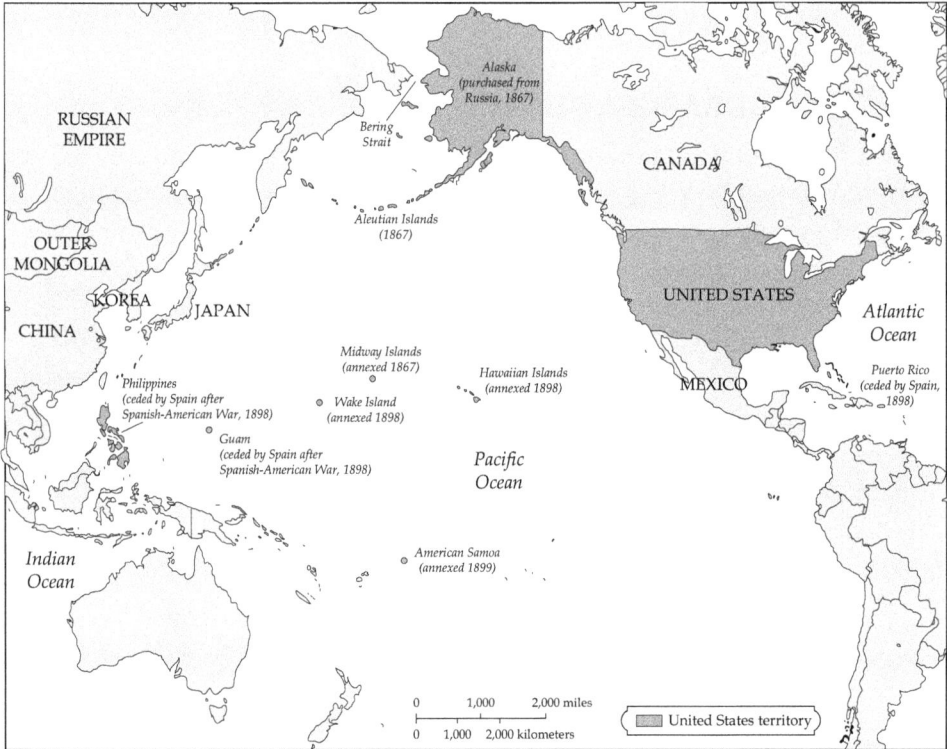

MAP 6.1 The American Colonial Empire, 1898

American capitalists and industrialists by the 1890s were also casting their eyes overseas in search of foreign markets and followed the dictum that "the flag follows the dollar," or vice versa. Hence, the United States did not become an imperialist nation in a vacuum.

MAP 6.2 The United States Interventions in the Caribbean, 1898–1934

SPANISH-AMERICAN WAR

The war in Cuba was fought by the United States in the name of supporting the indigenous Cuban rebels in their efforts to throw off the yoke of Spanish colonial domination, which had been declining for some time. On June 22, 1890, 17,000 U.S. troops landed in Cuba, and "this pleasant little war," as Secretary of State John Hay called it, lasted only three weeks. The Spanish surrendered on July 17. Curiously, the "yellow press" portrayed the Cubans as White freedom fighters when they were struggling to defeat the Spanish, and as submissive Blacks once the war was over. The racial composition of Cuba lent itself to a form of imposed segregation that conformed to American racial policy.

The conquerors provided the Cubans with the Teller Amendment, stating that they would have their own independent government. This dictum was compromised by the **Platt Amendment** (1901), which *required Cuba to allow the United States a naval base at Guantanamo Bay, and gave the United States the right to engage in military operations "to protect life, property, and individual rights," so defined.* This important document would serve as a cornerstone of American foreign policy and would later be extended and amended. Shortly after American troops conquered Cuba, the U.S. Army landed in Puerto Rico, also a Spanish colony, where they met only token opposition.

FIGURE 6.1 A 1899 cartoon from *Puck* showing Uncle Sam "civilizing" unkempt and unruly Black colonials while White Americans sit studiously in the back.

By means of the Treaty of Paris, signed on December 10, 1898, Spain relinquished its claim to Cuba, and the United States received Puerto Rico and certain Pacific islands, including Guam and the Philippines. The question of what to do with the Philippines loomed large. President William McKinley was said to have gotten down on his knees and prayed for a solution to this dilemma. In the end, he concluded that the United States must permanently occupy the islands and govern the native peoples "for their own good." The Filipinos didn't get the same message and embarked on a guerrilla war against the United States, which lasted until 1902, when superior American firepower finally tipped the balance. The Philippines remained under U.S. control until 1946.

For those who had climbed on the imperialist bandwagon, the Spanish-American War provided a series of outposts for future American economic domination. Senator Albert Beveridge of Indiana defended imperialism, stating that the economic future of the country would be based on trade with China, and that the possession of Oriental ports was vital to that future. "The Pacific is our ocean," he said. Beveridge also believed that the English-speaking Teutonic peoples were meant to be masters of the world and to establish order where chaos reigns. The Reverend Charles Ames, representing the anti-imperialist movement, offered a number of counterarguments, citing that imperialism puts the country in a state of perpetual warfare and that the American principles of liberty, equality, and self-determination were undermined by such a policy. He also stated that imperialism threatens to change the temper of a people by making them more arrogant, testy, and defiant of other nations.

FIGURE 6.2 Cartoon of President Theodore Roosevelt as the world policeman standing between the peoples of Europe and nonWhite colonials while waving his large stick at the latter group.

HEMISPHERIC IMPERIALISM

Charles Ames was correct in stating that imperialism leads to perpetual war. In the decades following the Spanish-American War, between 1900 and 1925, the United States intervened militarily in Latin America—no fewer than 24 times—to protect its economic interests, combat insurgents, and overthrow uncooperative governments. President Theodore Roosevelt issued what came to be known as the **Roosevelt Corollary**, stating that *the United States exercised the right to use police power to control the Western Hemisphere.* To back this up, he strengthened the American Navy and conspired with Panamanian rebels to defeat the ruling Colombian government, a prelude to securing rights to building the Panama Canal.

Presidents William Howard Taft and Woodrow Wilson were no less imperialistic. Taft landed troops in Honduras and Nicaragua in 1912 to protect American corporate interests; the U.S. presence remained there until 1925. Wilson, in response to political instability (resulting in several coups and an assassination), sent U.S. troops into Mexico to teach them "to elect good men." Wilson, the moralist, reiterated another pillar of American imperial policy, called the **moral imperative,** which was *to raise and civilize peoples in Latin American countries (and other places in the world) by instilling in them the lessons of democracy and free-market capitalism.*

FIRST WORLD WAR

On June 28, 1914, a Serb nationalist, Gavrilo Princip, assassinated Archduke Franz Ferdinand, the heir to the throne of the Austro-Hungarian Empire, which set off a chain of events leading to the First World War. The war was the culmination of growing militarism, national pride, colonial tensions, secret treaties, and an alliance system that pledged states within the alliance to declare war if a member state was attacked. The declaration of war by Austria-Hungary on Serbia triggered a reaction that led to Russian mobilization (in support of its Slavic neighbors). Germany, an ally of Austria, mobilized for war, which led its archenemy, France, to enter into battle on the side of Russia. After German troops marched into neutral Belgium, Britain joined the fray on the side of France and Russia. Soon all of Europe was at war. For the most part, the First World War would be a European war, although soldiers from the colonies of many combatant nations participated.

FIGURE 6.3 Anti-German propaganda poster during the First World War.

Initially, the United States saw no reason to become involved in what it considered to be a European conflict. Indeed, Woodrow Wilson was elected for a second term as president partly on the slogan, "He kept us out of war." As the war progressed, Germany took a more aggressive stance in attacking neutral shipping through submarine warfare. The 1916 sinking of the British ocean liner *Lusitania*, off the coast of Ireland, carrying American passengers along with military supplies, soured many Americans on Germany. This act, coupled with the relentless indiscriminate attack on shipping, neutral and combative alike, was the prime reason for the U.S. entry into the world war. There was also the matter of the Zimmermann telegram in which the German foreign minister, Alfred Zimmermann, sent a message to the Mexican government stating that in the event of a war with the United States, Germany would help Mexico recover the territories taken during the Mexican War. Moreover, it was revealed years later that several of the large commercial banks had loaned millions of dollars to Britain and its allies, which was an incentive to give these nations additional military support. Industrialists saw the possibility of profiting from the war through large government contracts, and so were willing to push Congress to declare war.

On April 2, 1917, President Wilson went before Congress to declare war on Germany. The war dramatically expanded the powers of the state, which gave itself intrusive powers to dominate whole spheres of domestic life. The Selective Service Act required all able-bodied men to register for the draft. New agencies appeared, including the War Industries Board, to supervise all aspects of war production; the Railroad Administration, to govern the nation's transport system; the Fuel Agency, which rationed coal and oil supplies; the Food Administration, to maximize and regulate farm production; and the War Labor Board, consisting of representatives of government and industry, to help stabilize the economy and ensure full employment. Demands put forth by organized labor for a minimum wage and shorter working hours were achieved in industries receiving government contracts.

Mobilization for war also brought into play an unprecedented amount of propaganda to convince the American people that joining forces with their allies was the right thing to do. There emerged a number of local patriotic societies that served to whip up war fever. President Wilson created the Committee on Public Information (CPI) to sponsor speakers to travel the country and talk up the war effort. The American Alliance for Labor and Democracy established 164 branches aimed at getting the labor movement behind the war effort. Patriotic symbols such as the American flag, the Statue of Liberty, and the Liberty Bell appeared on storefronts, in homes, and on public buildings. Much propaganda was directed against all things German, including German Americans, who, although constituting the second-largest ethnic group in the country, became the object of wide-scale discrimination—and in a number of cases, violence.

WARTIME COERCION AND THE QUESTION OF LIBERTY VS. SECURITY

Xenophobic nationalism and patriotic fervor challenged constitutional liberties. There are two sorts of patriotism. **Irrational patriotism** is *a blind acceptance of the proposition "my country right or wrong," coupled with a willingness to sacrifice moral considerations to the power of the state.* This kind of support is counterpoised by **rational patriotism,** which is *an appeal to a superior moral authority, and relates love of country to principles such as freedom, liberty, equality, and justice, all incorporated into the fundamental documents of the republic.* During the First World War, the higher standard of rational patriotism was swamped by a flood of irrational patriotism. Efforts to suppress dissent centered around two pieces of legislation: the **Espionage Act of 1917**, *prohibiting interfering with the draft and making false statements that might impede military success*, and the **Sedition Act of 1918**, which *made it a crime to speak out or print statements casting contempt or scorn on the American form of government or advocating interference with the war effort.*

These two laws were, by any logical standard, unconstitutional, and were used to silence and arrest not only ordinary citizens who opposed the war, but radicals, trade unionists, anarchists, and socialists such as Eugene V. Debs and Charles Schenck. In the case of Schenck, his appeal reached the Supreme Court. Chief Justice Oliver Wendell Holmes, in upholding Schenck's conviction, along with the other justices, put forth the "clear and present danger rule," in which it was argued that the constitutional right to free speech could only be abrogated when there was a just cause—meaning a direct threat to the country—and could not be used as a blanket justification to silence dissent. Debs was not so lucky. His appeal of a charge of obstructing the war effort was sustained by the Court.

The overflow of irrational patriotism created an avalanche of coercive measures. State and local governments enacted repressive acts aimed at rooting out war dissidents and those considered radical and unpatriotic. Schools and universities discouraged opposition to the war. A series of laws known as the Lusk laws, proposed by State Senator Clayton Lusk of New York, required public school teachers to obtain a license from the state showing that they were loyal to the "institutions and laws of the country." Another of the Lusk laws authorized the courts to remove from the ballot any political organization whose doctrines violated the state or federal Constitution or preached destruction of the U.S. government.

The Department of Justice in June 1917 sponsored the American Protective League, aimed at rooting out critics of the war. The Minnesota Commission of Public Safety closed saloons and theaters and tested people for loyalty. Even the U.S. Post Office Department began taking away the mailing privileges of newspapers and magazines that printed antiwar material. The zeal to eliminate people who were different furthermore led states such as Indiana to pass laws designed to sterilize those individuals classed as feebleminded.

The year after the war ended proved a depressing period in many respects. The Russian Revolution in 1917 unleashed a communist movement that threatened to undermine the vacuum in central and eastern postwar Europe caused by the disintegration of the

Austro-Hungarian and German empires. Fear of communism would be a source of consternation to capitalist countries for decades to come. There was a worldwide influenza epidemic that led to more deaths than the 11 million that died in the war. Within the United States, there was a series of strikes in the steel and shipbuilding industries and in the mines. Even the Boston police went on strike.

With lingering hatreds and the specter of communism in the air, the government (federal, state, and local) inaugurated a "Red scare," aimed at rounding up suspected Bolshevik sympathizers and so-called "undesirable aliens" for deportation—in direct violation of the U.S. Constitution. Attorney General A. Mitchell Palmer initiated more than 500 raids that netted 249 people of Russian descent who were sent back to their country of origin. In January 1920, the Justice Department, aided by the Boston police, staged a number of predawn raids of suspected radical immigrants. Underscoring these activities was the question of what constitutes Americanism. This question would be a point of contention in the coming decade.

BASEBALL

SPREADING BASEBALL ABROAD

Even before the advent of the 20th century, baseball had reached beyond its borders to other parts of the world. On March 20, 1888, the game's principal promoter, A. G. Spalding, announced he would take a group of baseball all-stars, including a number of men from his Chicago White Stockings team, on a world tour. Spalding's tour began in November 1888 and ended the following April. It included 28 games in a variety of countries. Although the tour did much to popularize the game abroad, it was a financial disaster. But from Spalding's perspective, his losses were compensated by new markets for his sporting goods.

Spalding organized another tour in 1913–1914, billed as the "tour to end all tours." Drawing some of the top players in the game, the five-month tour, which began in Cincinnati in October 1913, traveled first to Japan, where the players competed against some good Japanese clubs. From there, they moved on to Shanghai, China, then to Manila in the Philippines, and to Australia. Continuing, the tour moved to Ceylon, then to Cairo, where a game was played a game under the shadow of the Sphinx. After stopping off in Italy and several other European countries, the tour arrived in England. Although a number of English sportsmen looked upon baseball with some disdain, the game had some appeal and was more than just a curiosity. Members of the world tour arrived home the following spring aboard the *Lusitania*, the same ship that two years later would be torpedoed by a German submarine, which contributed to the United States entry into the First World War.

FIGURE 6.4 Genevieve Ebbets, daughter of Brooklyn Dodgers' owner Charlie Ebbets, throwing out the ball at the first game ever played at Ebbets Field, on April 5, 1913.

BASEBALL, IMPERIALISM, AND THE MILITARY

The penetration of baseball into Latin America was a case of the game following the flag. Even before the conquest of Cuba in the Spanish-American War, baseball had taken root in that country and was becoming part of the Cuban national identity. As the United States spread its influence into other Latin American countries, baseball quickly followed suit. According to Albert Spalding, "Baseball is war! It has followed the flag to the Philippines, to Puerto Rico, and to Cuba." Cap Huston, later the co-owner of the New York Yankees, played military baseball in Cuba.

The U.S. military establishment was a strong advocate of the national pastime, partly because it thought the game made good soldiers through its emphasis on training and drilling routines. The game also provided recreation and helped build troop morale. Furthermore, baseball was conducive to militarism in that both were offshoots of the cult of manliness prevalent at that time. Manliness emphasized, as did its counterpart, muscular Christianity, the virtues of rigor, toughness, and competition. The aggressive style of professional baseball that appeared in the 1890s, coinciding with the growth of the American empire and military ventures abroad, reflected the attitudes and values of the period. American League President Ban Johnson supported U.S. wars and military endeavors and was always eager to have baseball lend a helping hand.

The close association between baseball and the military was seen in the growth of Army-based teams and the intrusion of the armed forces into ballparks. Army units organized teams and leagues that played one another in formal competitions. Such teams frequently played major league clubs in exhibition games. In the run-up to the First World War, the military staged drilling exercises at big-league ballparks before regularly scheduled games. In some instances, players also took part in these drills.

BASEBALL AND THE FIRST WORLD WAR

After the United States entered the First World War—ostensibly "to save the world for democracy"—nearly five million men entered military service, of whom a million saw action on the Western Front.

Patriotic Fervor

The war was greeted by most Americans with patriotic enthusiasm. Organized baseball joined in the flag waving with great relish, and it was widely believed that never before had the national pastime been so equated with nationalism. By the end of the war, it was estimated that 55% of players under contract to American League clubs and 64% of those reserved to National League teams had served in the armed forces.

FIGURE 6.5 Detroit center fielder Ty Cobb (left) and Cleveland right fielder Joe Jackson (right), in 1913, two of the best hitters to ever play professional baseball.

Major league teams quickly jumped on the patriotic bandwagon. With the smell of war in the air, Captain ("Cap") T. L. Huston, co-owner of the Yankees, put forward a proposal, approved by American League President Ban Johnson, to set up training camps in the South for the purpose of putting players through a daily drill, under the watchful eye of a trained military officer. American League owners quickly adopted this proposal. Soon training stations, emphasizing military instruction and drill, were integrated into spring training.

FIGURE 6.6 The New York Female Giants, in 1913. They frequently played games against all-male competition.

With the opening of the regular season, Major General Leonard Wood threw out the first ball at the Polo Grounds before reviewing a military drill by Yankee players. Echoing the words of a future president during another world war, Wood stated that the highest military authorities believed that baseball should be continued as usual, "since the game maintains mental balance, instills patriotism, and arouses manly instincts, which were necessary if the nation was to stand up for its rights." Evangelist and former ballplayer Billy Sunday argued that no greater mistake could be made than to discontinue baseball because of the war. "That the great industry of baseball," he said, "was one of the worthiest industries and the war should not undermine the game in any way."

Disputes over Salaries

Prior to the start of the 1917 season, major league owners, sensing the inevitability of an impending war, sought to reduce the number of players under contract, which could save both leagues about $264,000. This decision added fuel to the existing fire of discontent. From the beginning of 1916, rumors were circulating about a possible strike by the fledgling Players' Fraternity on behalf of a number of disgruntled ballplayers.

The threatened strike became a reality when Players' Fraternity president, Dave Fultz, called for industrial action. The dispute was multi-causal but centered primarily on the spike in salaries resulting from the baseball war with the Federal League. With the anticipated expiration of war contracts at the end of 1917, the club owners were determined to reduce expenditures to what they considered parity.

"BEAN HIM!"*

*Note for ignorami—Hit him in the head

FIGURE 6.7 Cartoon supporting female suffrage, 1914.

Following the collapse of the threatened strike, the overwhelming response by the baseball owners was one of disdain. Terms such as "fire-eaters," "anarchists," and "weak-kneed pacifists" were directed by owners against players sympathetic to the Players' Fraternity. Connie Mack, manager of the American League Philadelphia Athletics, estimated that minor league salaries were 50% too high and in need of adjustment.

By the autumn of 1917, there was growing concern that the 1918 season would be in jeopardy if the war continued. This was despite signals from high officials in Washington that "the continuance of the national game should be encouraged." In addition to large operating expenses, the magnates were burdened with crippling war taxes that caused further hardship. When the American and National League magnates met independently in December to chart a course for the coming year, cost cutting was very much on their minds.

Baseball's National Commission proposed that a clause be added to each player's contract, stating that if the season ended early, salaries would be downgraded accordingly. The commission anticipated that such a move would cause an outcry from the players. Inevitably, the outcry led to agitation for a holdout, which was greeted with little sympathy. The *Sporting News* claimed that a hundred or more major league players were "trying to back their employers up against a wall on the salary proposition." In fact, there was a wide differentiation in pay between top stars such as Ty Cobb and Hal Chase and the many good, but less exalted, players, earning less than $4,000 a season.

Conscription and the War Against Slackers

The threat of holdouts and strikes were not the only problems affecting baseball. With the passage of the Selective Service Act, the ranks of the military drastically swelled, while teams were systematically depleted of players. From the start of the war, a policy of enforced patriotism was instigated from the national level down, aimed at rooting out dissenters, radicals, and slackers. Roundups of slackers, many of whom took refuge in large cities (particularly New York), along with people having inconvenient political views, routinely occurred. This was in defiance of basic constitutional rights and civil liberties.

While a number of players, reluctantly or enthusiastically, were pulled into military service, others sought exemptions to avoid conscription. There is no evidence that any ballplayer actively opposed the war; however, more than a few players broke their contracts and jumped to lucrative jobs in the shipyards and steel plants. Joe Jackson of the Chicago White Sox (who would later become implicated in the 1919 Black Sox scandal), despite being classified as fit for the draft, signed on with one of the shipbuilding companies and spent the duration of the war playing baseball. White Sox owner Charles Comiskey was so disgusted by Jackson's lack of patriotism that he tried to sell him to another club after the war. Not finding anyone prepared to meet his price, Comiskey decided, largely to his benefit, to keep him.

Matters changed drastically with the issuing of General Crowder's "work or fight order" in May 1918, which determined that all able-bodied men of eligible age be required to "join the colors," or engage in necessary war work. To the astonishment and disappointment of many, baseball was not considered an essential enterprise. "Slackers" in vital industries could now be seen as contributors to the war effort, though controls were implemented, with some success, to eliminate the recruitment of ballplayers at bank president salaries to be camouflaged as workers so they could play ball on company teams.

Dysfunctional Management

For some time, matters affecting major league clubs had been in a state of disarray. With the flight of players into war industries or the armed services, the owners were faced with the real possibility that professional baseball would be closed down for the remainder of the 1918 season, and perhaps beyond. Indecision, procrastination, and open hostility between the two leagues and within baseball's governing body led to widespread condemnation. Columnist Hugh Fullerton observed that the National Commission had been a joke for years. He referred to the falling-out between two of the commissioners, Ban Johnson and Garry Herrmann, and the breaking off of diplomatic relations between the two leagues as examples of this dysfunction.

The *Sporting News*, usually a dependable advocate of the owners' interests, pointed to the sorry plight of the game due to a lack of harmony between magnates of both major leagues. Some even suggested that a full season without baseball might not be a bad thing, since the game would ultimately rebound in a manner that would be more "business-like, sensible, and built around the principle of fairness."

With the war drawing to a close, the future of professional baseball remained uncertain. While expressing optimism that the game would revive, a writer for *Baseball Magazine* noted that the present state of the game was "very hazy, very chaotic." Ban Johnson was quoted as saying he would oppose any resumption of the game before the 1920 season, so that the sport could undergo a major housecleaning and readjustment.

The one point that united the magnates was that baseball would continue a policy of retrenchment. At their annual winter meetings, both leagues agreed to cut salaries, which would save the clubs more than $200,000. This would be done by chopping a month off the season, reducing the number of games played from 154 to 140, and thus pay players for five months' work instead of the usual six months. Having forfeited a month's wages during the 1918 season, the players almost certainly would have been outraged at their 1919 contracts. After the National League imposed a salary cap on each club of $11,000 a month for its entire payroll, some predicted that the players would force a big strike before or during the 1919 season.

But without a union to stand up for them, there was little they could do except hold out for more pay, which many did. Considering the demands of the Players' Fraternity two years before, the circumstances of baseball's employees with respect to their employers had just about returned to square one. Arguably, had the world war continued, the national game, for the immediate future, would have become one of its victims.

The premature resignation of Garry Herrmann, who was under fire from other magnates, signaled the end of the National Commission and baseball's "old order." The Dead Ball era did not pass away quietly, and the tumultuous war years, which nearly destroyed baseball, must be seen as the backdrop for the game's darkest hour, the Black Sox scandal of 1919 (see Chapter 7). Nevertheless, the close of the war alleviated many of the pressures that appeared life-threatening to professional baseball. With the appointment of Judge Kenesaw Mountain Landis as a sole commissioner with nearly dictatorial powers, coupled with a desire among the masses for more entertainment, baseball passed into a new "golden age" of vigor and prosperity.

SUMMARY

From the 1890s, the United States became an imperialist power, which has continued to be the case more or less and under widely different circumstances up to the present. As a consequence of the Spanish-American War, three basic principles were set in place that had future ramifications regarding American foreign policy. The Platt Amendment allowed the United States to engage in military operations in Cuba to protect life, property, and individual rights, The Roosevelt Corollary gave the United States the right to use its police power in the Caribbean to protect its own interests. Finally, Woodrow Wilson's moral imperative implied that imperialism was justified to raise "lesser races" to a higher standard of "freedom" and "democracy."

While the United States was late entering the First World War, it had a profound effect on American society. War fever and the expression of irrational patriotism led to the passing of coercive measures aimed at ending dissent and limiting basic constitutional freedoms. The passage of the Espionage Act (1917) and the Sedition Act (1918) were two such measures. Several court cases set a precedent that one's liberty could be suspended during war if there was a "clear and present danger." Whereas the Sedition Act was repealed in 1920, the Espionage Act is still on the books.

Baseball spread abroad with several world tours. It was also one of the consequences of American imperialistic ventures and was spread throughout Latin America. The "work or fight" order issued by the military after the United States entered the war meant that many players from both the major and minor leagues were either drafted into the military or forced to work in war-related industries. As a consequence, the major league season was cut short in 1918.

STUDY QUESTIONS

1. Based on the presented arguments, was the United States justified in entering the Spanish-American War? Give reasons.
2. Do you believe that the repressive legislation, including the Espionage Act and the Sedition Act, passed during the war and aimed at silencing dissent, was necessary in light of what Oliver Wendell Holmes and the Supreme Court judged to be a "clear and present danger"? Why or why not?
3. What affect did the Selective Service Act have on baseball during the First World War?

Credits

Fig. 6.1: Louis Dalrymple, "Uncle Sam Lecturing Four Children," *Puck Magazine*, 1899.

Fig. 6.2: Louis Dalrymple, "Theodore Roosevelt as World Policeman," 1905.

Fig. 6.3: H.R. Hopps, "Destroy this Mad Brute--Enlist," http://en.wikipedia.org/wiki/File:%27Destroy_this_mad_brute%27_WWI_propaganda_poster_(US_version).jpg, 1917.

Fig. 6.4: Bain News Service, "Genevieve Ebbets," http://www.loc.gov/pictures/item/ggb2005012717/, 1913.

Fig. 6.5: Louis Van Oeyen, "Ty Cobb and Joe Jackson," http://www.loc.gov/pictures/item/89714223/, 1913.

Fig. 6.6: Bain News Service, "New York Female Giants," http://www.loc.gov/pictures/item/ggb2005013524/, 1913.

Fig. 6.7: Donald McKee, "Bean Him!," http://www.loc.gov/pictures/item/93507578/, 1914.

CHAPTER 7

Excess and Celebrity in the 1920s

HISTORICAL BACKGROUND

In December 1918, Woodrow Wilson headed a delegation to Paris to enter into peace talks at the palace of Versailles in an effort to rebuild Europe at the close of the world war. Wilson brought with him a copy of his Fourteen Points, which he believed would be the blueprint for a permanent peace. The other allied nations thought differently, and in the end, the Fourteen Points were whittled down to one, which was the League of Nations. The idea behind this was that the nations of the world would come together to discuss matters of concern rather than fight over them. The League of Nations was doomed from the start, since a number of key nations, the United States being one of them, refused to give it support. The question: Could it be said that President Wilson's efforts to force his Fourteen Points on the postwar settlement was an illustration of American exceptionalism?

The Treaty of Versailles, which created the postwar settlement, imposed heavy penalties on Germany, which was forced to pay huge reparations and accept full responsibility for the war. The treaty did, however, set up a system of collective responsibility that would endure for a decade until it was severely challenged. Unlike the nations of Europe, the United States enjoyed a period of stability and prosperity during the 1920s that masked an undertow of conflicting forces.

FIGURE 7.1 A female telephone operator in the 1920s. The spread of telephones increased jobs for women while enhancing communications.

A NEW SOCIETY?

Frenchman André Siegfried, a frequent visitor to the United States, wrote an article for the *Atlantic Monthly in 1928*, in which he argued, "The basis of American civilization is no longer the same: a new society whose foundation rests upon entirely different principles and methods, has come to life; the geographical, the moral center of gravity of the country is no longer situated in the same place." Siegfried observed the coming to fruition of embryonic trends that had been maturing over a number of decades. The major trend that Siegfried noticed was the growth of a mass society characterized by mass production, creating the basis for a mass civilization. This was highlighted in part by the manufacture of consumer products to meet the desires of an expanding middle class. By 1929, the United States produced 40% of the world's manufacturing goods, including affordable automobiles, cosmetics, refrigerators, electric devices of all sorts, and new products such as the familiar Coca-Cola. What Siegfried saw was a society whose values and concerns were more materialistic, which was a departure from the past. In particular, a new culture had emerged.

New kinds of entertainment also abounded. Radio went on the air in 1920, and by the end of the decade, it had become a standard household product. Motion pictures, at first silent films and later the "talkies," developed widespread popularity and contributed to the rise of a celebrity culture. New sounds such as jazz and creative forms of artistic expression emerged. Likewise, games became more plentiful. Baseball and boxing were the dominant sports prior to the world war and continued to be so afterward, along with horse racing and college football. Moreover, professional football got its start in the 1920s. Athletes such as Babe Ruth, Red Grange, and Jack Dempsey dominated the sports pages of newspapers.

As Siegfried argued, there was a revolution in values. The Spanish philosopher José Ortega y Gasset observed the rise of what he called "mass man," described as disassociated from the past, in rebellion against social barriers, with pretentions to superiority, and easily susceptible to mass impression. Ortega y Gasset was likewise referring to the decline of standards in the postwar world. The formation of a youth culture—fueled largely by the emancipation of women from restrictive norms and the ennui brought on by despair following the world war—led to a collective defiance and questioning of older social restrictions. Social clubs, dance halls, and speakeasies offered new outlets for amusement and escape. The 18th amendment to the Constitution, supported by the **Volstead Act,** *outlawing the manufacture and sale of alcoholic beverages* gave rise to a decade of evasion and rebelliousness. While the "dry lobby" hoped to win over the middle classes to the cause of prohibition, its failure to do so weakened enforcement efforts. While visiting New York City in 1929, the mayor of Berlin, Gustav Boess, was taken on a tour of the city's hot spots and low places by Mayor James J. Walker. Before his departure, Boess asked the New York mayor, "When does Prohibition go into effect?" The problem was that Prohibition had been federal law for a decade.

FIGURE 7.2 Federal agents dumping confiscated liquor down a sewer during Prohibition.

The free market principle of supply and demand generated a sharp rise in lawlessness. Since the transport and sale of alcoholic beverages was illegal, the means for satisfying the craving of many Americans for booze gave rise to organized crime. As with other business ventures, criminals and criminal gangs staked out a market and territory. Turf battles over control of the liquor business led to violence that flourished in urban environments, particularly Chicago. Al Capone, the most notable celebrity criminal of the decade, made a fortune from the illegal liquor trade. But he was not alone. Prohibition gave immigrant Jewish, Italian, and Irish gangs more lucrative opportunities than they had ever experienced before.

A CHALLENGE TO CIVIL LIBERTIES

An assault on civil liberties and constitutional rights continued into the 1920s, which saw a marked upturn in mob violence and censorship. Lynching of Blacks, which had been an ever-present reality since the post-Reconstruction period, had been on the increase since the 1880s. The Ku Klux Klan (KKK) redefined itself in 1915 and expanded its agenda from intimidation of southern Blacks to include those groups not considered to be true-blue American, such as Catholics, Jews, the full range of political groups on the left, and alien ethnicities of all sorts. Riding on the wave of 100% Americanism, by the mid-1920s, the KKK claimed more than three million members nationwide. A northern city, Indianapolis, Indiana, was one center of Klan activity.

Censorship of art and literature, particularly relating to sexual themes, was widespread during this decade. The postal service refused mail broadly defined as obscene. Crusades against indecency, such as Boston's Watch and Ward Committee, excluded from bookstores a whole range of literature thought to be controversial. There was an attack on films in the wake of certain highly publicized Hollywood scandals. The adaptation of the Hays Code in 1922 prohibited films showing intimate scenes, adultery, negative depictions of the clergy, or a favorable treatment of criminals, foreigners, and Blacks. Censorship laws led many American writers and artists to move to Europe, particularly Paris, where the climate for artistic expression was more tolerant.

Beneath this wave of reaction, there were a number of progressive voices that became louder as the decade progressed. Holdovers from the Progressive Party such as Senator Robert LaFollette sought to limit the powers of the Supreme Court by allowing Congress to override Court decisions. He also favored requiring that justices obtain a 7–2 vote to make their decision binding. Neither of these proposals materialized, but their intent was to make a point.

Another progressive development was formation of the American Civil Liberties Union (ACLU) in 1917. Its founder, Roger Baldwin, represented a new breed of lawyers such as Arthur Garfield Hays and Clarence Darrow, who sought cases in which civil liberties were at stake. The ACLU actively worked to overturn a Kansas law that prevented people from criticizing the capitalist economic system. It was also instrumental in helping dispose of a Minnesota law restricting freedom of the press, and laws directed at individuals attending meetings advocating violent revolution. By the 1930s, pressure from the ACLU and others proved effective in reversing the ban on sending sexually related materials through the mail.

ETHNICITY, PLURALISM, AND ASSIMILATION

In the aftermath of the First World War, the United States encountered issues of self-identity. Massive immigration had sparked a nativist revolt during the war, which sought to classify aliens as radicals and undesirables. The knee-jerk reaction was to clamp down on immigration and establish policies of enforced assimilation at the state level. Some states such as Nebraska passed laws restricting the teaching of foreign language in schools. Other programs required compulsory military training, the teaching of civics, and patriotic rituals such as reciting the pledge of allegiance and honoring the flag. Congress passed a law in 1917 that required immigrants to be literate in English or another language.

Moreover, Congress stepped in to pass a series of acts limiting immigration and defining naturalization.

Congress, responding to the wave of anti-alien sentiment, enacted a series of immigration laws, culminating in the Quota Act. The **Quota/Immigration Act of 1924** *limited the number of immigrants allowed entry into the United States through a national origins quota. The quota provided immigration visas to 2% of the total number of people of each nationality in the United States as of the 1890 national census.* Quotas reflected a desire to bolster the Anglo-Saxon composition of the population, which the nativist element saw as "racially superior." The federal government permanently limited European immigration to 150,000 a year, according to national quotas and designed to restrict the flow of people from southern and eastern Europe. The law also barred Asians who were not residents of the Philippines. The 1924 Quota Act put no limit on Mexicans entering the United States, as they were needed as cheap farm labor. As such, the tide of immigration fell precipitously during the 1920s. The Cable Act of 1922 overturned a 1907 law requiring women married to foreigners to assume their husband's nationality. In its place, the Cable Act legitimized citizenship only to those aliens who were eligible to become naturalized U. S. citizens.

By the same token, the 1920s witnessed the coming of age for a new generation of immigrant children. While the country still was a patchwork of immigrant groups, many adhering to their own customs, religions, and superstitions, those of the next generation were becoming Americanized in their own peculiar fashion. Many immigrants had been driven by a desire to escape the poverty of the Old World and to seek a better life in the New World. The immigrant experience helped perpetuate the myth of the American dream—of the United States as a land of unlimited opportunity, which could be obtained through hard work, conformity to expectations, and a spirit of entrepreneurship. Since immigrants expected little or nothing from the government, the values of independence and self-reliance, characteristic of a settler mentality, were instilled and perpetuated into the progeny of newcomers and their offspring. While the idea that everyone has an equal chance is often contradicted by the severe social inequalities built into the fabric of social order, the American dream remains a strong and enduring myth.

THE FUNDAMENTALIST REVIVAL IN THE 1920S

Evangelical Protestants, whose numbers had been growing in strength since the 1870s, became a formidable political force in the 1920s. Evangelicals believed in the literal truth of the Bible as God's word, and felt that freedom meant that society should be based on moral law as the prototype for civil law. The defenders of "old-time religion" represented rural America, which saw the city, the immigrant, and the trend toward a secular society (modernism) as a threat to their idea of American exceptionalism based on traditional values.

As such, rigid evangelicals (termed fundamentalists) were staunch supporters of temperance (limiting the manufacture and sale of alcoholic beverages) and later Prohibition, the upholding of the Sunday observance, or blue laws, the promotion of censorship, and support for various measures aimed at social control. They also opposed the separation of church and state (in contrast with the intent of the first amendment to the Constitution) and the teaching of evolution in schools, which fundamentalists thought contradicted teachings in the Bible.

This last concern became the focal point for an important case that occurred in 1925. A science teacher in Tennessee, John Scopes, was encouraged by the ACLU to challenge the state law prohibiting the teaching of evolution in schools. Scopes was defended by Clarence Darrow. The case spoke to the validity of the Bible as a means of interpreting worldly matters. Darrow put the prosecuting attorney, William Jennings Bryan (former presidential candidate and secretary of state), on the stand as an expert on the Bible. Through cross-examination, Darrow proceeded to undermine the state's argument. Although Scopes was found guilty, this case signaled a change in the attitudes of the American people regarding the social and political roles of religion. Evangelism as a social force would eventually emerge again, but by the next decade, when the political climate changed due to the Great Depression, it had become a spent force.

In considering American society at any time there is always a conflict between progressive and conservative forces based on different interpretations of liberty and freedom. In the 1920s, with the country evenly divided between urban and rural areas, this conflict was acute. For city dwellers, whose population had expanded due to the influx of immigrants from abroad and migrants from the countryside, liberty meant liberation from restrictions of the past, especially for women, and the right to indulge in what had hitherto been considered forbidden activities. Those inhabitants of rural America, on the other hand, viewed liberty in moral terms as adhering to traditional norms and values. The Prohibition battle between wet and dry forces marked a clear bellwether as to where one stood in the culture war of this period.

THE NEW BUSINESS CULTURE

While the progressive era challenged runaway corporate trusts and the laissez-faire business culture, the pendulum in the decade of the 1920s swung back to a more business-friendly environment. The United States emerged from the war a solvent and prosperous country. High consumer demand generated a desire for manufactured goods, while European economies, particularly that of Germany, revived largely by loans from American banks. The image of business was enhanced by a resurgence of advertising and marketing techniques, coupled with the new field of public relations. The stock market, previously the playground of the rich, began to attract the small investor. Thus, a growing segment of the population identified with the capitalist system.

Business continued to enjoy a cozy relationship with government. The three Republican presidents during the 1920s, Warren Harding, Calvin Coolidge, and Herbert Hoover, saw their role as largely cheerleaders for business interests. Business leaders called on the federal government to lower personal and corporate taxes and maintain high tariffs. The Fordney-McCumber Tariff of 1922 raised taxes on imported goods to their highest level in history. The Harding administration in particular became noteworthy for government corruption, characteristic of the capitalist paradox, which exemplified the ongoing tradition of using public money for private gain at all levels of government. Charles Forbes, head of the newly formed Veterans Bureau, received kickbacks for the sale of government supplies. More important was the Teapot Dome scandal, in which businessmen bribed government officials to get oil leases on public land.

Republican appointments to agencies such as the Federal Reserve Board and the Federal Trade Commission ignored or weakened regulatory policies that also served the interests of the business community. Justices on the U.S. Supreme Court defended unrestricted free markets and tended to take a limited view of the role of government in economic affairs. As an example, in *Muller v. Oregon*, the Court struck down a minimum wage law for women.

While the middle class increased dramatically between 1910 and 1930 and a greater portion of the society was achieving affluence, there was a widening gap between rich and poor. Corporate profits rose faster than workers' pay, and by 1929, the income of the wealthiest 5% exceeded that of the bottom 60%. Forty percent of the population remained poor. On the other hand, the upper crust of American society functioned as a closed caste. Men such as William Durant, who formed the General Motors Corporation, and Charles E. Mitchell, president of National City Bank, amassed huge fortunes and exemplified the extravagant lifestyles of the top 1%. Mainstream newspapers chronicled the comings and goings of the propertied and affluent classes in their society columns.

For the first time, the number of Americans living in towns and cities exceeded those living on farms and in rural areas. Farm incomes, as those of the urban working class, were always susceptible to economic boom-and-bust cycles. During the 1920s, farmers began to experience a steady decline. The loss of income encouraged migration to cities and to other parts of the country. While the bulk of the population remained in the industrial Northeast and the Great Lakes states, the land boom in Florida and Southern California attracted many people to the South and West.

THE END OF AN ERA

While American affluence during the 1920s was a reality for a growing number of Americans, it rested on the illusion of endless growth and prosperity. This illusion was fueled by the stock market, which reached record heights in the course of the decade. Danger signs, however, began to appear. The main problem was that in the unregulated market, many investors were buying stocks on margin, meaning that they put down only a fraction of the cost, with the idea of covering themselves as the value of the stock increased. This was all well and good while investor confidence was strong. For whatever reason, greed for capitalizing on a mushrooming market had, by the end of the decade, turned into uncertainty and fear. The lack of investor confidence led to a desire to recoup assets in a falling market. After several months of market instability, panic ensued, bringing on the collapse of the stock market on October 21, 1929, which inaugurated the Great Depression.

BASEBALL

THE BLACK SOX FIX AND SCANDAL OF 1919–1920

As if the year 1919 wasn't bad enough—what with a global influenza outbreak that killed more people than the world war, widespread labor disputes, and political instability—baseball experienced its greatest scandal. The issue involved collusion between professional gamblers and eight members of the much-favored Chicago White Sox to fix the 1919 World Series against the Cincinnati Reds. Ironically, the case came to light following an investigation into a similar fix involving the Chicago Cubs the previous year. The case against the White Sox players came to court a year later, when

Joe Jackson, Buck Weaver, Eddie Cicotte, Lefty Williams, Swede Risberg, Happy Felsch, Chick Gandil, and Fred McMullin, along with New York gambler Arnold Rothstein and others, were indicted. Rumors of a World Series fix were not new and had surrounded the 1905 and 1908 fall classics. Previously, there had been so many documented cases of players throwing (or attempting to throw) games for money that under normal circumstances the Black Sox scandal would not have created such a fuss.

Nevertheless, times and values had changed, and the desire, coming from different quarters, to clean up the game and make a fresh start after the world war was over. The three-man commission that had been the governing body of Major League Baseball since 1903 was dissolved, and a single commissioner with dictatorial powers to make decisions was appointed. The new commissioner, Kenesaw Mountain Landis, had been a federal court judge and was a man of stern, unbending temperament. Landis wasted no time in banning the eight White Sox players from the game for life, despite the fact that not all of them were equally guilty. Buck Weaver knew of the fix but did not take part. Joe Jackson received some of the gamblers' money but played his heart out during the series. Lefty Williams, on the other hand, who won 23 games during the regular season and blew three games in the World Series, was clearly involved in the scheme.

NEW OWNERS

The breakup of the National Commission after the First World War was messy business. For many years, baseball had been governed by titans such as Brooklyn's Charley Ebbets, Pittsburgh's Barney Dreyfuss, Charles A. Comiskey of the Chicago White Sox, Clark Griffith of the Washington Senators, New York Giants Manager John McGraw, Cincinnati owner and National Commission Chairman Garry Hermann, and especially American League President Byron Bancroft (Ban) Johnson. Conditioned by decades of in-fighting and bickering, professional baseball at the commencement of the century's third decade resembled a patchwork quilt of feudal estates governed by barons, whose primary concern was the extension of their authority and the protection of their own turf.

New ownership changes altered the fortunes of a number of clubs. The New York Yankees, which had been largely a mediocre team during its first two decades of existence, became a powerhouse after Jacob Ruppert, who had been part-owner of the team, took over full command of the club. He hired an able manager in Miller Huggins, but more important, he was the beneficiary of Boston Red Sox owner Harry Frazee's fire sale. That netted Babe Ruth for the Yankees along with some other top players. Babe Ruth would become perhaps the game's greatest star. Frazee, who was in poor financial straits and had lost interest in baseball, sold the Red Sox in 1923.

FIGURE 7.3 Baseball game in Buffalo, New York, 1920.

The New York Giants, which had been a successful team, was sold by the estate of John T. Brush to three men: Charles A. Stoneham, a broker with unfortunate underworld connections; Judge Francis X. McQuade; and John J. McGraw. McGraw, known for his aggressive style of play with the National League Baltimore Orioles in the 1890s, carried over his fighting spirit to become the team's manager. He was the Giants' most successful manager, retiring at the age of 59 in 1932.

THE AUTOCRACY OF JUDGE LANDIS

No sooner did Landis assume office than he began to go after those who did not conform to his rigid—and often contradictory—sense of righteousness. In March 1921, the new commissioner banned from the game Gene Paulette, the former St. Louis Browns' and Philadelphia Phillies' infielder, for having associated with gamblers. Landis then also disbarred Benny Kauff of the Giants from playing professional ball. Kauff had been arrested for being party to an auto-stealing racket. Despite the fact that the case against him was *sub judice*, a point that Landis recognized, the commissioner held to his decision, citing Section 2, Article 4 of the major-minor league rules, making ineligible a player under indictment for a felony. Kauff was later acquitted.

Landis's high-handed arbitrariness was further demonstrated when he blacklisted Phil Douglas, who had been a valued member of John McGraw's world championship team of 1921. Douglas, a difficult man, was given to the ballplayer's common failing of constant inebriation. He had worn out the patience of a number of managers and was frequently the object of one of McGraw's tongue lashings. Late in the season, in a muddled state (caused no doubt from too much drink) and deeply annoyed with his manager, Douglas penned a letter to one of his former teammates, stating that he did not want the Giants to win the pennant. Called out on the carpet by the commissioner, Douglas admitted writing the incriminating words. Ignoring all the circumstances of the case, Douglas's admission of authorship was all Landis needed to evict the Giants' pitcher permanently from organized baseball.

Landis was confronted with yet another opportunity to assert the arbitrary power of his office. A scandal erupted later in the 1924 season, which again pitted Landis against Johnson. With only a few games left, the New York Giants were in a close battle with the Brooklyn Dodgers for the National League pennant. Apparently, before the first game of a double-header with Philadelphia, Giants' outfielder Jimmy O'Connell approached the Phillies' shortstop, Heine Sand, with an offer of $500 if he and his teammates would take it easy and, in effect, throw the game. Appalled by such a brazen proposal, Sand reported the bribe to his manager, Art Fletcher, who passed this information up the chain until it reached the ears of Landis. Naive and perhaps a bit stupid, O'Connell maintained that as an employee of the Giants, he was only doing what he thought management wanted. This explanation did not impress the commissioner, who, three days before the start of the World Series, banned O'Connell from the game for life, while exonerating the other star players whom he had implicated.

The Scandals of 1926/1927

Opposition to the dictatorial rule by Landis, largely from American League President Ban Johnson, was brought to a conclusion by two scandals during the winter of 1926/1927. Wheels began turning when early in September 1926, Dutch Leonard, a former pitcher of some note with the Red Sox and the Tigers, turned over to Johnson two letters outlining a betting scheme involving a couple of the game's most prominent players, Ty Cobb and Tris Speaker. The letters written by Cobb and former Red Sox and Indians' standout Joe Wood recounted a meeting between all four players that took place under the grandstand at Detroit's Navin Field on September 25, 1919, prior to a game between the Tigers and the Indians. While Cleveland had already secured second place in the American League, Detroit was battling the Yankees for a chance to end up in third place, and thus get some World Series money. It was intimated that the players might make some extra cash by laying down bets on a Tigers' victory. According to Leonard, Speaker and Wood each agreed to post $1,000.

FIGURE 7.4 Vice President Calvin Coolidge attending a game at Griffith Stadium, Washington, DC, in 1921.

FIGURE 7.5 St. Louis Browns' shortstop Wally Gerber slides home safely in a July 19, 1924, game against Washington at Griffith Stadium.

Meeting shortly thereafter in secret session with the American League directors, the magnates concurred with Johnson's decision that the player-managers of the Tigers and Indians (Cobb and Speaker) should be let go quietly, so as not to embarrass the league. That settled, the owners then turned over the letters and supporting documentation to Landis. On November 2, 1926, Cobb resigned as manager of the Tigers. A month later, Speaker quit the Indians, saying he desired to enter private business. The resignation of these two baseball immortals was headline news on sports pages across the country. Meanwhile, Landis was conducting his own investigations.

Four days before Christmas, readers of the daily newspapers were startled by front-page headlines announcing that Cobb and Speaker were implicated in a scandal to fix ballgames in 1919. Since he broke the story in early December, Landis had been noticeably silent on this matter; however, on January 19, 1927, he summoned all the club owners, along with Johnson and the attorneys for Cobb and Speaker, to a hearing scheduled for the 24th for the purpose of ascertaining what basis, if any, there was for a recent publication of the story "that neither Speaker nor Cobb could ever again play ball or manage an American League club." This ominous request came in the face of consultations between Landis and the players' attorneys concerning the secret meeting of American League magnates, called by Johnson in Chicago the previous September, resulting in the forced resignation of the two men. By then, the devious machinations of Johnson—coupled with embarrassing statements by the American League president regarding the commissioner's handling of the allegations, and his comments to the effect that both player-managers were forced to resign less for crookedness than for incompetence—proved to be the last straw as far as the magnates were concerned. By the time of the January 24 hearing, Johnson's removal from office was virtually a done deal

With Johnson out of the way, Landis moved to acquit Cobb and Speaker of any wrong-doing and to reinstate them as active members of their former clubs. Given the admitted evidence in this case, the leniency of the decision stood in contrast with the harshness meted out to others whose misdeeds were far less serious. Always claiming to be acting in the interests of baseball, Landis was sensitive to the winds of public opinion and to invasive actions of the federal government to interfere with what he believed should be the game's independent status. These factors, along with the charismatic power of Speaker and Cobb as baseball heroes, were clearly uppermost in the commissioner's mind in rendering his decision. For their part, the magnates, who in the words of a *New York Post* editorial, had hitherto "had a rather happy-go-lucky code of athletic morals," moved to tighten Section 24 of the major league rules dealing with conduct detrimental to baseball, and thus close a door on the somewhat tarnished practices of the Dead Ball era.

MEMORABLE SEASONS

As America entered the decade of the 1920s, the country's national pastime was never more popular. Attendance was up in all ballparks, and there was full coverage of baseball (along with other sports) in the media. After the trauma of the war years, Americans were content to look inward and enjoy life. The easing of restrictions against Sunday baseball in a number of states (New York in 1919) meant that more leisure time could be spent watching and participating in weekend games.

FIGURE 7.6 Cleveland Indians' bat boys posing outside the dugout at Griffith Stadium in Washington, DC.

Major league baseball provided a number of memorable seasons. The year 1921 saw the rise to prominence of the newly enhanced New York Yankees in the American League, who defeated the pennant winners of the previous year, the Cleveland Indians, in a close race. Their opponents in the World Series were their crosstown rivals, the New York Giants. The Giants won in eight games of a nine-game series and repeated again when the same two clubs met the following year. The Yankees finally got back at the Giants, beating them in six games in 1923, the same year the team moved from the Polo Grounds to their new home in the Bronx, Yankee Stadium.

FIGURE 7.7 Washington second baseman Bucky Harris giving his autograph to female fans, 1925.

The 1924 season has been considered by some to be baseball's greatest season. There were tight races in both leagues, with the surprising Washington Nationals (later known as the Senators) edging out the Yankees in the American League, while the unsurprising Giants had an equal amount of difficulty disposing of the Brooklyn Dodgers. With the Giants heavily favored in the World Series, the Nationals rode to victory in seven games behind the efforts of their star pitcher, Walter Johnson, one of the all-time greats. The Nationals would win the American League pennant again the next year, this time losing to the Pittsburgh Pirates in the World Series.

There is continuous debate over baseball's best team. A strong case could be made for the 1927 Yankees who ran away with the American League pennant, finishing 19 games up on the second-place Philadelphia Athletics. Moreover, this was the year that Babe Ruth hit his record-breaking 60 home runs. Ruth, the star of the show, was ably supported by an all-star cast of players, including Lou Gehrig, who himself hit 47 home runs, Earl Combs, and Tony Lazzeri, and on the pitching side Lefty Grove, Wiley Moore, and Herb Pennock. The Yankees went on to overpower the Pirates in four consecutive games in the World Series.

CELEBRITIES AND HEROES

Among other epithets, the 1920s could be characterized as the "age of celebrity." Magazines, newspapers, film, and the newest medium, radio, brought to the attention of the public a galaxy of stars and personalities, some of whom became social icons. The same medium also fed a growing desire for gossip and sensation news, including murders, high-profile divorces, and daring crimes. This was also an age of self-promotion, and nobody was a better self-promoter than Babe Ruth.

Ruth was born in Baltimore in 1895. An apparently difficult child, given to all sorts of youthful misdemeanors, he was placed in an orphanage. It was there that he learned how to play baseball and displayed some of the skills that would later elevate him to prominence. Scouted by a number of teams, Ruth signed with the Boston Red Sox as a pitcher and appeared in his first big league in 1914. Over the next four seasons, Ruth became the dominant left-handed pitcher in the American League. His greatness was overshadowed by his bad habits, a tendency for insubordination, and his yearly demands for more money than what the club was willing to pay. It was the combination of these factors, plus his relatively poor performance in the 1919 season, when the Red Sox descended into sixth place, that encouraged Frazee to sell Ruth to the Yankees.

FIGURE 7.8 Babe Ruth with some adoring young fans in 1921.

It was in New York where Babe Ruth—as a hitter, not a pitcher—made his mark. Indeed, it was Ruth who is credited with changing the focus of the game from "short ball" to "long ball," as his rate of home runs exceeded that of other teams. More than any other player, Ruth exemplified the freewheeling spirit of his age and became its leading celebrity. A man of gargantuan appetites, he overate, overdrank, overindulged in sexual affairs, and constantly played up to the media. He was no doubt the most photographed person of his time. With a nose for publicity, Ruth naturally attracted photo-ops, whether it was visiting sick children in a hospital, dressing in some outrageous costume, or, taking advantage of the rise in commercialization by selling products. Ruth hired an agent, Christy Walsh, who ran his business affairs and was constantly on the prowl for ways to promote the Yankees' star hitter. All this aside, it was his extraordinary talent as a baseball player that kept him in the news. More than any other player, he changed the game in a way that never happened before or has happened since.

SUMMARY

The 1920s was characterized by Andre Siegfried as a "new society." What he meant by this term was the advent of a mass civilization marked by the mass production of goods, popular entertainments, new values, and a challenge to the norms and mores of the pre-world war era. Society in the 1920s was largely fueled by Prohibition, which encouraged crime and rule-breaking and, indirectly, greater freedom for women.

Following this period of censorship and hostility to immigrants, modern ideas, and restrictive laws, the American Civil Liberties Union emerged, consisting of progressive lawyers who sought, often successfully, to challenge repressive laws.

Whereas large corporations prior to the First World War were under pressure for corrupt practices and undermining competition and free trade, they gained a new lease on life in the 1920s—thanks to an expanding economy and the demand for American goods. Federal, state, and local governments retreated from attempts to regulate business to passing legislation to promote business activity.

Baseball suffered through the Black Sox fix and scandal of 1919–1920 in which eight players on the Chicago White Sox were banned from the game for life. Major league owners hired Kenesaw Mountain Landis as the game's first commissioner, giving him dictatorial powers over baseball operations. Landis used his power in an arbitrary manner, and while he did not "clean up" the game in the manner that some people have suggested, the gambling plague that had griped baseball for decades abated somewhat by the end of the decade.

STUDY QUESTIONS

1. What is meant by the term "mass society"? In what ways did the United States become a mass society in the 1920s?
2. To what extent did big business in the United States during the 1920s personify the capitalist paradox?
3. In what ways might it be said that Babe Ruth symbolized and dominated the 1920s?

Credits

Fig. 7.1: Lewis Hine, "Female Telephone Operator," http://www.geh.org/fm/lwhprints/htmlsrc2/m197807500002_ful.html, 1922.

Fig. 7.2: "Agents Pour Liquor into Sewer During Prohibition," http://www.loc.gov/pictures/item/99405169/, 1921.

Fig. 7.3: "Baseball Game in Buffalo, New York," http://www.loc.gov/pictures/item/2009632650/, 1915.

Fig. 7.4: "Calvin Coolidge Attending a Game at Griffith Stadium," http://www.loc.gov/pictures/item/2009632650/, 1921.

Fig. 7.5: "Wally Gerber Slides Home Safely," http://www.loc.gov/pictures/item/npc2007011825/, 1924.

Fig. 7.6: "Cleveland Indians Batboys," http://www.loc.gov/pictures/item/npc2007006714/, 1922.

Fig. 7.7: "Bucky Harris Autographing Scorecards," http://www.loc.gov/pictures/item/npc2007006714/, 1925.

Fig. 7.8: Bain News Service, "Babe Ruth," http://www.loc.gov/pictures/item/ggb2006007797/, 1921.

CHAPTER 8

Race and Apartheid

HISTORICAL BACKGROUND

Until recently, the United States was divided into two nations: one Black and the other White. The habits of racial domination conformed to other patterns of hierarchy, whereby men dominated women, native Whites dominated Native Americans, mill owners dominated workers, and those with wealth ground down the poor. Implicit in these forms of domination was the distinction between those who were independent (and therefore people of consequence) and those who were dependent (and socially speaking, largely invisible). Slaves, being chattel property, were below the plateau of being considered fully human. One of the great achievements of the Civil War was to elevate African Americans to the status of citizens. Being citizens, they were entitled to the rights shared by others, but for another century, many Blacks would enjoy these rights largely in name only. Segregation, legal and otherwise, perpetuated the two-nation model, while mocking the values the Constitution sought to uphold. Thus, while African Americans obtained constitutional freedom with the end of slavery, to what extent were they free?

CREATING A SYSTEM OF SEGREGATION

While by federal law African Americans were no longer slaves, state laws known as Jim Crow laws emerged in the South after Reconstruction and were designed to obstruct the freedom of Blacks and keep them subordinate. This system, which was employed in South Africa, is known as **apartheid,** which is a *system of institutionalized racial segregation.* Subordination meant keeping the races apart by creating separate schools, clinics, public facilities, and institutions and living spaces, even down to separate cemeteries. What this amounted to was a duplicated society. At crossover points, when Blacks and Whites did come together, the laws always determined that the latter would enjoy superiority over the former. Segregation was both *de facto* and *de jure.* **De facto**

Segregation, meant *segregation by custom and practice, supported by a set of norms that were enforced by social pressure and existed throughout the country.* **De jure segregation,** which occurred primarily in the South, *mandated by law the separate roles and statuses of Blacks and Whites.* These were the Jim Crow laws.

Laws defining segregation were implemented by states over time. As with all things racial, there were a number of ambiguities, not the least of which was the question of who was of one race or another. This was all the more so, considering that, while slavery existed over the previous century, race mixing meant that many Blacks could claim White ancestors and vice versa.

THE MEANING OF LIBERTY AND FREEDOM IN A DIVIDED NATION

The question arises as to what freedom, meaning rights, and liberty, meaning individual autonomy, meant for those Blacks who had been liberated from the shackles of slavery. Certain points are obvious. African Americans were no longer tied to a plantation but enjoyed freedom of movement. Likewise, since they were no longer bought and sold as property, they could marry whom they wanted, live where they wished, and exercise the right to make choices within the constraints of their situation. Just as their White counterparts, they considered the right to own land as the basis of liberty.

FIGURE 8.1 Black children outside their schoolhouse following the Civil War.

Unfortunately, many of the promised liberties and freedoms were never fully realized. Most southern Blacks in the post-Reconstruction period were not landowners but made a living as sharecroppers. By this system, freedmen farmers were given small plots of land to cultivate, with part of their produce going to those who owned the land. Sharecropping spread quickly among Black farmers working the cotton fields in the South. Eighty percent of the cotton farms by 1880 had fewer than 50 acres, the majority of which were tilled by sharecroppers. Poorly paid and subject to the rules of segregation, many sharecroppers and other small farmers were attracted by the emergence of the farmers' alliance movement, which encouraged cooperatives as a means of challenging the railroads and other agencies within the capitalist system that victimized the agricultural worker.

One of the great conundrums in American history is how can liberty and freedom be fully achieved in a society that is grossly unequal. The constitutional guarantees of citizenship, equality before the law, and the right to vote, as articulated in the 13th, 14th, and 15th amendments, were ignored with respect to African Americans in the decades following Reconstruction. The prevailing attitude by Whites toward Blacks was not far removed from what it had been during slavery, and restrictions such as vagrancy laws, by which Blacks, if unable to account for themselves, could be arrested or entered into forced labor, were widespread. Given the prevailing degrading and demeaning attitudes entertained by many Whites toward Blacks, segregation was perhaps not the worst fate that could befall African Americans.

FIGURE 8.2 Large crowd in 1893 watching the lynching of a man accused of raping and murdering a young girl.

THE PLESSY V. FERGUSON DECISION

The landmark Supreme Court case that reinforced existing Jim Crow laws was the *Plessy v. Ferguson* decision in 1896. This case was brought to the Court by Homer Plessy, a Black man from Louisiana, who said he was entitled to ride first class on trains just as White passengers did. Arguing that he had the right to equal citizenship under the 14th amendment, Plessy stated that neither the state nor the railroad could discriminate against him based on color. In a 7–1 decision, the Court ruled against Plessy. Its reasoning was that while both races were entitled to equal political protection under the law, the Court could not govern social attitudes and conventions, which were the basis of discrimination. Justice John Marshall Harlan, the lone dissenter in this case, maintained that the Constitution was color blind, and that the 14th amendment guaranteed equality before the law to all citizens, regardless of race or background. This decision would sanction segregation for nearly 60 years.

BLACK CONSCIOUSNESS AND THE DEBATE OVER BLACK DESTINY

There were essentially three distinct perspectives put forward by black leaders over the role of African Americans. The first was articulated by Booker T. Washington, who had been born a slave in 1856. Washington, a southerner, worked his way through the Hampton Normal and Agricultural Institute, and was later instrumental in the 1881 founding of the Tuskegee Institute for Black students in Alabama. Washington preached accommodation to segregation. Through obedience to the existing social structure and by thrift and hard work, Blacks in time could, he thought, prove themselves worthy of inclusion into the mainstream of American society. White people, in turn, should provide Blacks with the rudiments of education and job training so they could eventually make this transition.

FIGURE 8.3 Octavius V. Catto, scholar, athlete, and civil rights pioneer. Among his many accomplishments, he helped found the Union League Association in Philadelphia and later became captain of the Pythian Baseball Club.

Washington's acquiescent view was challenged by W. E. B. Du Bois, who was born in 1868 and became the first Black man to receive his doctorate at Harvard College. Du Bois became a highly influential scholar and analyst of the African American experience. He saw Blacks under segregation as a nation within a nation, having to adapt themselves to two cultures, one White and one Black. He thought that African Americans should push forward and strive to achieve the rights and privileges owed to them as citizens. This could largely be achieved through education. Essentially, his message was one of struggle, not accommodation. Noting that there existed a stratification of social classes within Black society (as in the wider society as a whole), Du Bois thought it was the duty of the more educated and fortunate members of the Black community to give assistance and guidance to those who were less fortunate. He was one of the founders of the National Association for the Advancement of Colored People (NAACP), an interracial organization aimed at achieving greater equality for blacks.

The third perspective was put forward by Marcus Garvey, a Jamaican immigrant to New York City in 1919. Garvey founded the Universal Negro Improvement Association (UNIA), which became an activist organization designed to improve the lot of urban working-class Blacks. Unlike Du Bois, Garvey rejected the goal of racial integration, arguing that African Americans should turn their backs on White society and cultivate their own businesses and institutions to become more self-sufficient. Believing the country was hopelessly racist, he urged Blacks to return to greater freedom in their African homeland and to a more welcoming culture. Garvey enjoyed a fair degree of popularity among urban Blacks during the 1920s, but by the end of the decade, he fell afoul of federal law over a scheme to transport people and cargo from the United States to the West Indies and was consequently deported. It is safe to say that until the 1930s, the majority of American Blacks favored the path of accommodation.

URBAN MIGRATION DURING THE PROGRESSIVE ERA

While progressivism was hitting its stride during the first two decades of the 20th century, the consequences of segregation were also mounting. One indicator of the terrorism perpetuated by segregation was the increasing popularity of **lynching,** which means *the act of a mob to kill someone, especially by hanging, for an alleged offense with or without a legal trial.*

Ida B. Wells-Barnett, using social science research methods, documented mob violence against African Americans during the latter part of the 19th century. Her research showed that the number of lynchings in the South rose from 52 recorded instances in 1882 to 169 instances in 1891. Most were for the suspected rape of a White woman or for suspected murder. These figures do not tell the whole story, since an untold number of Blacks, who were already marginalized, just disappeared and could well have been murdered by persons unknown.

The escalating incidences of violence against Blacks were one of the sparks that fueled growing migration from the South to the industrial cities in the North. Another obvious reason was the demand for unskilled (and skilled) workers to fill positions in an expanding industrial economy. The demand for workers accelerated during the world war, as millions of men (including some Blacks) were drafted into military service. Within a short period, the demographics of urban areas changed, as Blacks moved en masse into the South Side of Chicago, into the region north of Central Park in New York City, into the Homestead region around Pittsburgh, and in significant numbers into Detroit, Cleveland, Newark, New Jersey, and other industrial centers. These newly arrived Black workers quickly adapted to the rhythms of city life. Wrote Langston Hughes of Chicago in 1918: "Midnight was like day. The street was full of workers and gamblers, prostitutes and pimps, church folk and sinners."

Blacks displaced those living in low-rent areas, many of whom were immigrants who congregated in the ethnically polarized neighborhoods of large cities. Clearly, the newly arrived Black migrants were not welcome. Discrimination forced Blacks into tightly packed ghettoes. Rising racial tensions led to violence. On July 2, 1917, White mobs competing for housing and jobs attacked African Americans in East St. Louis, resulting in many deaths and loss of property. There was a race riot in Chicago in 1919 as African Americans encroached upon the predominantly Irish district. Additionally, there were 26 bombings of African American residences on Chicago's South Side between 1917 and 1919. Another such riot took occurred in Tulsa, in 1921. Whereas the discrimination of Blacks in northern industrial cities could be seen as marginally less harmful than the constant threat of terrorism in the South, their lives were still hard and problematic.

THE EMERGENCE OF A BLACK POPULAR CULTURE

African American migration continued into the 1920s. Nearly one million blacks moved north during that time. By the same token, some 150,000 immigrants from the West Indies also came to the United States between 1900 and 1930. While most of these new arrivals survived as best they could working as shoe shiners, day laborers, or at other menial jobs, a smaller group formed an emerging Black middle class, operating small businesses in Black neighborhoods or providing an array of educational, medical, and legal services. A dominant institution in Black neighborhoods (as it was in the South) was the Black church. One newspaper source estimated that within the 150-block area of Harlem, there were 140 Black churches, many operating out of storefronts staffed by preachers who came north with the Great Migration.

Of importance was the tremendous contribution of Blacks to popular culture. African American culture at the turn of century had largely consisted of Black minstrels (many of whom were white men with black faces) singing "coon songs" that reinforced racial stereotypes. By the 1920s, Black popular culture was coming into its own. Jazz, an innovative musical form, grew out of small Black clubs in New Orleans, Chicago, and Kansas City, and thanks to radio, spread to become the dominant musical form of the age. Jazz underscored the Harlem renaissance, where Black entertainers performed for large audiences at such venues as the Cotton Club, the Savoy, and the Apollo Theater. There was also a plethora of Black writers such as Langston Hughes, dancers such as Bill Bojangles Robinson, and singers such as Billie Holiday. The popularity of Black culture reflected the growth of Black consciousness. By the end of the 1920s, a strong independent spirit was emerging within the Black community.

BASEBALL

CREATING THE COLOR LINE IN BASEBALL

The history of Black baseball in the United States mirrored the patterns of segregation in the wider society. There is scattered evidence of Blacks playing baseball before the Civil War, but the first recorded games took place in northern cities during the Reconstruction period. In October 1867, the Uniques of Brooklyn hosted a team from Philadelphia called the Excelsiors in what was advertised as "the championship of colored clubs." At about the same time, an application was made by another Black Philadelphia team, the Pythians, to join the National Association of Base Ball Players, which was the newly formed governing body of organized baseball. The Pythians' application was unanimously rejected, accompanied by an admonition barring "any club which may be composed of one or more colored players." Two years later, the Pythians became the first Black team to play against an all-White club. Overall, at least 70 Blacks played organized baseball in the late 19th century. About half played on all-Black teams, while the other half were part of integrated clubs.

By the late 1880s, only a handful of Blacks played on White professional teams before the color bar fully closed. One such club was the minor league Syracuse Stars, which holds the distinction of being the last professional White team to field a Black ballplayer prior to the self-enforced apartheid that lasted until Jackie Robinson broke the color barrier anew in 1947. The last Black player on the Stars was Moses Fleetwood Walker. Walker, as did most educated African Americans during segregation, lived in the twilight zone of two worlds. A student at Oberlin College, followed by a brief legal education at the University of Michigan, Walker entered professional baseball in 1883 as a catcher for the Toledo ball club. One of a handful of Black players in professional baseball, Walker suffered a multitude of physical and emotional indignities from White opponents and teammates alike. In the mid-1880s, there were about 20 Black professional ballplayers, but by the time Walker arrived in Syracuse in 1888, he was virtually the last. The unwillingness of White teams to play against a club with a Black player—and the unwritten agreement among club owners that athletes of color were no longer wanted—ended the century's brief chapter of integrated baseball.

FIGURE 8.4 A Black baseball team from Danbury, Connecticut, ca. 1880.

EARLY BLACK TEAMS AND LEAGUES

Shunned by White leagues and players, African Americans developed their own institutions and created a rich baseball culture. In 1887, the National Colored Baseball League was formed, which was the first (and short-lived) attempt to create a Black professional league. In 1889, the Middle States League included a number of noteworthy Black teams, including the Cuban Giants, the most famous Black team of the period. The Giants had a 55–17 record that year. A year later the Giants shifted to the Eastern Interstate League, but that league folded in mid-season. Their final appearance occurred the next year (1891), this time in the Connecticut State League. Shortly thereafter, both the league and the Giants went out of business. The instability of baseball leagues and teams during the late 19th century was extremely volatile, much more so for Black baseball.

Faced with constant financial troubles, a lack of suitable venues, and all the restrictions imposed by segregation, Black (or Negro) league teams and leagues lived hand to mouth. As such, they were constantly on the move, barnstorming from town to town, playing against local (and often hastily formed) teams before moving on to the next town. Since Blacks were frequently denied sleeping accommodations in hotels and lodging houses, they often had to spend nights in their game uniforms on traveling buses or, in extreme cases, in open fields. Many places did not serve Blacks, so players had to grab food whenever and wherever they could. Barnstorming involved playing two or three games a day, sometimes in separate towns. In a number of instances, the money gained barely covered expenses. Such was the life of Negro league baseball players throughout the decades of Jim Crow.

To attract more fans, Black ball teams would stage additional entertainment. The Page Fence Giants, founded by a man named Bud Fowler, in 1895, attracted attention by riding through the streets on bicycles before taking the field. Four years later, in 1899, Fowler created the All-American Black Tourists, who would arrive in town dressed in full suits with top hats and silk umbrellas. Singing and vaudeville-type shows performed by Negro league players were not unknown. The visit by a company of minstrel showmen to Auburn, New York, in 1913 produced an added benefit since members of the company were also baseball players. Before their evening performance, they took on a local team for the benefit of a local charity.

In an effort to skirt around the rules imposed by segregation, major league managers would sometimes try to pass off lighter-skinned Black players as Whites. In his final season with the Baltimore Orioles, in 1901, Manager John McGraw sought to camouflage Charlie Grant, a Black second baseman with the Columbia Giants, as an Indian named "Chief Tokohama." The ruse worked until Chicago White Sox owner Charles Comiskey got wind of the scheme and threatened to expose the deception. Grant was forced to return to his paying job as a bellhop, where he remained until he died. The Cincinnati Reds in 1911 tested the waters by signing two light-skinned Black Cubans named Armando Marsans and Rafael Almeida. Despite suspicions leaked by the press that the players were really Blacks, the Reds' management maintained that the two players were "genuine Caucasians." The inclusion of light-skinned players from Latin America (mostly Cubans) would continue for the duration of the Negro leagues. As far as darker-skinned players were concerned, that was another matter.

FIGURE 8.5 Ballplayers from Morris Brown College in Atlanta, Georgia, 1899.

As black migration out of the South to northern cities accelerated after the turn of the century, Chicago emerged as the center of Black baseball. Teams such as the Leland Giants and the Chicago American Giants rose to prominence. Other cities featured recognized Black professional teams such as the Lincoln Giants in New York, another team called the Giants and the Hilldale Club in Philadelphia, the Indianapolis ABCs, and the Bacharach Giants of Atlantic City. These teams sported good players with colorful names such as Smokey Joe Williams, Cannonball Dick Redding, and John Henry Lloyd. Such players were much in demand, and frequently they would jump from one team to another, depending on who paid the most money.

The first important entrepreneur in Black baseball was Andrew "Rube" Foster, born in Texas in 1879. In his early 20s, Foster signed on to pitch for the Chicago Union Giants. Shortly thereafter, he moved on to pitch for other clubs, and soon became the top pitcher in Negro league baseball. Foster was best known, however, as a manager, promoter, and master strategist. In 1911, he joined with a Chicago saloonkeeper to form the Chicago American Giants. With his managerial and organizational skills, coupled with the financial backing of his partner, the Giants established, for a time, a permanent home in Chicago and attracted many of the best Black players. While Foster controlled Black baseball in Chicago, access to other venues was often in the hands of White booking agents, who charged Black teams exorbitant rates to play in suitable ballparks. Several attempts by Foster and others to create a viable Negro league were of short duration.

Foster's most successful effort was the formation of the Negro National League in 1920. His idea was to merge Black clubs into a single league and place those clubs under the control of African Americans. Realizing that Blacks played in a parallel universe to Whites, he felt strongly, in the tradition of W. E. B. Du Bois, that Black organizations should look after their own kind. There were exceptions, however. Foster included the Kansas City Monarchs (which would prove to be a powerhouse in Black baseball) into the league, even though its owner, J. L. Wilkinson, was White, in order to keep the Negro National League alive. The short-term success of the league encouraged others to get in on the act. Soon, the Negro Southern League and the Eastern Colored League came into existence. In 1924, the first Negro World Series was played, with the Kansas City Monarchs defeating the Hilldale Daises from the Philadelphia area, five games to four. Foster became ill in 1926, and without his leadership, the Negro National League folded.

Black Baseball in Pittsburgh

The focus of Black baseball then shifted to Pittsburgh. Two men, Cumberland (Cum) Posey and Gus Greenlee, who would become legends within the Black community, formed teams that would become baseball powerhouses. Posey's team, the Homestead Grays, represented a steel town just south of Pittsburgh. Posey rose to become a wealthy Black businessman, and used his money to sign top Black athletes, among them Oscar Charleston, Judy Johnson, Martin Dihigo, and Cool Papa Bell, all now enshrined in the National Baseball Hall of Fame.

FIGURE 8.6 Black groundskeepers preparing the diamond at Griffith Stadium, October 3, 1924.

Greenlee accumulated his fortune from gambling and hid his money from the Internal Revenue Service by siphoning the profits under the table into baseball. He made his team, the Pittsburgh Crawfords, a top-notch club, largely by luring players from other teams, particularly the Homestead Grays. Greenlee sought to unify franchises by reviving the Negro National League, which helped keep Black baseball alive during the Great Depression. Greenlee's other claim to fame was creation of the East-West Game in 1933, which drew large crowds—both Black and White—to Comiskey Park in Chicago to watch the best of the Black baseball stars perform. The East-West Game, and Negro league baseball in general, benefitted from a lively Black press that promoted and reported on ballgames.

SATCHEL PAIGE

Whereas Babe Ruth dominated White organized baseball, Black baseball had its share of superstars, the most prominent being Satchel Paige. As was Ruth, Paige was born into poverty and spent part of his youth in an industrial school where he developed baseball and character skills. As a pitcher, Paige had a tireless arm, and was able to throw a baseball in ways that seemed uncanny. Having a "gift for the gab," Paige coined a number of pithy phrases and home truths such as "fried foods make the blood boil." He soon came to the attention of promoters such as Posey and Greenlee, who coveted his services. Although the date of Paige's birth remains unknown (and was never revealed by the man himself), by his mid-20s, Satchel Paige was the one of the biggest names in Black entertainment, ranking with boxer Joe Louis and jazz musician Louis Armstrong.

Along with Ruth, Paige had a clear understanding of his talent and monetary worth. As such, he spent much of his career following the money, jumping from team to team, as determined by his inclination and the fee guaranteed for his services. It was said that any team that got into trouble would send for Satchel to pitch. Almost single-handedly, Paige propelled an obscure North Dakota team to the national semiprofessional championship. He also pitched in the Dominican Republic at the behest of dictator Rafael Trujillo and played in Mexico against a team of major league all-stars. And similar to Ruth, Paige had a taste for the high life and enjoyed driving fast in expensive cars, hanging out with celebrities, wearing fine clothes, and running around with attractive women. Part showman, he would frequently dazzle audiences with his pitching prowess.

Paige, as did many Black ballplayers, always hoped to make it to the big leagues once the color bar was lowered. Most Black stars, however, ended their careers during baseball's segregation years, or were passed over by major league teams that still clung to a racist perspective of the game. This was not the case with Paige, who, toward the end of his playing career, pitched for the Cleveland Indians, where he was named "rookie of the year" in 1948, and then had a stint with the St. Louis Browns. After Jackie Robinson broke the baseball's color line in 1947, other Black players were signed by major league teams.

Less fortunate was Josh Gibson, a power-hitting catcher for the Homestead Grays. Gibson is considered to be the best home run hitter of all time, and while statistics on Black baseball are sketchy, some have estimated that he may have hit as many as 800 home runs during a playing career that stretched from 1930 to 1946. The closest he came to the major leagues was when Clark Griffith, owner of the Washington Senators, called him and another Black slugger, Buck Leonard, into his office and asked them if they wanted to play in the big leagues. They naturally answered in the affirmative, but never heard from Griffith again. Gibson died in January 1947, a few months before the major leagues were finally integrated.

SUMMARY

With the end of slavery, African Americans remained in a dependent and servile status due to the institution of segregation. Black apartheid was reinforced by the *Plessy v. Ferguson* Supreme Court decision confirming that segregation was constitutionally legal.

Three Black leaders, Booker T. Washington, W. E. B. DuBois, and Marcus Garvey articulated different visions for African Americans. Washington believed that Blacks should learn a trade and accommodate themselves to segregation. DuBois saw the problem of Blacks in psychological terms and believed in struggle to achieve racial justice. Garvey preached self-help for Blacks, and considered the country to be hopelessly racist. He urged Blacks to return home to Africa where life would be freer.

With the coming of the progressive era, many Blacks left the South for jobs in northern industrial cities and hopes for a better life. Although they were free from segregation, the threats of lynching, and loss of one's livelihood, life in the North was problematic and Blacks were still victims of bigotry and racism. This culminated in a number of race riots after the First World War.

In the 1920s, northern Black ghettos saw the rise of a cultural renaissance that featured new innovative sounds such as jazz along with creative literature and poetry. Black entertainment was popular among both African Americans and Whites.

Black baseball, as the rest of society, was segregated. After 1890, when Blacks were driven out of organized baseball, they formed their own leagues and barnstormed around the country. The most celebrated Black baseball player was Satchel Paige, a dominant pitcher, who plied his trade for many Black teams and freelanced his skills as well. Paige was one of the first Black players to join the major leagues after the integration of baseball was realized in 1947.

STUDY QUESTIONS

1. Discuss the reasons why the U.S. Supreme Court in *Plessy v. Ferguson* agreed that segregation was in line with the 14th amendment that stipulated equality before the law?

2. Discuss the role of Blacks as articulated by Washington, Du Bois, and Garvey. Which perspective was the most prevalent during the period of segregation, and why?

3. In what ways was the doctrine of "separate but equal" contradicted by the condition of Black baseball players in segregated America?

Credits

Fig. 8.1: "Schoolhouse Following the Civil War," http://www.virginiamemory.com/blogs/out_of_the_box/2011/05/18/mapping-segregation-in-arlington-county-public-schools/, 1895.

Fig. 8.2: "Large Crowd Watching Lynching," http://www.loc.gov/pictures/item/cph32337/, 1893.

Fig. 8.3: S. Fox, "Octavius V. Catto," *Harper's Weekly*, 1871.

Fig. 8.4: Edward David Ritton, "African American Baseball Team," http://www.loc.gov/pictures/collection/gld/item/2008677253/, 1880.

Fig. 8.5: "Ball Players from Morris Brown College," http://www.loc.gov/pictures/item/95507100/, 1899.

Fig. 8.6: "Preparing the Diamond for World Series," http://www.loc.gov/pictures/item/npc2007012299/, 1924.

CHAPTER 9

Depression and a New Deal

HISTORICAL BACKGROUND

The general prosperity and good times of the 1920s were brought to a sudden end by the Great Depression, which lasted nearly a decade. American capitalism was prone to frequent boom-and-bust cycles, but never had the economy endured a continuous state of depression. The wisdom of classical economics was that the economy was self-correcting. This implied that the role of government would be limited to largely to law and order functions and that the economic life of the country would be run by private enterprise. In other words, a strict interpretation of liberty.

After the stock market crash in 1929, the whole system began to collapse and conditions only got worse. No sphere of life remained untouched by the Depression. Further hardship was experienced by farmers in the southern Plains states, who—after years of overcultivation with the prospect of a quick return—experienced the worst drought in American history. The dust bowl drove many farmers into bankruptcy. Thousands of "Okies" were forced to abandon the Plains and start a new life in California. It was these matters that provided the context for life during the 1930s.

The Depression, which lasted throughout the 1930s, would bring into question the whole relationship between the private sector and the federal government. The question to be considered: Was President Franklin D. Roosevelt's New Deal solution to the Depression a partial or complete revolution? **Revolution** meaning *an overthrow of a social order, in favor of a new system.* Whether for better or worse, the New Deal cast a long shadow over American society ever since.

COLLAPSE OF THE ECONOMY

When the market collapsed, banks were compelled to call in their loans, which forced businesses that relied on credit to lay off workers or go into bankruptcy. The same was true for cash-strapped city governments. Bank failures, the lack of credit, and unemployment affected homeowners who could no longer afford to pay their mortgages, and thereby lost their homes or farms. Moreover, since many European countries had supported their relative prosperity through large loans from American banks, the American banking crisis caused a global depression that would have profound political and social effects.

The scale of the Depression can be seen statistically. Between 1929 and 1933, nearly every index of economic activity showed a dramatic decline. The gross national product shrank from $104.4 billion in 1929 to $72.2 billion in 1933. Bank failures went from 640 in 1928 to 2,294 in 1931. During the same period, the income of farmers dropped by two-thirds. By 1932, a quarter of the American workforce had lost their jobs and struggled to survive without relief.

President Herbert Hoover, elected in 1928, thought that the Depression, as previous ones, would remedy itself and so responded to the crisis in a piecemeal manner. The Agricultural Marketing Act of 1929 established a Federal Farm Board to encourage cooperatives to pool resources for producing and distributing crops. Hoover also encouraged creation of a National Credit Corporation aimed at aggregating financial resources. Furthermore, he backed the Reconstruction Finance Corporation along the same lines. On the other hand, Congress passed the Hawley-Smoot Tariff Act, which raised import duties, causing further harm to foreign economies. Many people, homeless and out of work, congregated in "Hoovervilles," which were shantytowns on the outskirts of cities such as Seattle. At the depth of the Depression, in 1932, 20,000 "Bonus Marchers" set up camp in the nation's capital, demanding the veterans' bonus promised them for their services during the First World War. The encampment lasted several months, ending when Attorney General William D. Mitchell ordered the veterans removed from all government property. The Bonus Marchers and their families were driven out by the Army, supported by six tanks.

FIGURE 9.1 Police attacking Bonus Marchers at their encampment in Washington, DC, in July 1932.

RELIEF AND RECOVERY

The presidential election of 1932 brought to office Franklin D. Roosevelt, a former New York governor from an old, propertied family. Roosevelt knew that something out of the ordinary had to be done to jump-start the economy, put people back to work, and help relieve the misery of the many. Roosevelt was a pragmatist. He had no ideological blueprint of what to do so he took the trial-and-error approach. The new president gathered around him a coterie of experts such as Frances Perkins, Harry Hopkins, and Harold Ickes, who had experience working with relief and welfare agencies, to brainstorm on what to do.

Consequently, the first hundred days of what Roosevelt promised would be a New Deal saw the appearance of a whole range of laws and agencies designed to stop the financial hemorrhaging and put people to work. The Emergency Banking Act stabilized the private banking system; the Agricultural Adjustment Act established production controls and price supports for farmers, backed also by the Emergency Farm Mortgage Act, which allowed for refinancing farm property. The Home Owners' Loan Act did the same for those facing foreclosure. The Civilian Conservation Corps (CCC) and the Public Works Administration (PWA) were designed to put men back to work, while the Glass-Steagall Act, the Securities Act, and the Federal Deposit Insurance Corporation (FDIC) sought to bring regulation to Wall Street investment firms and the banks.

At the heart of efforts to revive American industry was the National Industrial Recovery Act (NIRA), which created an agency that sought to halt the decline of wages and prices, and expand employment opportunities by suspending antitrust laws and authorizing industries to draft codes setting quotas, price policies, and wage rates. The act also gave labor the right to organize unions and to engage in collective bargaining. Despite the fact that the NIRA was exploited by business interests for their own ends, the Supreme Court, taking a narrow interpretation of the role of government, declared the act unconstitutional.

ROOSEVELT AND HOOVER

In his speech to the Democratic National Convention in 1936, President Roosevelt laid out his vision for a second New Deal. In denouncing economic tyranny brought on by what he termed "economic royalists," he went on to say that "necessitous men are not free men," meaning that persons in want of the basic necessities of life could not enjoy the blessings of freedom. He further commented that freedom is no half-and-half affair, meaning that one could not have equal opportunity in the polling place without freedom in the market place. Here Roosevelt was using both the language of liberty and freedom. By liberty he was referring to personal freedom to better oneself without restrictions imposed by monopolies and the inequities of the capitalist system. By freedom he meant economic security whereby each citizen had the right to a "safety net" as protection from the calamities of life and extreme poverty.

Herbert Hoover, who Roosevelt defeated in the 1932 election, became the chief spokesman against the New Deal. He said that it had no philosophy, that it was sheer opportunism, the muddle of a spoils system, emotional economics, and a host of other pejorative names. His central argument was that the New Deal was a significant departure from traditional economic law and experience that had guided the republic from the beginning. Hoover's meaning of the word liberty was unrestricted free enterprise that placed no limitations on individual aspirations. What separated Hoover from Roosevelt was the concept of economic justice, which Hoover ignored, and Roosevelt felt was essential for a free society.

THE SECOND NEW DEAL

By 1935, the multitude of relief-and-recovery acts passed by Congress was beginning to show some effect. This encouraged the president to start thinking about moving beyond temporary measures to more permanent solutions. Roosevelt's vision was to create a society that would provide security for the poor and vulnerable. This idea was a significant departure from the role of government in the past. During the progressive era, government (mostly state governments) sought to impose greater efficiency and correct the abuses brought on by a lack of regulation, trust-busting being a case in point. What Roosevelt proposed was the embryonic basis of a welfare state, in which the federal government would ensure minimum standards to meet basic human needs and create a fairer and more just society. This notion of industrial freedom espoused initially during the progressive era was put into action during the New Deal.

The first step in this direction was the **National Labor Relations Act.** *It was a foundational statute of United States labor law that guaranteed the right of private-sector employees to organize into trade unions, engage in collective bargaining, and take collective action such as strikes.*

Hardship brought on by the Depression was the genesis of widespread strikes in a variety of industries. The Wagner Act (named after Senator Robert Wagner, who drafted the act) guaranteed a worker's right to organize unions, engage in industrial action, and prohibit employers from adopting unfair labor practices, such as firing union activists and forming company unions that sought to do the bidding of employers. "Labor's Magna Carta," as it was called, because it incorporated the workers' inherent right to freedom, also contained provisions to enforce workers' rights, prevent coercion by employers, and to oversee union elections. Through the efforts of the United Mine Workers' president, John L. Lewis, unskilled workers were organized into the Congress of Industrial Organizations (CIO), which covered workers within an entire industry.

FIGURE 9.2 Civilian Conservation Corps workers doing forest reclamation at Yosemite National Forest in 1935.

Another more significant step of long-range importance was the creation of Social Security. The **Social Security Act** was *a law enacted in 1935 to create a system of transfer payments in which younger, working people support older, retired people.* This act contained three parts. The first was workmen's compensation, providing some benefits to those who lost their jobs. The second provision was a form of old-age pension, which set up a fund that one paid into through payroll taxes during that person's working years. Retirees would then receive back in measured amounts the money paid into the system when they stopped working. Excluded from this provision were agricultural workers (including sharecroppers) to appease White southern segregationist Democrats who controlled key committees in Congress, and domestic workers, encompassing mostly women. Together, these two groups represented about one quarter of the workforce that would not be covered by Social Security.

The final piece of the Social Security Act was the Aid to Dependent Children (ADC) program. ADC was designed to provide for women who had children, but no husband. Hence, the funds were to pay for the children's needs, assuming that the parent was able-bodied and could work. This program was never intended to provide a recipient with permanent assistance, but to tide them over until they could find employment. Prejudice against the poor (specifically Blacks and other minorities) soon created a set of moral attitudes that unfairly equated welfare recipients with laziness and other demoralizing characteristics. What the New Deal effectively did was to partly fulfill the promise of industrial democracy articulated by John Mitchell and others during the progressive era.

Significant also was the Rural Electrification Act (1935), which overrode the reluctance of private companies to extend power lines to the countryside because it was not profitable. Under this act, electric power was provided to the 90% of farms that previously could only use oil or kerosene lanterns and wood fires.

OPPONENTS OF THE NEW DEAL

The fact the New Deal redefined to a limited extent the relationship of the state to the nation, it was a cautious, piecemeal, and pragmatic development, concerned with supporting the capitalist system and stabilizing existing institutions. Hence, it was far from being revolutionary. This is not how it was perceived by many people, particularly business leaders. The most severe challenges to Roosevelt came from conservative groups and individuals. After a brief acquiescence to some of the relief efforts of the New Deal, business and financial leaders coalesced to combat what they considered to be government intrusion into the private sector, an undermining of classical economic theory, and "creeping socialism." The wealthy were further incensed that one of their own class was challenging their interests through regulations and higher taxes. In 1934, right-wing business leaders and politicians formed the **American Liberty League**, *which was primarily a group of wealthy business elites and prominent political figures who were conservatives opposed to the New Deal of President Roosevelt. Its principles emphasized private property and individual liberties.* Its intention was to combat all forms of radicalism by defending private property and upholding a narrow interpretation of the Constitution. A Liberty League sympathizer actually approached Marine General Smedley Butler in November 1934 with the idea of organizing a military coup against Roosevelt, to be replaced by a fascist-style government. Happily, Butler, in the strongest possible terms, refused to go along with this plot.

The 1930s replaced the adherence to business prosperity and religious fervor of the 1920s with a focus on political and social issues, both on the left and the right. The Communist Party, which constituted a small group of adherents in the United States after the Russian Revolution in 1917, reached its zenith of popularity during the 1930s, counting several hundred thousand members. Party members were active in organizing workers into unions, backing rent strikes, and standing up for those who were oppressed, and often ignored, by other organizations. The various socialist parties also gained supporters. With the rise of dictatorships in Europe, especially the ascension of Adolf Hitler and the Nazi Party in Germany, there emerged a strong undertow of fascism in America, which brought to the surface a wave of anti-Semitism. Not surprisingly, both the communists and the fascists were critical of the New Deal, but for very different reasons.

FIGURE 9.3 Resettled workers playing baseball at the Rimrock Camp in Oregon, 1936.

There were other people who felt that the New Deal did not go far enough in remedying the country's industrial and social problems. Huey Long, governor of Louisiana, put forth his Share-Our-Wealth program in 1934. This program took direct aim at the New Deal by promising to end poverty and unemployment, and extending welfare services much further than Roosevelt was prepared to go. Father Charles Coughlin, a Catholic priest from Detroit, used the radio to promote his plan for a National Union for Social Justice. Francis Townsend, a retired California physician, proposed a pension plan that would extend benefits to anyone over the age of 60.

END OF THE NEW DEAL

In the presidential election of 1936, Roosevelt was returned to office in a landslide victory over his Republican opponent, Alf Landon. Perhaps overconfident with this win, Roosevelt made several crucial mistakes that cost him much political capital. Sensing that the economy was improving by 1937, the president sought to cut government spending and return to a balanced budget. The loss of government revenue forced the economy to go into a recession, which compromised some of the gains of the previous years.

The next mistake was his attack on the Supreme Court. Constantly vexed over the narrow approach of the Court in striking down the provisions of the New Deal, Roosevelt proposed that for every judge over the age of 70 who did not retire, he would appoint an additional judge, thus expanding the Court from nine to a limit of 12 justices. Clearly, the newly appointed members to the Court would have a more favorable opinion on New Deal legislation. This proposal was challenged not only by Republicans—predictably—but by members of Roosevelt's own party, who saw it as a self-serving political attempt to undermine the principle of checks and balances underscoring the Constitution. Ultimately, Roosevelt was forced to back down from this plan, but luckily for him, several of the more conservative justices elected to retire, which changed the political complexion of the Court.

Lastly, Roosevelt sought to purge his party of those elements who were hostile or indifferent to his New Deal programs. The Democratic Party at that time was an odd and often incompatible coalition of White southern Democrats, labor unionists, Blacks (who switched over from being Republicans in the 1930s), Catholics, and social reformers. This fragile coalition became more fragile through such heavy-handed actions as packing the Supreme Court. As war clouds loomed on the horizon, Roosevelt would need all the support he could get to prepare the country for the coming titanic life-or-death battle, so as to ensure the nation's security.

BASEBALL

ECONOMIC HARD TIMES

Understandably, the Great Depression affected baseball in a number of significant ways. There was, however, a delayed reaction after the stock market crash in 1929. In 1930, major league attendance reached an all-time high of about 10.1 million fans. A year later, hard times began to catch up with baseball, resulting in salary reductions for players and a tailing off at the gate. Players, who on average earned about $7,500 during the 1920s, saw their salaries decline by 25% the following decade. Even high-end players such as Babe Ruth, Joe Cronin, and Chuck Klein were forced to take a salary cut. As the Depression worsened, ticket prices, which now included a federal amusement tax, were out of reach for many would-be customers.

Opening day of the baseball season in 1932 drew only 121,000 fans for all eight games. The Yankees and Athletics, the American League's two most successful clubs, hosted a mere 16,000 fans, while the St. Louis Cardinals began defense of their World Series title in front of only 7,000 supporters. By 1935, attendance at big-league ballparks reached a total of six million, a huge jump from the previous two years. From that point on for the rest of the decade, attendance figures continued to climb, which reflected an overall improvement in the economy.

FIGURE 9.4 Members of the local Cedar Grove team relaxing outside a store near Chapel Hill, North Carolina, on July 4, 1939.

A BRIEF DYNASTY

Whereas the New York Yankees were the dominant American League team for most of the 1920s, they were replaced by the Philadelphia Athletics from 1929 to 1931. The team's president and manager, Connie Mack, known to be a shrewd judge of baseball talent, had amassed a formidable array of stars that included power hitters such as first baseman Jimmie Foxx, outfielder Al Simmons, Mickey Cochrane—one of the best catchers to ever play the game—and a trio of exemplary pitchers, Lefty Grove, George Earnshaw, and Rube Walberg. The Athletics went on to win the World Series in two of their three championship years: 1929 and 1930.

Mack was also known for being financially tight. After the Athletics fell to third place in 1933, and with declining gate receipts, the Philadelphia manager sought to recoup his losses by selling off his top players. Over the next three years, Mack unloaded $590,000 worth of talent by sending Cochrane to Detroit, Earnshaw to the White Sox, and Grove (and later Foxx) to the Red Sox. The Athletics would never recover, and were consistently a second-division team while they remained in Philadelphia.

BRANCH RICKEY AND CREATION OF THE MINOR LEAGUE FARM SYSTEM

From the early years of the century, the minor leagues existed as independent organizations within the structure of organized baseball. They were subject to the reserve clause and the same territorial restrictions that governed the major leagues. Within the structure of minor league baseball, teams were grouped hierarchically from the AA level to Class D, depending on the quality of talent. Big-league teams wishing to acquire a minor league player would be required to pay a purchasing price. Some major league teams had working relationships with minor league clubs, but those franchises operated as separate entities. One caveat to the major-minor leagues' working agreement was that a limited number of players were eligible to be drafted.

Within organized baseball, the minor leagues were more vulnerable to wider economic conditions. In 1928, there were 31 minor leagues, which by 1933 had been reduced to 14 leagues. Some leagues during these troubled times failed to finish the season. From this low point, the number of minor leagues rebounded and doubled in number between 1935 and 1941. The St. Louis Cardinals alone in 1930 either owned outright or had working agreements with seven minor league teams. By 1936, two-thirds of all minor league clubs had major league affiliations.

A significant reordering of the relation between the major and minor leagues was the implementation of the farm system. The originator of the farm system was Wesley Branch Rickey. He was born in 1881 on a farm in southern Ohio and educated at Ohio Wesleyan College. Later, he received a law degree from the University of Michigan. In 1913, Rickey went to work for the St. Louis Browns, and in 1917, he moved over to the Cardinals as president. From 1919 to 1925, Rickey was the team's field manager. Thereafter, he ran the club from the front office.

Knowing that he could not compete with the well-heeled New York teams or the affluent Chicago Cubs, Rickey developed a grand scheme of hiring more scouts than anybody else. These scouts would comb the country for prospects, and then sign them for little—if any—money. The signed players were then placed on the Cardinals' affiliated teams, where they would be held, promoted, and discarded accordingly. One of Rickey's quotable axioms was, "Out of quantity comes quality." His system produced a steady flow of talent that provided the basis for the Cardinals' success over several decades. Gradually, other franchises adopted the farm system.

A block in the road was Commissioner Kenesaw Mountain Landis, who objected to the farm system on two counts. First, he thought that the minor league franchises should be localized operations for the benefit of their hometown fans and not for a major league team. His second concern was that a big-league team could keep a prospect in the minor leagues indefinitely, without the possibility of advancement to the majors or high minors. The attempt by St. Louis to cover up draft-eligible players so irked Landis that in March 1938 he made free agents of 91 Cardinal-controlled players.

THE COMING OF NIGHT BASEBALL

Another consequence of the Depression was the introduction of night baseball. Since baseball was played most every day during the summer, working people often had little chance to watch weekday games. The cash-strapped minor leagues were the first to embrace night baseball. By mid-summer 1930, according to one newspaper, there were more night games than day games. Altogether, 38 minor league teams in 14 leagues had installed lights by the early 1930s. The Kansas City Monarchs led the way among Negro league teams by carrying with them a portable system of lights that could be mounted on poles as they barnstormed through the Midwest.

FIGURE 9.5 Young fans at a Tigers' game at Briggs Stadium in Detroit.

The Cincinnati Reds were the first major league team to incorporate night games. Consequently, their attendance improved, and the franchise turned a $50,000 profit. Other National League clubs, with the exception of the New York Giants and the Chicago Cubs (which delayed installing lights until 1988), soon followed suit. At the American League winter meetings, team executives voted to include in their schedules a limited number of night matches, minus the Yankees, who said they wouldn't play night games anywhere.

ETHNIC IDENTITY AND BASEBALL

Clearly, the composition of professional baseball reflected the migration and demographic structure of the country. As the new wave of immigrants from southern and eastern Europe became assimilated into the United States, some of their sons, representing the next generation, made their way into organized baseball. While the majority of players still came from the British Isles and Germany, a growing number, reflected by names such as Ogrodowski, Kreevich, Vosmik, Tamulis, and Medwick, were of different nationalities.

A noticeable number of ballplayers during the 1930s were of Italian descent. The most famous was Joe DiMaggio, known as the Yankee Clipper, and his two brothers, Vince and Dominic, both big-league players. The Yankees' Frank Crosetti, the Cubs' Phil Cavaretta, and the Pirates' Cookie Lavagetto were other notable players with an Italian heritage. Hank Greenberg, the star first baseman of the Detroit Tigers, came from a Jewish background, as did Moe Berg and Harry Danning.

Some players from immigrant backgrounds changed or altered their names after they entered professional ball. Aloys Szymanski became Al Simmons, Peter Jablonowski changed his name to Pete Appleton, and Cleveland first baseman Hal Trotsky previously went under the name of Harold Troyavesky. The modification of names not only reflected a desire on the part of players to have more pronounceable Americanized names, but also to avoid the ethnic and racial stereotypes that abounded during this time. In a socially less sensitive time, when prejudice against those who seemed different was stronger, ethnic slurs such as "dago," "hunky," "kraut," and "sheeny," were commonly thrown around by players in ordinary banter, and especially by those who sought to "ride" their opponents.

NEW STARS AND THE SECOND YANKEES' DYNASTY

No one team dominated the National League in the years 1932 to 1939. The Chicago Cubs (1932, 1935, and 1938) and the New York Giants (1933, 1936, and 1937) each won the pennant three times, while the St. Louis Cardinals (1934) and the Cincinnati Reds (1939) rounded out the league winners. With the exception of three seasons (1933–1935), the Yankees not only dominated the American League, but all of baseball, winning the World Series five times. While the 1930s found Babe Ruth in his declining years, finally closing out his career with the Boston Braves in 1935, he was soon replaced by another superstar, Joe DiMaggio, purchased by the Yankees from the Pacific Coast League San Francisco Seals in 1934 for $25,000. It would prove to be one of the greatest baseball transactions of all time.

Some of the most celebrated names in baseball history appeared on the scene in the 1930s. The Cleveland Indians signed a 17-year-old fastball pitcher from rural Iowa named Bob

Feller, who would go on to become one of the greatest strikeout artists of all time. The St. Louis Cardinals were certainly one of the game's most colorful teams. They were known as the Gashouse Gang, boasting characters such as Dizzy and Paul Dean, Rip Collins, Frankie Frisch, Pepper Martin, and Joe Medwick. The New York Giants possessed one of baseball's best pitchers in Carl Hubbell and position players in Mel Ott. The Boston Red Sox, for over a decade one of the poorest teams in the American League, rose to respectability after the club was purchased by South Carolina millionaire Tom Yawkey. His most significant acquisition was the best player in the history of the franchise, Ted Williams, who arrived on the scene in 1939.

LOU GEHRIG

The end of the decade was epitomized by a tragic moment for one of baseball's greatest stars. First baseman Lou Gehrig, who entered the Yankees' lineup in 1925 and was a dominant fixture, teaming with Babe Ruth to become the best one-two punch in baseball, entered the 1939 season having played a record-breaking 2,130 consecutive games. He performed reasonably well in 1938, though his numbers were down from the previous year. During spring training in 1939, however, Gehrig knew something was wrong. Tests at the Mayo Clinic revealed he was suffering from a rare neuromuscular disease, amyotrophic lateral sclerosis. Knowing that his career—and probably his life—was over, Gehrig appeared at Yankee Stadium for the last time on June 4. There he uttered the immortal words, "I consider myself the luckiest man on the face of the earth." Such humility exemplified a quality of character that marked his life.

SUMMARY

In response to the collapse of the American economy in the 1930s, President Roosevelt introduced a series of legislative measures aimed at providing relief, recovery, and reform. The so-called First New Deal was designed to put people back to work and deal with some of the structural issues that forced the collapse of the economy. The Second New Deal was aimed at putting into place permanent programs such as Social Security and the Wagner Act to correct the worst abuses of the free market capitalist system.

While Roosevelt enjoyed immense popularity within the country, he was strongly opposed by industrialists and persons of wealth who saw the New Deal as a direct assault on their liberty, so defined. Opposition also came from those who felt that Roosevelt had not gone far enough to restructure the economy. Herbert Hoover saw the New Deal as a direct assault on what he saw as traditional economic law and experience. It is worth pointing out that while Roosevelt and Hoover made constant reference to liberty and freedom, they often had different interpretations of these words.

The Depression also affected baseball. Dwindling crowds forced teams to sell off star players and to cut costs. One such approach was night baseball. The farm system of minor league teams was introduced by Branch Rickey of the St. Louis Cardinals' organization. The New York Yankees dominated the sport in the latter years of the decade. This was also a period when the sons of immigrants, largely from Italy and eastern Europe, began to enter the big leagues.

STUDY QUESTIONS

1. Discuss some of the ways that the New Deal changed the relationship of the federal government to its citizens. How was it different from the progressive era 20 years earlier?
2. Considering the upheaval brought on by the Depression, could the New Deal be considered an unqualified achievement, a limited success, or a failure? How so?
3. What effect did the Great Depression have on organized baseball in the 1930s?

Credits

Fig. 9.1: U.S. Army Photographer, "Bonus Marchers," http://en.wikipedia.org/wiki/File:Bonus_marchers_05510_2004_001_a.gif, 1932.

Fig. 9.2: "Civilian Conservation Corps in Yosemite," 1935.

Fig. 9.3: Arthur Rothstein, "Baseball Game at the Resettlement Administration Rimrock Camp," http://www.loc.gov/pictures/item/fsa1998019402/PP/, 1936.

Fig. 9.4: Dorothea Lange, "Cedargrove Team," http://www.loc.gov/pictures/item/fsa2000003541/PP/, 1939.

Fig. 9.5: John Vachon, "Young Fans at a Tigers Game at Briggs Stadium," http://www.loc.gov/pictures/item/owi2001009329/PP/, 1942.

CHAPTER 10

Second World War

HISTORICAL BACKGROUND

From the time Adolph Hitler and his Nazi Party took over in Germany (1933), the balance of power in Europe, which was based on collective security within the League of Nations, began to crumble. After the First World War, fascist governments and dictatorships emerged in Italy (and later Spain) and most of the newly formed nations in eastern Europe, which were created by the collapse of the Austro-Hungarian and Russian empires. Upon becoming chancellor of Germany, and then assuming dictatorial power, Hitler tore up the Treaty of Versailles and began a program of military rearmament. Next, Hitler pursued a policy of expanding German territory. In 1938, with virtually no opposition from Britain and France, the German army marched into Austria. Later the same year, after the two allies refused to support Czechoslovakia, Hitler co-opted the Sudetenland region of that country, populated mostly by ethnic Germans. Soon he took over the whole of Czechoslovakia. When Hitler attacked Poland on September 1, 1939, Britain and France declared war on Germany two days later. Question: To what extent was the Second World War merely an extension of the First World War with a 20-year truce?

AMERICAN NEUTRALITY

While the storm clouds of war were gathering in Europe, the United States adopted a policy of strict neutrality. Many people believed the country had been tricked into the First World War, which proved to be a futile war that benefited only the war profiteers and sowed the seeds for future conflict. For most Americans, the 1920s were a time of introspection and, for some, self-indulgence. Personal hardship, which cut across all classes (caused by the Great Depression of the 1930s), pushed foreign affairs into the background. While President Franklin D. Roosevelt was aware of the emerging dangers (Japan's invasion of Manchuria in 1931, Italy's invasion of Ethiopia in 1935, the Spanish

Civil War of 1936–1939, and Hitler's aggression), the vast majority of Americans were opposed to any sort of foreign involvement. From 1935 to 1937, Congress passed a series of neutrality acts prohibiting the United States from making loans or extending credit to nations at war.

Following the sweep of Nazi forces into western Europe and the fall of France in May 1940, the Germans turned their attention to the British Isles. Knowing Britain's desperate need for supplies and military help, yet aware of the isolationist mood of the country, Roosevelt put forward a policy of Lend-Lease. The proposal was that the United States would lend Britain the weapons it needed, which would be returned at the end of the war. This was a preposterous idea, but Congress and the American public bought it. A combination of American supplies, British resolve, and Hitler's mistakes saved Great Britain from a Nazi takeover.

VISION FOR A NEW WORLD ORDER

In his State of the Union address to Congress on January 6, 1941, President Roosevelt enunciated his "Four Freedoms" that would serve as a vision for the postwar world. These simple statements cited: freedom of speech and expression; the freedom to worship God in one's own way; the freedom from want, meaning the securing of an adequate standard of living; and freedom from fear, which, translated into world terms, meant the reduction of armaments to such a degree that no nation would be in a position to attack another. Each of these statements concluded with the phrase, "everywhere in the world," making the Four Freedoms a global vision. It could be said that these four statements were the most complete expression of freedom hitherto given.

There were other voices that set forth a vision for the postwar world. Henry Luce, an influential magazine publisher, thought that the coming century would be an American century, by which the United States, through its economic and military power, would shape and, to a large extent, dominate the postwar world. Clearly, this was a restatement of American exceptionalism. Henry Wallace, who was Roosevelt's secretary of agriculture and vice president from 1940 to 1944, noted that future U.S. policy must be based on the Four Freedoms. He characterized the postwar world as the century of the common man, meaning that everyone will have the opportunity to enjoy a comfortable life and live in a relative degree of freedom.

Seven months after Roosevelt delivered his Four Freedoms speech, he met with Prime Minister Winston Churchill on the British ship *Prince of Wales* in the North Atlantic where they put forth a declaration of common principles, which they hoped would be the basis of a better world. The *Atlantic Charter* reiterated a number of the proposals that had been included among President Woodrow Wilson's "Fourteen Points." This encompassed self-determination for people in choosing their form of government, freedom on the high seas, and the removal of economic trade barriers. The eighth and last point of the Charter related to the last of the Four Freedoms, calling for a permanent condition of disarmament.

The vision of a New World Order for the Allies stood in stark contrast to that of their enemies. The Nazi world order was one of German domination, in which conquered states would be subordinated to the status of dependents—or in the case of those at the bottom of the racial hierarchy, as slaves to be worked to death or eliminated. Japan sought to impose a military dictatorship over Southeast Asia, which would serve the interests of the mother country.

PEARL HARBOR AND AMERICA'S ENTRY INTO THE WAR

America's splendid isolationism came to an abrupt end on December 7, 1941, when Japan attacked and destroyed the entire Pacific Fleet of the United States, stationed at Pearl Harbor, Hawaii. Calling this a "day of infamy," President Roosevelt declared war on Japan the next day. Shortly thereafter, Hitler, for reasons of his own, declared war on the United States. Britain and the United States were now officially at war against the Axis powers of Germany, Italy, and Japan. Almost overnight, American industries were converted to war production. As millions of men were drafted into the armed services, and many more millions of government dollars were pumped into the economy, the Great Depression was now over.

FIGURE 10.1 Destruction caused by the Japanese attack on Pearl Harbor, December 7, 1941.

MAP 10.1 Military Action in the Pacific Theatre, 1941–1945

During the course of the war, the United States became the "arsenal of democracy," supplying not only its own military needs, but also supporting those of Britain and its other ally, the Soviet Union, which became part of the antifascist coalition after Germany invaded Russia in June 1941. While Russia experienced unimaginable destruction and hardship from the massive German onslaught, Britain and the United States plotted joint operations in what was now a two-front war.

During the early months of 1942, the war in the Pacific went badly as the Japanese swept through Southeast Asia, capturing territory that was part of the British, Dutch, French, and American empires. A turning point came with the Battle of Midway in June, whereby a sizable number of Japanese carriers were sunk. This battle effectively gave the United States air and sea control of the Central Pacific region. For the next three years, Allied troops were engaged in a grueling and bloody island-hopping campaign, tediously dislodging Japanese troops from one stronghold after another in some of the more memorable battles of the war.

MAP 10.2 Military Action in the European Theatre, 1942–1945

THE HOME FRONT

With the country at war abroad, the American economy went through an unprecedented transformation.

As in the First World War, though to a much greater extent, the federal government exercised controls on the economy for the duration of the war. Unlike the First World War, many of the structural changes to the economy remained permanent. The **military-industrial complex,** which is *a country's military establishment and those industries producing arms or other military materials, is regarded as a powerful vested interest.* Thus, many large industries, particularly on the West Coast, received large military contracts. War contracts created 17 million new jobs. Many new industries emerged outside the traditional industrial

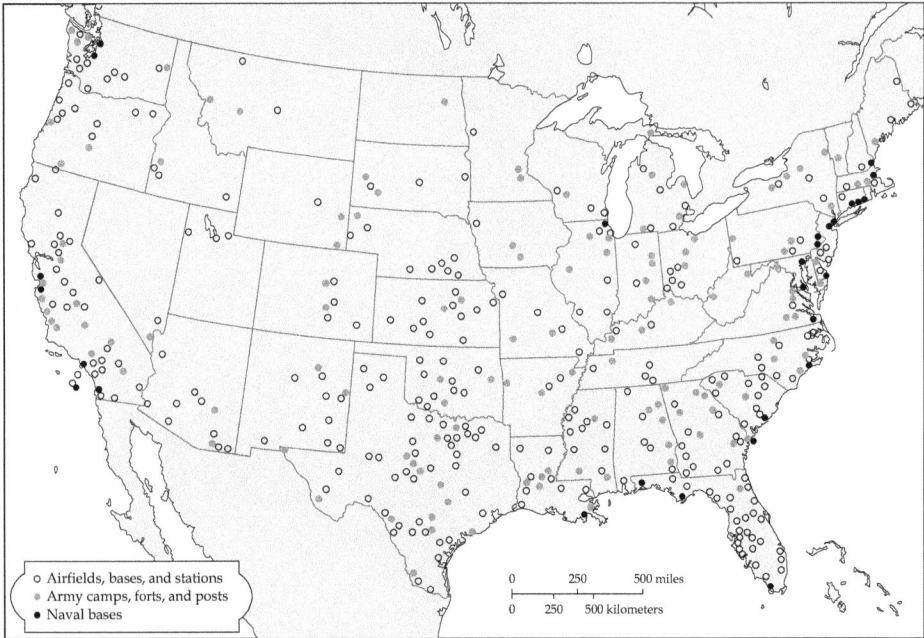

MAP 10.3 Military Bases and Airfields During World War II

regions of the country in places such as Mobile, Alabama, Wichita, Kansas, and San Diego, California. The federal government, which had always favored balanced budgets, now used deficit spending to expand the economy. Between 1939 and 1945, the federal budget rose from $9 billion to $106 billion. At the same time, astronomical goals were set for wartime production. Over the course of the war, American industry provided nearly two-thirds of all the Allied military equipment produced, including: 297,000 aircraft, 193,000 artillery pieces, 86,000 tanks, and two million Army trucks. In four years, America's industrial production, already the largest in the world, nearly doubled.

The war gave a boost to women, who put on work clothes and headed to the factories to fill much-needed positions. Some 350,000 women also joined the armed forces and served in a variety of noncombatant positions. The fact that many women were now taking on jobs that hitherto had been reserved for men, old stereotypes of femininity and women's supposed physical limitations were called into question. The pay for those working in plants that received government contracts was good. There was a downside, however. According to one source, workplace safety was often the main point of contention: "Quite literally, during the first few years of the Second World War, it was safer for Americans to be on the battlefield than it was for them to work on the home front of the arsenal of democracy. Workplace deaths during the war averaged yearly between 17,800 and 20,100; 1943 saw the highest number of wartime workplace deaths. Further, according the Bureau of Labor Statistics, a staggering 2 million workplace injuries and/or disability occurred each year during the war." The war was good for labor as a whole. With high-paying jobs and favorable government regulations, the ranks of organized labor swelled from 10 million in 1941 to nearly 15 million in 1945.

Due in part to the lack of sufficient adult supervision, juvenile delinquency increased during the war, as did gang violence. Ethnic and racial tensions remained high, as witnessed by the Zoot Suit Riots against Mexican Americans in Los Angeles and the 1943 race riots in Detroit.

THREE CONTROVERSIAL DECISIONS

Internment of Japanese Americans

Shortly after the Japanese attack on Pearl Harbor, Roosevelt issued a controversial executive order (9066) mandating the expulsion of Japanese Americans from the West Coast into internment camps. **Internment** *means putting a person in prison or other kind of detention, generally in wartime.*

Military zones were created in California, Washington, and Oregon—states with a large population of Japanese Americans—and Roosevelt's executive order commanded the relocation of Americans of Japanese ancestry. This action, motivated by fears of possible espionage, revived important concerns over the extent to which a government can suspend fundamental human freedoms during wartime. Fred Korematsu, a native of California and of Japanese ancestry, sued the federal government, charging that this enforced internment violated his civil rights as an American citizen, which was clearly unconstitutional. The Supreme Court, in attempting to ensure public safety, sided with the government in citing the principle of a clear and present danger. Justice Robert A. Jackson in his dissent argued that if any fundamental assumption underlies our system, it is that guilt is personal and not inheritable. This meant that Korematsu was convicted not for committing a crime but because he was of Japanese descent. Jackson also raised the point that the president's decree was a military order and that a court cannot enforce such an order if it clearly violates the Constitution. Racism may have also affected this decision. Despite the fact that Germany was the Allies' number one enemy, the Germans were seen in a different light from the Japanese, who, as Asians, were considered by many Americans to be racially inferior. This controversial decision is still debated among historians.

The Holocaust

Technically speaking, the world war was a holocaust with an estimated death toll of between 70 million to 85 million killed, or roughly 3% of the entire world population in 1940. **Holocaust** means *destruction or slaughter on a mass scale*. More specifically, the

Holocaust refers to the systematic liquidation of the Jewish populations of Europe during the Second World War. A consequence of the German totalitarian state was the rounding up of people and confining them to **concentration camps,** which are *a place where large numbers of people, especially political prisoners or members of persecuted minorities, are deliberately imprisoned in a relatively small area with inadequate facilities, sometimes to provide forced labor or to await mass execution.*

Those put in such places were persons who did not fit into the Nazi new world order, including political opponents (particularly socialists and communists), those with unconventional lifestyles, and religious opponents, particularly Jews. Overall, about 80% of those in such camps were non-Jews.

The philosophy of the Nazi state was predicated on race and racial purity. The Jews, who are essentially a religious and ethnic category of people, were classified under the Nazi system as a race, which was endowed with every negative association one wished to ascribe to it. Throughout the 1930s, it was Nazi policy to marginalize the Jews from German life through restrictive laws, essentially depriving them of citizenship and making them a convenient scapegoat. This was a step-by-step process (not a preconceived plan, as some historians have suggested), which became over time more radicalized. It should be pointed out that anti-Semitism was rife throughout Europe at this time, which was an important factor in bringing about the Holocaust.

After the start of the war, as German troops pressed into eastern Europe where the majority of Jews lived, the problem developed as to what to do with them. Massive killings in Poland and Germany took place by *Einsatzgruppen* (killing squads), with considerable help from the largely anti-Semitic public. Two years into the war, the idea emerged of a more systematic way of getting rid of the Jews and other "antisocial types." Consequently, a number of death camps were built (mostly in Poland) that streamlined the killing process in assembly-line fashion up to the end of the war.

While all this was going on, countries that could have been safe havens for those fleeing the Nazis did relatively little to help them. The pope, who knew what was occurring and exercised considerable influence over believing Catholics, said and did little to help the Jews. President Roosevelt directed that all resources should go to winning the war and not be diverted to other matters, e.g., bombing railroad lines leading to the concentration and death camps. Moreover, the pronounced anti-Semitism within the American government prevented a modification of the 1924 Quota Law, which placed strict limits on the number of Jews and other nationals who could enter the country. Despite these restrictions, 200,000 Jews found their way to the United States between 1933 and 1945. Bolivia opened its doors, allowing Jewish refugees to enter the country from 1938 to 1941.

The Atomic Bomb

In December 1938, two German physicists stunned the scientific world by splitting the atom, making the creation of an atomic bomb possible. Knowing that the Nazis would be developing this technology, President Roosevelt secretly directed that a group of American scientists be put to work on creating an atomic bomb, which was accomplished by the end of 1942. Two weeks after Roosevelt died, on April 12, 1945, Harry Truman, now president, was informed that the atomic bomb was ready for use.

The decision to drop the atomic bomb on Japan was controversial, to say the least. Many signs pointed to the fact that the Japanese military machine (not to mention the Japanese economy) was on the verge of collapse, and it was widely thought that the Japanese government would be willing to surrender, provided that Emperor Hirohito be retained as head of state. Those favoring use of the bomb thought that the only alternative to employing the bomb would be a costly invasion of the Japanese homeland. Moreover, they figured that its use would prove decisive. They were right. Truman decided to go with the bomb. On August 6, 1945, an atomic bomb was dropped on the city of Hiroshima, killing outright a quarter of the city's 280,000 residents. By the end of the year, half the population was dead. A second bomb was dropped on the industrial city of Nagasaki, with similar devastation. Japan surrendered unconditionally shortly thereafter.

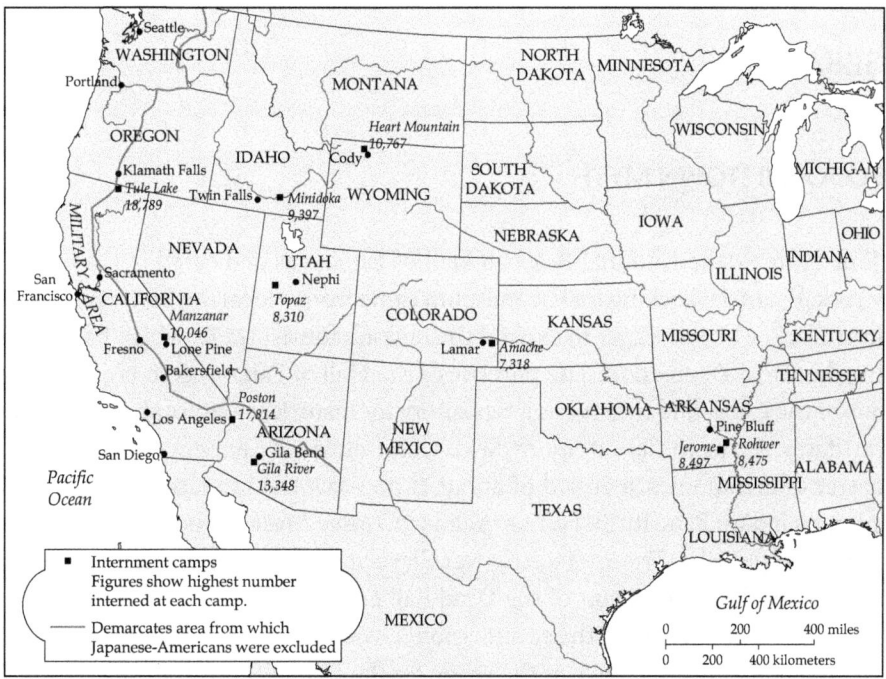

MAP 10.4 Japanese-American Internment Camps, 1942–1945

TURNING POINTS AND THE END OF THE WAR

The Second World War provided a number of significant battles that determined its outcome. The Battle of Britain was one such crisis; another was the combined victory by Allied forces in North Africa. Perhaps most important was the defeat of the German Sixth Army at Stalingrad in Russia in January 1943. Russia, which had suffered the brunt of the fighting and casualties, had been pressing Roosevelt and Churchill since 1942 for help by opening a second front in western Europe. Following a number of delays, the Allies launched the Operation Overlord (known as D-Day) attack across the English Channel to the heavily guarded coast of France on June 6, 1944. By then, the tide of battle had turned. Rome was liberated on June 5, 1944, and Paris fell to the Allies two months later. By mid-1944, Russian troops were pushing into Poland and eastern Europe. A year later, the Allies entered Germany from the west, while the Soviet army moved in from the east. The Germans surrendered on May 2, 1945, which effectively ended the war. Hitler was not around to witness the end—he had committed suicide in his underground bunker as the Russians closed in. With the conclusion of the war in the west, Russia, as previously promised, entered the war against Japan. By then, the Japanese army had largely been pushed back to the mainland. Japan formally signed surrender terms on September 2, 1945.

BASEBALL

THE COOPERSTOWN MYTH

On June 12, 1939, the National Baseball Hall of Fame was dedicated in Cooperstown, New York. Financial backing for the museum came from a local tavern owner, Stephen Carlton Clark, who was eager to expand the region's tourist trade, which had fallen off during the Great Depression. The purpose of the Hall of Fame was to honor the great players of the game, and to serve as a repository for historical memorabilia, documents, and artifacts. At the initial ceremony, with Commissioner Kenesaw Mountain Landis as master of ceremonies, a crowd of about 11,000 saw the induction of 10 heroes of the past, including Babe Ruth, Honus Wagner, Connie Mack, Napoleon Lajoie, Walter Johnson, George Sisler, Tris Speaker, Grover Cleveland Alexander, and Eddie Collins. Ty Cobb, perhaps the greatest star of the Dead Ball era, boycotted the ceremony to avoid having his picture taken with the commissioner, with whom he had issues.

The selection of Cooperstown as the venue for the Hall of Fame was not accidental. In his speech to the gathering, Landis remarked, "Nowhere other than at its birthplace could this museum be appropriately situated." This, of course, was a convenient myth, given the unclear origins of the game, which played into a nostalgic desire to reaffirm the national pastime's purely American beginnings. The date was also significant, insofar as it marked a hundred years from the alleged creation of the game in Cooperstown, in 1839. The dedication ceremony occurred unintentionally two months before the start of the Second World War, marking another important transition in the history of baseball.

THE 1941 SEASON

Even before the United States entered the war, Major League Baseball enjoyed one of its most remarkable seasons. The game that year was highlighted by the feats of its two brightest stars: Ted Williams and Joe DiMaggio. Starting on May 15, DiMaggio hit in a record-breaking 56 consecutive games, which ended on July 17 against the Cleveland Indians. During that time, the Yankees' centerfielder had a .408 batting average, with 91 hits and 15 home runs. DiMaggio's hit record has never been duplicated.

Meanwhile, Williams was blistering the baseball and hitting at an astonishing .400 clip for most of the season. Through September 11, he was batting .413, and then "slumped." Entering the last two games of the season against Philadelphia, the Red Sox slugger was batting .400. Advised by his manager, Joe Cronin, to sit out the double-header so as to preserve this milestone average, Williams refused. He went on to get three hits in the first game and four hits in the second game, to finish with a .406 average. Rarely in the history of baseball had such a feat been accomplished.

JUDGE LANDIS AND THE APPROVAL OF PRESIDENT ROOSEVELT TO CONTINUE BASEBALL

Shortly after the United States entered the war, Judge Landis, despite his dislike for Roosevelt and his policies, wrote a tactful letter to the president asking about the fate of wartime professional baseball. The president responded, saying he felt that keeping baseball going would be in the best interests of the country, even though people would have to work harder and give full exertion to the war effort. Roosevelt noted that while able-bodied ballplayers would be expected to serve in the armed forces, older players might take their place so as to provide entertainment for the public.

Within days after the Japanese attack on Pearl Harbor, players flocked to join the colors. Cleveland fire-baller Bob Feller was one of the first to sign up and saw duty throughout the war in the Navy. Soon, many of the game's other stars such as Ted Williams and Joe DiMaggio were in uniform. By 1943, more than a hundred major league players had joined the armed forces, along with 1,400 minor leaguers. The following year, the number had increased to 500 and 5,000, respectively. Some players avoided military service by engaging in war production jobs. There were others who did not meet the physical requirements. Cleveland's Lou Boudreau was rejected by the draft board due to bad ankles and was classified as 4-F, unfit for service. This did not stop Boudreau from playing, and the following year (1944) he led the league in hitting, with a .327 batting average.

Despite the inconveniences and the shortages of gasoline needed for the war, major league teams decided to play a full schedule. The clubs did, however, curtail travel to the South for spring training, preferring to stay closer to home. The Dodgers trained, sometimes in the snow, at Bear Mountain, north of New York City, while other teams prepared for the season in armories or indoor arenas. Broadcasters and reporters were told not to comment on the weather, lest this information reach the enemy. While initially discouraged because of the fear of air raids, night games were encouraged to boost attendance. The Chicago Cubs planned to install lights at Wrigley Field, but donated them to the war effort instead. Most night games were, in fact, twilight games, due to "dim-out" regulations to save energy and because of year-round daylight saving.

BASEBALL AND THE RENEWED WAVE OF PATRIOTISM

As with the First World War, organized baseball waved the flag of patriotism and supported patriotic causes. Players in a number of ballparks would march to the flagpole before a game and join in singing the National Anthem. Patriotic symbols were also employed. Commissioner Landis required all clubs to display the American flag on their uniforms. The Chicago Cubs put a War Department emblem on the uniforms of players returning from military service. Reenacting what had taken place in ballparks during the First World War, Philadelphia Phillies' players marched with bats, simulating rifles, on their shoulders during spring training games to show solidarity for the war effort.

Ball teams demonstrated their support for the war in more practical ways. The minor league Louisville club promoted a Waste Fat Night, in which fans donated thousands of pounds of grease that would be converted to glycerin to make powder for shells. In Cincinnati, a game was held in which the cost of admission was cigarettes, which were sent to the troops. Philip Wrigley, owner of the Chicago Cubs, sent free gum to the soldiers and refrained from using aluminum foil to wrap his gum so it could be used in war production. Major league teams were also active in promoting war bonds and raising money for relief efforts. Baseball was often used by politicians, businesses, and other agencies to rally support for the war by promoting "Americanism."

Blacks living under apartheid had less cause to back such efforts, even though most supported the war, and many fought gallantly in a segregated U.S. military. The Negro leagues provided both soldiers and entertainment. An example of how segregation played out during wartime baseball was the rule that Blacks were rarely allowed to play games with Whites within the United States but were permitted to do so when stationed abroad. Larry

Doby was denied the opportunity of playing for the Great Lakes Navy team, even though he was one of the best Black players in the country, if not one of the best players in all of baseball. Commissioner Landis, praising baseball as a symbol of the United States and a "melting pot," clearly took into account only those players with white skin. While the war, as far as baseball was concerned, reinforced segregation, it gave a boost to ethnic diversity. As sports page celebrities, Detroit's Hank Greenberg and Joe DiMaggio inadvertently contributed to greater acceptance of Jews and Italians.

REPLACEMENT PLAYERS

Clearly, the loss of major and minor league players to the military greatly compromised the quality of organized baseball during the war. Some older players such as Babe Herman, Pepper Martin, and Jimmie Foxx came out of retirement to fill positions on major league rosters. Joe Nuxhall, at the age of 15, became the big league's youngest player. Disabled players such as Pete Gray, who had only one arm, also found a spot in the majors. Depleted rosters created an even playing field that allowed poorer teams to compete at a higher level. By the 1944 season, when the greatest numbers of players were off to war, the St. Louis Browns—for decades the perennial doormat of the American League—found themselves in the World Series against the Cardinals, their hometown rivals. Despite the fact that the Cardinals won the all–St. Louis series four games to two, the Browns achieved a moment of glory they would not experience again.

THE ALL-AMERICAN GIRLS PROFESSIONAL BASEBALL LEAGUE

As male professional clubs dwindled during the course of the war, Chicago Cubs' owner Philip Wrigley hit upon the idea of fielding a professional women's baseball team, consisting largely of women softball players. This was the genesis of the All-American Girls Professional Baseball League (AAGPBL) that commenced operations in 1943. The teams were situated in medium-sized Midwest cities such as Rockford, Illinois, South Bend Indiana, Racine, Wisconsin, among others. The AAGPBL played a high caliber of baseball, and generated a following of fans of both sexes. They even drew interest from GIs overseas. While women's professional baseball helped to alter the standard feminine stereotypes at that time, league rules required the players to act and dress in a ladylike manner, attend charm school, and appear glamorous. In addition, the AAGPBL women were recruited to sell war bonds. Their games featured numerous funds and charities aimed at promoting the war.

MILITARY BASEBALL HOME AND ABROAD

Major and minor league players not only fought in Europe and the Pacific but carried on their occupations in military leagues. As far as the military was concerned, baseball was not just recreation, but an important part of their training program that honed physical skills, along with instilling competition and team spirit. Foremost among the stateside military leagues, which were active on all bases, was the naval Great Lakes Training Center, which featured a number of big-league stars. The composite Great Lakes team compiled a record of 188 wins and 32 losses during the war years.

FIGURE 10.2 Game between servicemen stationed at Amchitka Island, Aleutians, in June 1943.

Service baseball was extensively played overseas. By 1943, with nearly a million American soldiers stationed in Britain, baseball leagues quickly formed. The London International Baseball League, for instance, faced challengers in Britain, Northern Ireland, and France. Wherever the troops were situated, overseas military baseball flourished. Games were played under the Leaning Tower of Pisa in Italy, on the spacious parks in Paris, and in fields and pastures near towns that had been liberated. Baseball was played extensively in North Africa, where it was promoted heavily by former big leaguer Zeke Bonura. It was the same story in the various Pacific theaters. An unusual story concerned Moe Berg, who played on a number of major league teams. As a person of extremely high intellect who could speak 12 languages, Berg served as a spy for the American government in a variety of capacities. On a tour with all-star players to Japan in 1934, he secretly took military-sensitive photos of sites that were later helpful to pilots carrying out bombing missions over Japanese cities.

Baseball was also played in prisoner-of-war camps as a form of recreation. There were dozens of teams in such camps. The Germans not only allowed baseball to flourish, but even permitted shipments of equipment supplied by the Red Cross as a means of keeping the prisoners active and out of trouble. In Japanese camps, which were far more brutal, there was less tolerance for inmate baseball, and camp personnel were known to confiscate equipment provided to prisoners by charitable organizations.

Baseball was played in all the Japanese American internment camps, most particularly at the 18-square-mile Tule Lake facility in Northern California. At that camp, there were at least 24 baseball fields, which provided for dozens of teams that formed into American and National leagues. The inmates, from whom there were a number of excellent players, held tryouts for their teams. Not only did they play among themselves, but also against White teams composed of players outside the camps. It was noted that a composite Tule Lake club won two games against a California All-Star team. The internment camps remained open for seven months after the war, and baseball continued at Tule Lake until October 1945. Baseball in these facilities, and elsewhere around the world during the war, served as a positive force, in contrast with the raging hostilities elsewhere.

SUMMARY

As with the First World War, when hostilities initiating the Second World War commenced in 1939, the United States was a neutral nation. This changed after the Japanese bombed the American fleet at Pearl Harbor on December 7, 1941. The country immediately entered the war on the side of the Allies (Britain and Russia) against the Axis powers of Germany, Italy, and Japan. Now in the war, the United States quickly mobilized the home front, turning industries producing profitable consumer goods to war production. With millions of men fighting abroad, women entered the workforce in large numbers, challenging traditional gender roles.

In defense of the Allied war efforts and a vision for the postwar world, President Roosevelt gave forth his "Four Freedoms," which were intended statements of humanity's inherent rights.

The war brought to light three major issues that would have important consequences. For reasons of national security, many Japanese Americans living on the West Coast were forced into internment camps until the end of the war in violation of their constitutional rights. The Holocaust perpetrated against the Jews in Europe challenged other nations to intervene on their behalf. The response for various reasons was far from adequate. Toward the end of the war, with the Japanese military pushed back to its homeland, the United States faced a crucial decision over whether to use atomic weapons against that nation. The dropping of two atom bombs on Japan ended the Second World War.

Baseball supported the war effort in a number of ways with many major and minor league players joining the colors. Where the soldiers went about the globe, they took baseball with them. The decimation of the professional leagues opened the door for retired players and those unqualified for the draft to take their place. At the same time, the All-American Girls Professional League was formed, which offered a good brand of baseball in cites throughout the Midwest.

STUDY QUESTIONS

1. In what way was President Roosevelt's "Four Freedoms" a vision for the postwar world? Was it a realistic goal, as Roosevelt indicated?
2. Was the internment of Japanese Americans justified? Did Roosevelt's executive order meet the requirement of a "clear and present danger"?
3. What were some of the ways baseball served the war effort?

Credits

Fig. 10.1: "Pearl Harbor Attack," http://www.loc.gov/pictures/item/owi2001045668/PP/, 1941.
Fig. 10.2: "Baseball Game at Amchitka Island," 1943.

CHAPTER 11

Postwar America—Challenges and Prosperity

HISTORICAL BACKGROUND

At the close of the Second World War, the balance of power in Europe shifted eastward to the Soviet Union and westward to the United States. Britain and France were largely bankrupted by the war. Losing political prestige, they were faced with the clamor for independence from nationalist groups within their colonies. Germany was decimated and divided into sectors under the control of the three victorious Allies: Britain, the Soviet Union, and the United States, along with France. The question is to what extent did developments in the postwar world conform to the vision set forth by President Roosevelt's "Four Freedoms"?

CREATING THE POSTWAR WORLD

A series of conferences toward the end of the war helped to shape the postwar world. At the Bretton Woods (New Hampshire) Conference in June 1944, the Allies agreed to replace the British pound with the American dollar as the basis of foreign currency. New financial organizations such as the International Monetary Fund (IMF) and the World Bank were created to ensure global economic balance and stability. At the Yalta Conference in February 1945, the three victorious Allied Powers agreed to demand the unconditional surrender of Germany, allow for free elections in eastern Europe, and that Russia would enter the war against Japan. At a later conference, the Allies laid plans for creation of the United Nations to replace the defunct League of Nations.

Roosevelt and Soviet Premier Joseph Stalin recognized the need for the Russians to be surrounded by a ring of friendly states in eastern Europe for its security. While Roosevelt and Stalin wanted to continue friendly relations, this was not to happen. In July, when the Allies met again at Potsdam, Roosevelt was dead, and Harry Truman was now president. Shortly after taking office, he was informed that the atomic bomb was ready for use. Armed with this knowledge, Truman sought to deny the Soviets the economic and territorial concessions they had been promised at Yalta.

COMMENCEMENT OF THE COLD WAR

Soon after the war, relations between the Russians and its former allies deteriorated rapidly. The Cold War, as it was called, was largely a psychological and perceptual conflict of incompatible economic and ideological systems. The question thus arises as to whether the Cold War was inevitable. The answer: not necessarily so. Both Roosevelt and Henry Wallace (the vice president from 1941 to 1945) hoped to maintain cordial relations with the Soviets. Wallace was dropped from the ticket in 1944 for political reasons, enabling more hawkish individuals to direct policy. At the same time, the Russians retreated into a more nationalistic posture. The Cold War might have been averted if each side had respected the security and national interests of the other, devoid of ideological zealotry.

But this did not come about. Hatred of communism, dating back to the Russian Revolution (1917), resurfaced after the war, perpetuated by defenders of the status quo in the West who wished to reassert their power. There followed a series of events that only reinforced (from the American perspective) the ill will and expansionist tendencies of the Soviets.

In February 1946, George Kennan, the American ambassador to the Soviet Union, expressed his belief in a long telegram that the Soviets were not to be trusted, and there could be no peaceful coexistence between Russia and the United States. Magazines and newspapers picked up the message, and the American reading public was flooded with a wave of anti-communist and anti-Soviet reports and stories that disseminated throughout the culture.

Reacting to a civil war in Greece, instigated by pro-communist Greek insurgents, President Truman issued what came to be called the Truman Doctrine, which stated that the United States would "support free peoples who are resisting attempted subjugation by armed minorities or outside pressures." The doctrine was, in many ways, a restatement of the Platt Amendment and the Roosevelt Corollary, reserving to the United States the right to use military power to protect its own interests. The Truman Doctrine also justified a permanent military presence after the war, paid for by deficit spending and federal borrowing.

FIGURE 11.1 Senator Joseph McCarthy showing map of alleged communist organizations operating in the United States. Many of McCarthy's allegations proved to be false.

As the British and French colonial empires dissolved into independent nations, the United States used its military and economic power to step into the vacuum and act as a global policeman. The world war had greatly expanded the size of the federal bureaucracy, which contained a new security apparatus, inclusive of the Central Intelligence Agency (CIA) and the National Security Council (NSC). This marked a significant departure from the past, when the military operations of the United States had remained within their own hemisphere. Now they would become part of a global strategy.

In June 1947, Secretary of State George Marshall announced a "European Recovery Plan" aimed at combating suffering and the economic and social desolation of postwar Europe. This plan, apart from its humanitarian purpose, had the intention of limiting the appeal of communist parties in western Europe. Money from the Marshall Plan used for capital projects was issued in the form of credits to American corporations, which of course benefited the U.S. economy.

DIVIDING THE WORLD EAST AND WEST

There were other events that reinforced Cold War attitudes. On June 24, 1948, the Soviets cut off rail traffic to Berlin through Germany's eastern sector, due to the violation of prior agreements by the United States. This act instigated an around-the-clock airlift of food and supplies to the British, American, and French sectors of West Berlin. The airlift finally ended in May 1949. Soon afterward, the United States was instrumental in forming the North Atlantic Treaty Organization (NATO), which was a military arrangement among European anti-communist forces under U.S. control. The Soviets later engineered their own military alliance, the Warsaw Pact, in 1955.

Toward the end of 1949, the Chinese Communist Party, which had been building up support since the 1920s, gained control of China. Although the Chinese Communists were a separate entity from the Soviets, policy makers in the West saw them as part of an international communist conspiracy. The inability to distinguish political ideology from national interests would cloud American foreign policy for decades to come.

Further trouble emerged in 1950, when North Korean communist forces in the divided peninsula invaded South Korea and challenged the American-installed dictatorship there. The American-led United Nations force quickly adopted a resolution opposing this aggression, which resulted in the Korean War. This costly, difficult, and strategically unimportant war lasted until an armistice was established on June 27, 1953. Ironically, this back-and-forth struggle hardly changed the boundary between the two countries.

By 1950, Soviet scientists effectively produced an atomic bomb of their own, which shifted the Cold War into another phase. The threat of nuclear war would cast a shadow over the world for decades to come and would produce insane scenarios such as Mutually Assured Destruction (MAD) that was entertained during the 1950s. The thinking behind

MAD was that if the Soviets launched an all-out attack on the United States, the favor would be returned, causing the mutual destruction of both civilizations. Essentially, all foreign policy calculations and decisions, until the end of the Soviet Union in 1991, would be made in light of the Cold War.

McCARTHYISM AND THE NEW RED SCARE

Thanks in large part to the growing hysteria that characterized Cold War America, there emerged a new "Red scare" and its consequent disregard for civil liberties and constitutional rights. In many ways, this was a repeat of the post–First World War attack on radicals and nonconformists. Heightened fears about communism—mixed with irrational patriotism—led to a witch hunt against those on the political left who challenged the status quo. The House Un-American Activities Committee began hearings into organizations suspected of having communist sympathies. Republican Senator Joseph McCarthy from Wisconsin spearheaded a number of investigations into communist activities, making wild and inaccurate accusations against a number of innocent people.

These attacks were based on largely questionable suspicions that important government officials had been guilty of passing atomic bomb secrets and other sensitive information to the Soviets. One such suspected person was Alger Hiss, a high State Department official, who was eventually convicted of perjury. Another high-profile case involved Julius and Ethel Rosenberg, a Jewish couple and admitted members of the Communist Party, who were convicted of treason—on doubtful evidence—and sent to die in the electric chair at Sing Sing Prison. Many well-intentioned Americans, who had joined the American Communist Party in the 1930s, were denounced, even though most had disavowed their previous affiliation.

The Red scare put a premium on loyalty and conformity. The McCarran Internal Security Act of 1950, similar to the Sedition Act of 1918, banned people with "Communist sympathies" from entering the United States, and forced "subversive" groups to register with the government. Police departments in a number of cities used "Red squads" to gather information on certain political groups. In New Rochelle, New York, suspected communists were required to register with the police. Educators were forced to sign loyalty oaths upon threat of losing their jobs. In *Dennis v. United States*, the Supreme Court upheld the jailing of Communist Party leaders. Throughout the country, increased powers were given to the FBI to root out alleged nonconformists. The vague and arbitrary allegations of communism enabled business leaders to smear labor unions. White supremacists also used the communist label to attack civil rights groups.

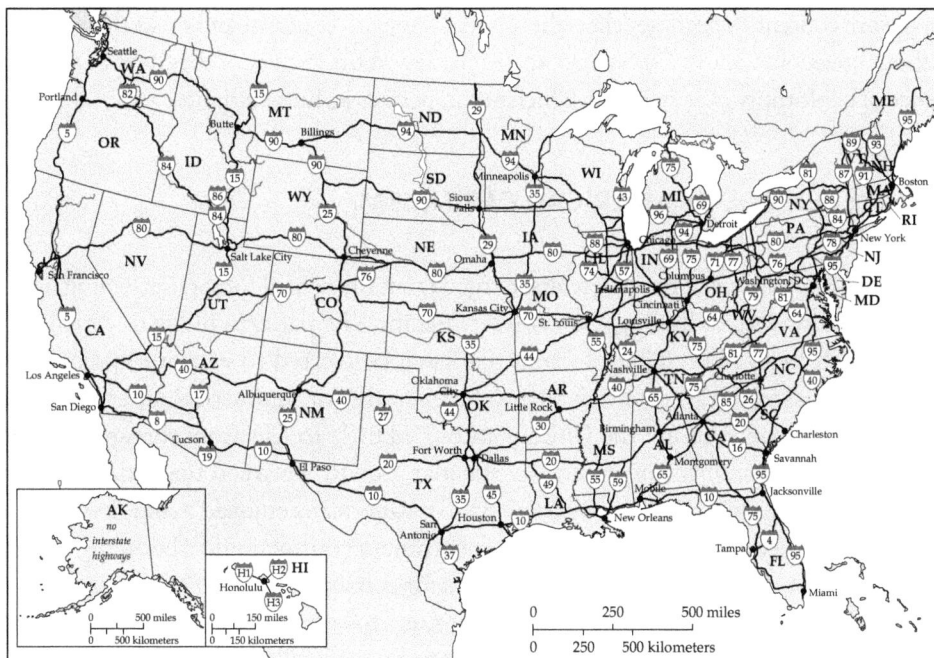

MAP 11.1 The Interstate Highway System Begun in 1956 and Completed in 1993

FREEDOM AND CONFORMITY

In 1947, historian Henry Steele Commager wrote an influential article for *Harper's* magazine, titled "Who is Loyal to America." In the article, Commager argued that those who claimed to be loyal were disloyal to American principles, and that the new loyalty was actually conformity, or the uncritical acceptance of America's political and economic institutions as a finished product. He noted that the pressure of conformity stymied curiosity and intellectual freedom, rejecting inquiry into the race question, socialized medicine, public housing, or the validity of America's foreign policy. By the same token, those defined as loyal were the ones who spouted bigotry, held anti-union beliefs, sought to restrict voting rights, and in other ways subverted the Constitution. In other words, Commager saw loyalty as the opposite of freedom. Commager's arguments would set the tone for much of the 1950s.

Writing a decade later, sociologist C. Wright Mills argued that since freedom is the opportunity to choose between sets of alternatives, it cannot exist without an enlarged capacity for human reason. He noted that the issue of freedom is a problem because, at that time (1959), many people did not naturally want to be free, meaning that they did not want to accept the responsibilities that freedom imposes on one. Therefore, the mass of unthinking people are content to become "cheerful robots," happy to conform and do as they are told without question. Clearly, Commager and Mills viewed the temper of the times as the prevalence of conformity over freedom, which put in peril basic human rights.

THE GOLDEN AGE OF AMERICAN CAPITALISM

After the war, millions of men were discharged from the armed forces. Returning home, they looked forward to finding a job and settling into the patterns of life to which they were accustomed. Many factories that had been converted to war production now reverted to making all kinds of salable products. As the lone industrial superpower (far ahead of the Soviet Union), the United States had little to fear from foreign competition; hence, its economy underwent spectacular growth. Between 1946 and 1960, the gross national product doubled. By 1960, 60% of Americans enjoyed a middle-class lifestyle. The new economy was sustained by government contracts and a booming private sector, brought about by high rates of demand for consumer goods. Defense industries that had developed during the world war continued to be engines for growth in regions of the South and the West Coast. The number of white-collar workers surpassed the number of manual blue-collar workers for the first time. While the percentage of those employed on farms diminished during the 1950s, agricultural production increased.

Greater prosperity triggered a desire for space, which contributed to the growth of suburbs. By 1960, suburban families for the first time outnumbered those in rural areas and the inner cities. Home construction doubled during the 1950s. Of the 13 million new homes built between 1948 and 1958, 85% were constructed in the suburbs. The country witnessed a demographic shift, as newer service industries took root in cities such as Houston, Phoenix, and Los Angeles. Furthermore, there was a significant increase in population, thanks to the postwar baby boom. Large numbers of children led to the building of new schools and playgrounds. By the end of the decade, children born just after the war were entering their teenage years, leading to new styles of music (rock and roll), dancing, and more informal lifestyles. There was also an upsurge in juvenile delinquency.

CHANGES IN LIFESTYLES

The 1950s marked the predominance of the automobile. Large auto and rubber corporations colluded to buy up streetcar and railroad companies and put them out of business, paving the way for the car culture. Massive road construction, including freeways and interstate highways, responded to the multiplication of auto traffic. By 1960, 80% of American families owned at least one car, while 14% of families possessed two or more cars. The domestic auto industry was booming.

Changes in the physical landscape (suburbs, roads, cars) contributed to changes in lifestyle. A few people noticed that many Americans no longer wished to take the time for formal meals, which gave rise to the fast-food industry. McDonald's opened its first hamburger stand in 1954. Drive-in restaurants and movie theaters, and the emergence of shopping malls, illustrated the close relationship between changing lifestyles and the automobile.

As in the 1920s, but even more so, the 1950s were a time of expanded consumerism and material concerns. Most significant was the arrival of television. By the end of the decade, nine out of 10 families owned a television, which structured the way Americans used their leisure time. Television created a culture all its own, including a cast of celebrities and personalities, in addition to expanding one's visual horizons. Television reinforced an emphasis on the home as the center of activity and entertainment. Women, who had contributed greatly to the wartime economy, lost their jobs and were encouraged by the media to focus their energies on home and family. The comfortable middle-class world of the 1950s, reinforced by conformity, prosperity, and consumerism, led to a cultural and intellectual sterility, what sociologist C. Wright Mills called a nation of "cheerful robots" that would provide ammunition for future social critics.

New ideas of freedom and liberty also appeared. Clark Kerr, president of the University of California at Berkeley, argued that industrial society had created a consensus culture that provided for a common core of beliefs, ideas, and value judgments. He further argued that society expanded freedom by creating more leisure time and promoting higher standards of living. This materialist perspective of freedom was matched by the comments of David Lilenthal, chairman of the Atomic Energy Commission, who contended that big business was not the enemy of freedom. Rather, large economic units coupled with free enterprise expanded freedom through creating greater consumer choice.

OVERT AND COVERT OPERATIONS ABROAD

By the mid-1950s, the Cold War, which had emerged in a climate of fear, suspicion, and hatred, had become institutionalized, both in the United States and the Soviet Union. Large military establishments on both sides, plus the close association between an expanding military and defense industries, created a powerful institutional structure that perpetuated building up arms for their own ends. The Central Intelligence Agency (CIA) in the United States drew upon American military superiority to engage in covert actions against suspected (loosely defined) communist regimes in places such as Iran, Guatemala, and Indochina (Vietnam), the latter of which had been part of the French empire. The United States moved into Vietnam after the French were pushed out, in order to combat the communist/nationalist forces in the north under the leadership of Ho Chi Minh. The steady commitment of U.S. forces at the behest of the military was the basis for the Vietnam War.

BASEBALL

A NEW COMMISSIONER

A year before the end of the war (1944), Commissioner Kenesaw Mountain Landis died at the age of 78. Judge Landis had ruled baseball for 24 years with an iron fist, and while his rulings were often arbitrary, he did help bring order and respectability to the game. Landis has often been condemned for opposing the entry of Blacks into the major leagues. It is true he was something of a bigot, but this dubious honor he shared with a number of the owners who fought to maintain the status quo and thus preserve the "gentlemen's agreement" that big-league baseball should remain White.

To replace Landis, the owners sought a person with a strong public image and someone who would not interfere with their business decisions. Moreover, they wanted an efficient administrator to carry out the policies they wanted, and to lobby officials to further their interests with the government in Washington, DC. The man they selected, Albert B. "Happy" Chandler, a former U.S. senator and governor from Kentucky, fell short of all these expectations. Despite his $50,000 annual salary, Chandler acted more as a glad-handing politician desiring to please everyone rather than someone who would give vision and direction to organized baseball. Before the end of his seven-year contract, due to expire in 1952, the owners did not hesitate to fire him. They then selected one of their own, Ford Frick, the former National League president, who served as commissioner until 1965.

THE RESURGENCE OF BASEBALL AFTER THE WAR

In the years after the war, 1946–1949, the popularity of professional baseball reached another high point. The wartime sacrifices brought on by rationing, long hours of work, and various other hardships left the majority of Americans starved for entertainment and with a desire to return to comfortable and familiar pastimes.

The late 1940s witnessed some of the game's best baseball and most exciting pennant races. As ballplayers exchanged their military uniforms for baseball suits, the game again became more competitive. The first club to rise to predominance was the Boston Red Sox, which had begun to compile winning records in the years prior to the war. With a star-studded lineup, the Red Sox won 104 games in 1946, marred only by Boston's loss to the St. Louis Cardinals in the World Series. The Yankees returned to form in 1947, easily winning both the pennant and the World Series, defeating the Brooklyn Dodgers in seven games.

The 1948 season was one of the most climactic in American League history. Three teams—the Boston Red Sox, Cleveland Indians, and New York Yankees—pushed the pennant race down to the wire. As the season ended, the Red Sox and the Indians were tied, forcing a one-game playoff, which Cleveland won. They completed their triumph by defeating the hitherto hapless Boston Braves, who had not played in the World Series since 1914. The following season presented another cliff-hanger involving the Red Sox and the Yankees. With two games left and Boston in first place, the Red Sox only had to win one of those games to become the league champions. They lost both, and the Yankees went on to the World Series.

While attention was focused on the American League race, the Dodgers and the Cardinals were battling it out in a similar fashion in the National League. Traditionally the weakest of the New York franchises, the Brooklyn club under General Manager Branch Rickey had patiently put together a farm system that rivaled St. Louis. Staffed with good homegrown players and coupled with elite players from the Negro leagues, thanks to integration, the Dodgers were now in a position to become the dominant National League team for a decade.

THE MEXICAN LEAGUE AND CHALLENGES TO THE RESERVE CLAUSE

While major league teams were providing excitement on the field, organized baseball was confronted with a number of difficult problems. The first concerned a challenge to its supremacy. One of the most politically powerful families in Mexico decided to upgrade baseball in that country by paying major league players large salaries to ply their trade south of the border. In February 1946, eight big-league players were lured to Mexico, the most prominent of whom was Mickey Owen, the Dodgers' catcher. Both Ted Williams and Bob Feller turned down gigantic offers of $100,000 to play. In all, 27 U.S. players joined teams in the Mexican League, including Browns' shortstop Vern Stephens, who was paid $250,000, but found living in Mexico to be intolerable.

The commissioner and the owners took a dim view of the players who had jumped ship. When Owen returned to the United States and asked for reinstatement, he was turned down on the basis that he, as others, had violated the reserve clause, which gave teams the right to keep a player under contract as long as ownership wished. New York Giants' outfielder Danny Gardella took his case to court in 1947, challenging the reserve clause. Eventually, the case made its way to the U.S. Supreme Court, which upheld the 1922 decision exempting baseball from antitrust legislation, and thus legitimizing the reserve clause. In the end, Gardella received a sizable cash settlement for his troubles. Two years later, George Toolson, a minor league player, also challenged the reserve clause, and again the Supreme Court upheld it, citing precedent. Clearly, the Court did not wish to overturn baseball's traditional way of doing business. If changes were to be made, the justices believed that Congress should legislate on the status of the game.

More astute players and observers began to see organized baseball as a kind of plantation system, by which the magnates (plantation owners) extracted full benefits from their players (field hands), giving little back in return. Without a union, professional baseball athletes remained in the subordinate position they had occupied for decades. While union membership in other industries soared after the war, modest efforts were made to organize ballplayers. In 1946, Robert Murphy, an attorney, sought to create an American Baseball Guild among players on the Pittsburgh Pirates. His call for a strike vote fell short of the two-thirds needed for union certification. From that point, talk of a union was dead.

SHIFTING TEAMS AND DEMOGRAPHICS

In the following decade of the 1950s, the burst of enthusiasm underscoring the revival of baseball attendance in the late 1940s began to fade away. As with other institutions, baseball had to adjust to changing demographics. While increasingly more people moved from the inner cities to the suburbs and experienced a different lifestyle, they established new contacts and found a greater diversity of activities to occupy their time.

The primary diversion was television. Baseball had, for several decades, been a radio sport that commanded a broad listening audience. Television opened a whole new avenue for watching baseball. Big-league teams benefited from television revenues and club owners profited from deals with local networks. Teams collected between $15,000 and $75,000 for television rights. In 1949, the Gillette Razor Company signed a $200,000 seven-year deal with Major League Baseball to sponsor the World Series. While the owners accumulated greater profits, they refused to share this income with their players and kept it to themselves. Throughout this period player's salaries stagnated. The dependence on outside revenues at the expense of gate receipts marked an important shift in baseball financing.

The traditionally worst teams in both major leagues were the hardest hit by the dwindling fan base. Struggling to avoid bankruptcy, the St. Louis Browns hired Cleveland General Manager Bill Veeck, a person with great imagination who was well known for his promotional skills, to try and beef up fan attendance. Crowds at Browns' games often numbered in the hundreds, not thousands. One of Veeck's more outrageous stunts was to hire a midget, Eddie Gaedel, to bat in a game against Detroit. The 3-foot-7 Gaedel walked on four pitches and then was taken out of the game. While this stunt may have humored the fans, it did not amuse the commissioner or the owners, who had Gaedel's name stricken from the record books. Gaedel later joined a circus but died at the young age of 36. Veeck's attempt to move the franchise from St. Louis to Baltimore was blocked by the other owners, who disliked him. After he sold the club, the magnates approved the transfer.

The move to Baltimore was one of several shifts of franchises that occurred in the 1950s. The Boston Braves were the first when owner Lou Perini moved his club to Milwaukee, where the team was successful initially. The Philadelphia Athletics fell victim to management squabbles after the death of Connie Mack, who had been Major League Baseball's longest-serving manager. Unable to raise the necessary revenues and find a local buyer, the team was eventually sold, with league approval, to Chicago businessman Arnold Johnson, who relocated the club to Kansas City. Johnson, who previously bought the Kansas City territorial rights from the New York Yankees, turned his club into a virtual farm team for the Yankees during the 1950s. What these franchise shifts revealed was that two-team cities, which were losing population, could only support one club. Consequently, within a few years, the geographic arrangement that had lasted since 1903 changed.

Low attendance affected the minor leagues as well. In four years, from 1949 to 1953, the number of fans at minor league games declined by half, from 42 million to 22 million. Similarly, the number of leagues fell from 59 to 38 over the same period, with a reduction of (mostly independent) clubs from 243 to 150. By the 1950s, all major league teams had a farm system. Realizing that they could get by with fewer clubs, the minor leagues further dwindled. When major league expansion began in 1961, there were only 19 leagues left in the minors.

THE DOMINANCE OF NEW YORK BASEBALL

Throughout the 1950s, Major League Baseball was dominated by teams from New York. With the exception of 1950, when the Philadelphia Phillies won the National League crown, and the pennant-winning teams in Cleveland (1954) and Milwaukee (1957–1958), New York clubs in both leagues appeared in the World Series every year prior to 1959. The New York Yankees were again the dominant team, winning the World Series from 1949 to 1953, and again in 1956 and 1958. Their main rival was the Brooklyn Dodgers, who appeared in the fall classic in 1952, 1953, 1955, and 1956.

Several writers and commentators have referred to this decade as the "last golden age" of baseball, and it certainly had its share of highlights. Most notable was the 1951 playoffs between the favored Dodgers and the Giants, who had been trailing for much of the season. With a four-run lead in the ninth inning, the Dodgers looked poised to win the pennant. In the bottom of the inning, however, the Giants fought back, adding a run. With two men on base, Bobby Thomson hit a home run to left field to win the game. Years later, it was revealed that the Giants had developed an elaborate spying network to pick off the signs from the opposing catcher, thus enabling the Giants' hitters to know what pitch to expect. This, no doubt, contributed to the team's surprising success. The Dodgers would get their revenge on the baseball world, particularly the Yankees, by winning the World Series in 1955 for the first time. A year later, opposing the Yankees in the Series again, the Dodgers were victim to a perfect game pitched by Don Larsen.

While the Yankees continued to roll, the Dodgers and Giants were declining teams with aging players, finishing in third and sixth place, respectively, in 1957. More important events, however, were taking place off the field. Needing a new ballpark, Dodgers' owner Walter O'Malley was willing to use his fortune to build a stadium in Brooklyn. His ambitions were thwarted by a grand scheme for the redevelopment of the borough, put forward by a man named Robert Moses, who exercised extensive authority over the operation. While negotiations with the planners dragged on, O'Malley was courted by influential people in Los Angeles, who wanted a big-league franchise and were willing to give the Dodgers' owner what he wanted. O'Malley then persuaded Giants' owner Horace Stoneham to shift his team to San Francisco. With the start of the 1958 season, both clubs were playing in California, leaving only the Yankees in New York. Hence, Major League Baseball now reached across the country, and it marked the start of a new era.

SUMMARY

The postwar era witnessed dramatic changes that would alter the course of modern America. The Cold War that emerged immediately after the Second World War dominated geopolitical thinking until the 1990s and beyond. Characteristic of the Cold War was the arms race between the United States and the Soviet Union, which was overshadowed by the buildup of atomic weapons on both sides. The hatred of communism fueled by the Cold War laid the basis for a "new Red scare" that mimicked the one at the end of the First World War, and challenged constitutional rights and civil liberties.

The 1950s, drawing upon American economic dominance, created wide-scale prosperity for a large segment of the population. Affordable cars, housing, and a healthy standard of living underscored this prosperity. Television came on the scene, which transformed people's lifestyle habits, along with fast-food restaurants and a host of other modern conveniences. The construction of a national highway system facilitated transportation.

Baseball witnessed a revival after the war, characterized by racial integration and several failed challenges to the reserve clause. Demographic changes within the national and urban environment resulted in lower attendance at ballgames, as more people moved from the inner city to the suburbs, along with population shifts to cities in the South and West that lured weak teams from cities that had more than one baseball team. Televised games also contributed to reduced attendance at games; however, revenues from television made the owners richer.

STUDY QUESTIONS

1. To what extent did the Cold War foster a climate of conformity in America? What was the effect of this conformity?
2. In what ways did developments in the postwar period limit and enhance liberty and freedom?
3. Discuss some of the reasons why the resurgence of baseball after the Second World War was stalled during the 1950s.

Credit

Fig. 11.1: "Welch-McCarthy Hearings," http://en.wikipedia.org/wiki/File:Welch-McCarthy-Hearings.jpg, 1954.

CHAPTER 12

Integration and Civil Rights

HISTORICAL BACKGROUND

Although the New Deal helped many families and individuals across the board, the condition of African Americans remained precarious, thanks largely to continuing segregation. Not only were Blacks excluded from many welfare programs such as Social Security, they faced discrimination at the workplace. Unions often made half-hearted efforts to organize Blacks, and tensions mounted between Black and White workers, who were often vying for the same jobs in factories still in the grip of the Great Depression. In the South, where discrimination was routine, not much had changed. Blacks were still liable to serious consequences if the rules governing segregation were violated. Question: Could it also be said that integration and the civil rights movement liberated Whites and gave Blacks greater freedom? If so, how?

THE FIRST PHASE OF THE CIVIL RIGHTS MOVEMENT

THE COMMENCEMENT OF CIVIL RIGHTS

It is erroneous to assume that society and its institutions remain static. The institution of segregation from the 1930s was challenged, often subtlety, by advocates for Black rights and those favoring integration, or the assertion of freedom. Noticeable changes were facilitated by the Second World War. As in so many other ways, the war engendered profound changes in American society that would gradually alter race relations in America. Given that the war was fought for the preservation of high ideals, Black leaders saw an opportunity to use this conflict against fascism to stage a campaign against racial prejudice and discrimination at home. **Prejudice** is defined as *a preconceived opinion that is not based on reason or actual experience.* **Discrimination** is *prejudicial treatment of different categories of people or things, especially on the grounds of race,* *age, or sex.* Even after the start of the war, many African Americans were excluded from wartime industries and were marginalized in the segregated federal government. In 1941, labor leader A. Philip Randolph threatened to assemble 10,000 Blacks for a march on Washington and to hold a rally in front of the Lincoln Memorial to demand equal rights and access to employment. The threatened march attracted the support of a number of civil rights leaders, which put pressure on the president to do something. To avoid the embarrassment that a high-profile event would have in exposing to the world America's own "dirty laundry," Roosevelt issued an executive order that forbade discrimination in defense industries. He also established a Fair Employment Practices Committee to handle complaints of unfair treatment. This was a first important step in what would become the civil rights movement, but there was a long way to go. The military remained segregated throughout the war, and African American units were largely deployed in noncombatant roles.

TENTATIVE CHALLENGES TO THE JIM CROW LAWS IN THE 1940S

Challenges to segregation occurred during the 1940s in a piecemeal fashion. A series of Supreme Court decisions confronted the iniquitous position of African Americans. In *Smith v. Allwright,* in 1944, the Court banned Whites-only primaries, which were common in the southern states. Two years later, the *Morgan v. Virginia* case ruled that interstate bus companies could not segregate passengers. In *Shelley v. Kraemer*, the Court struck down the practice of private agreements among property owners not to sell houses to African Americans and other minorities. While these decisions punched large holes into the institution of segregation, enforcing them would prove to be difficult, especially since many people saw that the federal government had only a limited role regarding Jim Crow laws.

In the meantime, civil rights organizations such as the NAACP and the Congress of Racial Equality (CORE) were putting pressure on state and local governments to end racial discrimination. While such pressures had no effect in the South, 30 cities and 12 states had by 1953 adopted fair employment laws. While the national Democratic Party was reluctant to actively press for an end to racial discrimination, given that White southerners constituted an important part of the party's coalition, President Harry S. Truman took the courageous step in calling for strong federal action against lynching, voter suppression, and other civil rights violations. When the Democrats included a civil rights plank in their national party platform in 1948, the southern White faction bolted the party (at least temporarily) and formed the short-lived Dixiecrat Party.

THE LANDMARK BROWN V. BOARD OF EDUCATION DECISION

By the 1950s, knowledge of the horrors of segregation was becoming mainstream, due to more press coverage and a number of celebrated cases. One incident in particular involved a 14-year-old boy named Emmett Till, who had gone to Mississippi from Chicago to visit his relatives and, innocently, broke one of the rules of segregation by speaking fresh to a White woman. Till was soon abducted by the woman's husband and brother, beaten to death beyond recognition, and dumped into a river in Money, Mississippi. To no one's surprise, the all-White jury at the trial acquitted the two men of murder. This case was covered in the media and dramatized the horrors of Jim Crow.

The attention of those opposed to segregation had already begun to focus on the question of segregated schools. About 40% of American schoolchildren went to segregated schools, which were uniformly inferior to White schools and severely underfinanced. Looking for a test case, lawyers for the NAACP highlighted the case of a seven-year-old Black girl named Linda Brown, whose parents wanted to send her to a White public school in Topeka, Kansas, that was closer to home instead of the Black school farther away. Thurgood Marshall, arguing the case for the NAACP, contended that segregation was inherently unequal, since it imposed serious psychological and social harm on Black children. The opposition pointed to a consistency of legal decisions over the years that supported the *Plessy v. Ferguson* decision. After some debate, the Supreme Court—in a unanimous 9-0 decision—declared that segregation in public schools was unconstitutional under the 14th amendment to the U.S. Constitution. While the *Brown v. Topeka Board of Education* decision was directed specifically toward segregation in schools, it brought into question the whole institution of racial inequality. Far from bringing the matter to closure, this decision would take several decades to become fully implemented, as the backers of the status quo dug their heels in to defend "their traditional way of life." In many ways, the battle for integration and civil rights had only begun.

THE MONTGOMERY BUS BOYCOTT

By the mid-1950s, greater numbers of Blacks, especially in southern cities, were chafing against Jim Crow-mandated local ordinances. Rules dictating that Blacks sit in the back of city buses and defer to White passengers were especially onerous. On December 1, 1955, Rosa Parks, an NAACP activist, tested the law by boarding a bus in Montgomery, Alabama. Parks refused to give up her seat to a White person and was arrested. This act galvanized the Black community, which boycotted the city buses for nearly a year, preferring to walk or carpool instead. The boycott was held together by mass meetings at local Black churches. The movement was further helped by the arrival of a 26-year-old preacher, the Reverend Dr. Martin Luther King, Jr. Along with other ministers in the

Southern Christian Leadership Conference (SCLC), King gave leadership to the movement. Black solidarity and loss of revenue finally forced the bus line and city officials to capitulate. In November 1956, a court declared segregated buses to be unconstitutional.

While King is generally given the major credit for the success of civil rights in the South, in truth, the movement was carried out by large numbers of people (Blacks and Whites) in hundreds of venues who were no longer willing to put up with the indignities of segregation. Many civil rights workers were young, and in a more general sense reflected a generation coming of age that was pushing against imposed conventions. The strength of the movement was in its nonviolent approach, meaning that acts of violence or intimidation would be met with passive resistance. This tactic created a moral divide between those who wished to hang on to the old discriminating practices of the past, and those who sought to invoke the higher ideals of the republic to further justice and equality.

ENFORCING SCHOOL INTEGRATION

The Supreme Court decision on school integration was put to a test in 1957 after the school board in Little Rock, Arkansas, accepted a federal court order to integrate the city's Central High School. Opposition came from the state's governor, Orval Faubus, who called out the Arkansas National Guard to prevent nine black students from enrolling. Segregationist sympathizers, many from out of state, came to Little Rock, which only complicated the issue. President Dwight D. Eisenhower, who was lukewarm toward civil rights, was put in a difficult position. Knowing that the federal government was being challenged, he sent in federal troops to protect the students.

A similar case of defiance occurred five years later (1962), when the governor of Mississippi, Ross Barnett, personally refused to allow a Black student, James Meredith, to enroll at the University of Mississippi. President John F. Kennedy, who also preferred to take a low-key approach to civil rights matters, was put into the same position as was his predecessor. After numerous failed attempts to negotiate with Barnett, Kennedy sent in federal marshals to ensure the court mandate was upheld. With the arrival of federal troops, the campus erupted into rioting, resulting in two deaths and more than one hundred people wounded. Order was restored, but the scale of anger and hostility to integration was plain for all to see.

THE INTENSIFICATION OF CIVIL RIGHTS

As the country moved into the 1960s, protests against segregation spread throughout the South. In 1960, a group of Black students from North Carolina A & T College began a series of sit-ins in the all-White sections of the lunch counters in the local Woolworth stores. This tactic spread and encouraged formation of the Student Nonviolent Coordinating

Committee (SNCC), in 1961. SNCC, along with other civil rights groups, began voter registration drives in Mississippi, where they encountered harassment and violence.

That same year, Whites and Blacks commenced the "Freedom Rides" by traveling south together on interstate buses. **Freedom Riders** were *civil rights activists who rode interstate buses into the segregated southern United States in 1961 and subsequent years to challenge the nonenforcement of U.S. Supreme Court decisions.* The Supreme Court had already declared segregated interstate bus travel to be illegal, but once buses crossed the Mason-Dixon Line, the rules of Jim Crow came into effect. The freedom riders defied these laws and were beset with physical violence and intimidation in the Deep South. As others joined in the Freedom Rides, with the help of federal marshals, interstate buses were desegregated.

Defying Jim Crow and nonviolently accepting arrest was the goal of the civil rights movement. The idea was that once the jails were filled with anti-apartheid protesters, then local officials would have to negotiate. This tactic was put to a test in Birmingham, Alabama, in 1963, in perhaps the most segregated city in the South at the time. Eugene "Bull" Connor, the public safety commissioner and a classic racist, not only overwhelmed the jails with hundreds of people seeking to integrate local stores but turned police dogs and fire hoses on Black demonstrators, many of them young children. Shocking pictures of this brutality were televised and provoked international sympathy. One of those arrested in Birmingham was Martin Luther King, Jr., who was placed in solitary confinement. From his cell, he wrote his "Letter from Birmingham Jail," which contained a number of powerful statements, the most memorable being, "We must come to see . . . that justice too long delayed is justice denied."

Four months later, King led a march on Washington, DC, which brought together a crowd of nearly 200,000 people, including 50,000 Whites. Speaking from the steps of the Lincoln Memorial, King uttered his famous "I have a dream" speech, which envisioned unity for all people—Blacks and Whites—even in the most segregated bastions of the country. The power of this speech, which exemplified freedom in its broadest sense, empowered the huge congregation of people willing to stand against the southern Jim Crow system. It revealed that the nonviolent civil rights movement had reached full maturity.

In response, violent opposition continued. White and Black college students in the North directed their attention the following year to voter registration drives in rural Mississippi. Freedom Summer, as it was called, also sought to educate Blacks about their political rights, teach basic literacy and other skills, and work to form a new political party, the Mississippi Freedom Democratic Party. This effort to educate Blacks, especially in rural areas of the state, about their rights was often dangerous. Three such college students were arrested for a minor violation and put in jail. Upon release late at night, the young men disappeared. Their bodies were found in a ditch weeks later. While not experiencing a similar tragic fate, many Freedom Summer volunteers were beaten, threatened, jailed, and abused in a number of ways.

Following the assassination of President Kennedy in November 1963, Vice President Lyndon B. Johnson became the new president. Johnson entered the White House determined to give legislative support to civil rights. In January 1964, the 24th amendment to the

Constitution was passed, which outlawed poll taxes that had habitually been used to keep Blacks from voting in the South. Two important pieces of legislation legally ended *de jure* segregation in the South. The Civil Rights Act (1964) outlawed racial discrimination in all public places, and the Voting Rights Act (1965) gave teeth to the 24th amendment and swept away all restrictive barriers imposed by Jim Crow laws regarding the right to vote. These acts, plus a significant shift in popular opinion on racial matters, were a major step in the effort to achieve equal rights that had begun during Reconstruction.

THE SECOND PHASE OF THE CIVIL RIGHTS MOVEMENT

While the war in Vietnam was holding center stage, the struggle for civil rights entered a new phase. Having enforced legal integration in the South, attention then turned to the social and economic conditions in the country as a whole. Blacks, many of whom lived in the ghettos of northern cities, suffered the most from poverty and discrimination.

URBAN RIOTS AND BLACK POWER

As Black people became more aware of injustices, the movement turned increasingly militant and violent. Young African Americans rejected the nonviolent approach of the SNCC and the SCLC, preaching instead Black Power, which was another perspective for obtaining freedom. **Black Power** is defined as *a movement in support of rights and political power for Black people, especially prominent in the United States in the 1960s and 1970s.* The call was for Blacks to defend themselves—with violence, if necessary—against the police and those they identified as the "White establishment." The Black Panthers, organized by Huey Newton and Bobby Seale in Oakland, California, saw African American ghettos as internal colonies in need of protection and self-determination. They organized self-help efforts and confronted directly those they deemed hostile. Another approach was taken by the Nation of Islam, a religious movement founded in Detroit, which rejected racial integration and favored Black separation, seeing White society as the enemy. They sought to form Black institutions and supported the Islamic religion, in opposition to the White man's Judeo-Christian churches and sects.

Even before the emergence of new organizations within the Black community, anger and frustration that had been building for decades boiled over into rioting. Violence broke out in the Watts neighborhood in Los Angeles in August 1965, which brought before the public images of looting, rioting, and arson. The Watts uprising had been preceded by riots the previous year in Rochester, New York, New York City's Harlem district, and Brooklyn, and were followed by violent outbursts in Newark, New Jersey, and Detroit in 1967. Fears of race war and civil strife that swept across the country cost the civil rights movement much of the goodwill it had garnered during its nonviolent phase. Martin Luther King, Jr., believed that the whole system of capitalism served to keep Blacks in the basement of American society. As cries for economic and social justice became louder, many White middle-class people saw threats to their own status and self-interests. Political rights and liberties were one thing, but economic justice and equality were not a priority for many Americans.

THE WAR ON DRUGS AND 'THE NEW SLAVERY'

The "war on drugs" was a response to the widespread use of illegal substances such as marijuana, cocaine, and psychedelic drugs that grew out of the countercultural movement of the 1960s. States passed new laws mandating harsh custodial sentences for even the possession of a small quantity of illicit drugs. These laws, intentionally or unintentionally, were directed at Blacks, which led to the incarceration of a large number of African-Americans in the early 1970s and thus depriving them of their freedom. Throughout the 1970s, Blacks were approximately twice as likely to be arrested for drug offences as were Whites. Activist Angela Davis, writing in 1970, contended there was a vicious circle linking poverty, the police courts, and prisons as an integral aspect of ghetto existence. Unlike the mass of Whites, she argued, prisons are deeply rooted in the imposed patterns of Black existence.

The expansion of the prison population, comprising a majority of minorities, increased tensions within those institutions. This was coupled with a long laundry list of deprivations and abuses that threatened to trigger violence. On September 9, 1971, more than a thousand prisoners at the Attica Correctional Facility in western New York rose up against what they considered brutal conditions and took a number of guards hostage. Both Black and White inmates joined to issue a set of demands aimed at improving conditions in the facility. Governor Nelson Rockefeller refused to consider these demands, and on September 12 he ordered in state police and the National Guard, which resulted in the death of 32 prisoners and 11 guards. The heavy-handed use of the law to incarcerate Blacks has led to the conclusion by some of an imposed new slavery. By definition, prison is a form of involuntary servitude.

BASEBALL

INITIAL EFFORTS TO INTEGRATE THE MAJOR LEAGUES

By the end of the 1930s, pressure to integrate Major League Baseball was growing. The Negro leagues had achieved stability and were drawing large crowds to games played at big-league ballparks such as Forbes Field in Pittsburgh and Griffith Stadium in

Washington, DC. Huge crowds gave familiarity to Black players, who became known to the White community. In 1942, there were several serious attempts to bring about integration in baseball. Jackie Robinson, who would later sign for the Dodgers, got an audition from White Sox Manager Jimmie Dykes, who was impressed with what he saw. With the start of the war, however, the matter went no further. The Pirates gave Negro league catcher Roy Campanella a tryout, but the Baltimore Elite Giants' player never heard back from the club. The same thing occurred after the owner of the Washington Senators approached two of the biggest stars in the Negro leagues, Josh Gibson and Buck Leonard.

Paul Robeson, a singer and supporter of equal rights, tried to talk with baseball owners at their winter meetings. Commissioner Kenesaw Mountain Landis, sensing what the conference was about, ruled that the subject of integration would not be discussed. The issue was raised again when the Philadelphia Phillies ball club went on the market in 1943, after finishing in last place for five consecutive seasons. Bill Veeck, Jr., a baseball entrepreneur and the son of a popular baseball executive, claimed that he offered to buy the team and fill the roster with players from the Negro leagues (though a number of researchers have denied the verity of this claim). Veeck remarked that he made the mistake of informing the commissioner ahead of time of his intentions. The next thing he knew, the Phillies were not for sale; however, shortly thereafter, the team was sold to Bill Cox, described as a New York sportsman. Cox liked to gamble and wagered bets on the Phillies. When Landis found out, he banned Cox from baseball for life. The team was then sold to Bob Carpenter Jr., a member of the fabulously wealthy DuPont family. Carpenter had no interest in signing Black players, which no doubt pleased the commissioner and many of the other owners. As for Veeck, he would go on to make a name for himself in the game, as an innovator and promoter, and an advocate for racial integration in baseball. During the years 1942 to 1943, minor league clubs were eager to sign Black ballplayers, but knew that Commissioner Landis would block their efforts.

INTEGRATION OF THE MAJOR LEAGUES

At the end of the 1942 season, the president of the Brooklyn Dodgers, Larry MacPhail, resigned. He was replaced by Branch Rickey, who had just left his post with the Cardinals. Rickey almost immediately notified the Brooklyn directors that he planned to sign Black players in the near future. After the war, he was ready to take action, but he stood alone. In August 1946, team executives met to discuss the race question, and concluded that integration would "lessen the value of several major league franchises."

Rickey knew he had to approach integration carefully. Racism was predominant throughout the country, and Black players entering the major leagues would face virulent and constant abuse. He therefore set about looking for a player who could handle what was thrown at him (literally and figuratively) and strengthen the Dodgers on the field. Rickey believed he found his man in Jackie Robinson, who had served in the military and was a three-sport all-star at UCLA. After scouting Robinson closely, he was signed by the Dodgers and posted to the team's top farm club in Montreal. Prior to the signing, Rickey carefully interviewed Robinson and required him to give assurances that he would not respond in word or deed to the inevitable abuse that he would receive. Shortly after Robinson entered the Dodgers' system, four other Black players, including future stars Roy Campanella and Don Newcombe, were signed and sent to the minors. On opening day 1947, Jackie Robinson was in the Dodgers' lineup playing first base. He was quick to show off his set of baseball skills and finished the season with a .297 batting average. He also led the league with 29 stolen bases. For his achievements, Robinson was voted Rookie of the Year in the National League.

Other Black players were soon on the way. Campanella joined the Dodgers the following year. So did Larry Doby, the first Black player in the American League, and the famed Satchel Paige, both of whom were signed by Bill Veeck, Jr., now general manager of the Cleveland Indians. These men were immediately placed on the team. Interestingly, the Dodgers and the Indians set attendance records in 1948. Over the next few seasons, the influx of Black players into the majors was slow but steady. The New York Giants joined the integration bandwagon in 1949 by signing future Hall of Famer Monte Irvin and Hank Thompson. At the same time, Veeck signed two more Black players, the Cuban Orestes "Minnie" Minoso and first baseman Luke Easter. The Boston Braves acquired Sam Jethroe from the Dodgers in 1950 and installed him in their lineup a year later. By the end of the 1953 season, the benefits of integration had become apparent to a number of teams, even though 10 of the 16 major league clubs still had no Black players. Future Hall of Fame stars such as Hank Aaron, Willie Mays, and Ernie Banks were now plying their trade with the Braves, Giants, and Cubs, respectively.

FATE OF THE NEGRO LEAGUES

This first generation of Black players to integrate organized baseball was largely drawn from the Negro leagues. They brought with them a style of play that emphasized speed and agility that was characteristic of Black baseball. As more and more players entered the minor and then major leagues, the Negro leagues gradually faded away. As early as 1947, attendance at Negro league parks dropped drastically. By 1951, the Negro American League was reduced to six teams. Two year later, the league comprised only the Memphis Red Sox, Birmingham Black Barons, Kansas City Monarchs, and Indianapolis Clowns, all in non-major league cities. Several teams from the Negro National League such as the Newark Eagles and the New York Black Yankees were soon gone. This trend continued throughout the 1950s. In 1963, the last East-West All-Star Game was played in Kansas City. By 1965, only the Clowns remained as a reminder of segregation era baseball.

While the integration of baseball has been universally seen as a positive step, the negative consequences to the Negro leagues were widespread. Black baseball was a complex and far-reaching institution that employed many people in the Black community, from team executives and promoters to those who looked after the grounds, sold concessions, and did more menial tasks. There was also a popular Black press that reported extensively on the games. When the Negro leagues crumbled, so did the employment that they generated. Effa Manley, the Black woman owner of the Newark Eagles, lamented the lost livelihoods and careers of 400 Negro league players and the effect this had on their families. To add insult to injury, major league owners treated the Negro league teams with contempt, and often refused to compensate Black teams for the players they signed away. A case in point was the high-handed manner in which Branch Rickey signed Jackie Robinson away from the Kansas City Monarchs, giving nothing back in return.

SECOND-GENERATION BLACK PLAYERS

Insofar as the first generation of Black players in the major leagues were pioneers who suffered the inequities of segregation and ill treatment by bigoted fans and the public at large, the second generation was less willing to put up with abuse and persistent Jim Crow policies. Black players on the Dodgers united to challenge the lodging arrangements in cities such as St. Louis, which did not allow Blacks to stay in the same hotels as their White teammates. Their opposition forced modest changes in some of the hotels' restrictive policies. Leading the fight was Jackie Robinson, who as a player had become a force in the struggle against racial discrimination. When Robinson retired in 1956, he spent the rest of his life championing the cause of civil rights.

Blacks suffered from even greater acts of discrimination in the South during spring training. Pressure from both Black and White teammates was one of the considerations that led the Dodgers to construct a special spring training facility at Vero Beach, Florida, that would allow players of both races to live together and share the same facilities. Second-generation Black players on the Cardinals, including Bill White, Curt Flood, and Bob Gibson, led the fight against the segregated arrangements at the team's site in St. Petersburg, as did a number of Black players on the Braves, including Hank Aaron, who found such conditions intolerable. Some teams chose to train in Arizona, where the racial climate was less restrictive.

As more Black players reached the upper echelons of baseball, long-held records began to fall. In 1962, Maury Wills, shortstop for the Los Angeles Dodgers, stole 104 bases—surpassing Ty Cobb's record of 96 set in 1915. Twelve years later, outfielder Lou Brock stole 118 bases and eclipsed Cobb's previously held career record. Frank Robinson of the Cincinnati Reds was named National League Rookie of the Year in 1956 and became the fifth Black player—after

Campanella, Mays, Aaron, and Banks—to win the Most Valuable Player award, which he did in 1961. Frank Robinson would become the first player to win that award in both leagues, achieving this recognition with the Baltimore Orioles in 1966. While talented Black players became a dominant force in Major League Baseball, those of lesser ability often found their path to the top blocked by prejudices and the subtle patterns of institutional discrimination. Front-office and management positions for all major league teams remained largely all White for decades. The first token Black manager was Frank Robinson, who was hired by the Cleveland Indians in 1975.

THE CURT FLOOD AFFAIR

A serious challenge to organized baseball's reserve clause came from Cardinals' outfielder Curt Flood. On October 7, 1969, the Cardinals traded Flood to Philadelphia. Having business interests in St. Louis and not wishing to go to a city with a history of racial discrimination, Flood refused to be traded. Writing to Commissioner Bowie Kuhn, he stated, "After 12 years in the Major Leagues I do not feel that I am a piece of property to be bought and sold irrespective of my wishes." He went on to say that such a system violates his basic rights as a citizen and is inconsistent with the laws of the United States and of several states. In so doing, Flood was asserting his liberty as an individual citizen, and advancing the cause of freedom by advancing the rights of African American players to be free from the reserve clause that bound them to the wishes of the team who held their contract. Kuhn replied by denying that a trade violated Flood's constitutional rights.

With the support of the newly formed Players' Association, Flood initiated a $4.1 million antitrust suit in federal court against Commissioner Kuhn and the 24 team owners, charging that the reserve system constituted "slavery." He also gave up his $90,000 annual salary by retiring and refusing to join the Phillies. The case was heard the following year. Judge Irving Ben Cooper saw no reason to overturn the reserve clause, stating that such changes should be accomplished through negotiations between players and owners. He also denied Flood's claim for damages. Flood's lawyers then took the case to the U.S. Supreme Court. In a 5–3 vote, the Court turned down Flood's appeal, citing baseball's 1922 antitrust exemption. It was the decision of the Court that the reserve clause could only be changed by an act of Congress or through collective bargaining. Challenges to baseball's preferred status and the exploitive power of the owners were occurring simultaneously and would surpass what the baseball establishment and the players thought possible.

SUMMARY

Integration and the struggle for civil rights in America occurred gradually over a number of decades. The civil rights movement can be divided into two phases. The first phase dealt with overturning the Jim Crow laws in the South that enforced racial segregation. This was a mass movement, led largely by Black ministers, and widely supported by mostly young college-age people of both races. An important characteristic of this phase was that it emphasized nonviolent protest as a way of awakening the moral conscience of the nation. This culminated in the Civil Rights Act of 1964 and the Voting Rights Act of 1965.

The second phase of the civil rights movement was directed against economic and racial injustice in northern cities. The second half of the 1960s decade witnessed riots in a number of cities including Detroit and Newark, New Jersey, causing much destruction of property and loss of life. Simultaneously, there emerged a number of groups dedicated to advancing Black Power, which sought to confront police violence and racism directly. State laws directed at combatting the rising use of drugs were used largely against Blacks, leading some to suggest this was a new form of slavery.

Black baseball players after the Second World War, starting with Jackie Robinson, were finally integrated into Major League Baseball. Gradually over the decade racial restrictions, such as segregated hotels, were challenged and overcome. Labor organizer Marvin Miller gave new life to the previously ineffective Players' Association and began to take on the owners over a number of issues. After he was traded from the St. Louis Cardinals to the Philadelphia Phillies, Curt Flood refused to report to the Phillies and launched a challenge to organized baseball over the reserve clause. The case went to the U.S. Supreme Court but was denied by the justices.

STUDY QUESTIONS

1. Discuss the primary differences that distinguished the first phase of the civil rights movement from the second phase.
2. After the passage of the Civil Rights Act and the Voting Rights Act (1964 and 1965, respectively), Martin Luther King, Jr., in a 1967 speech titled "Where Do We Go From Here?" said, "We must honestly face the fact that the movement must address itself to the question of restructuring the whole of American society." What did he mean by that statement?
3. What affect did the integration of Major League Baseball have on the Negro leagues?

CHAPTER 13

The 1960s—A Time of Change

HISTORICAL BACKGROUND

Although on the surface the early 1960s appeared to be a continuation of trends in the previous decade, the mood of the country was becoming receptive to change. The quickening pace of civil rights was one such element, but another driving force behind social transformation was in the arena of foreign affairs, particularly the U.S. involvement in Vietnam. Question: What was the impetus behind the rights movements of the 1960s?

THE KENNEDY ADMINISTRATION AND CUBA

The presidential election of 1960 matched Vice President Richard M. Nixon with Senator John F. Kennedy. Both men campaigned as strong Cold Warriors, and in terms of policy, there was not much dividing them. Kennedy won one of the closest elections in American history.

Before the election, there had been a revolution in Cuba (1959), where the American-backed dictator, Fulgencio Batista, was overthrown by Fidel Castro. The new Cuban leader, not wishing his country to become a client state of the United States, soon approached the Russians for support and declared himself to be a communist. The CIA began plotting against the Castro regime, and hatched a plan to use Cuban émigrés to launch an invasion of the island. The invasion, which took place in April 1961, was a complete fiasco, in which most of the 1,400 exiles were killed or captured. President Kennedy took responsibility for this operation, even though he had neither authorized nor given it support.

A more serious problem occurred a year later. American spy planes observed that the Soviet Union was building missile-launching sites in Cuba for short-range and intermediate-range nuclear weapons, in response to a similar deposit of American missiles in Turkey and in Europe. Kennedy decided to use a naval blockade around Cuba to prevent Soviet missiles from reaching their destination. Tensions mounted as Russian ships carrying the missiles headed for Cuba. A number of military leaders strongly urged the president to invade Cuba, which he refused to do. While the world waited for what could have been the start of a nuclear war, the Soviet leader, Nikita Khrushchev, backed off before negotiating an agreement with Kennedy. Accordingly, the Americans would dismantle their missile sites in Turkey and respect the independence of Cuba. Both leaders learned important lessons from the Cuban missile crisis, and together sought to ban nuclear testing and find ways to reduce Cold War tensions.

The chief accomplishment of Kennedy's domestic program was creation of the Peace Corps. This program was designed to send Americans possessing certain skills to poorer countries to combat illiteracy, help build homes, roads, schools, and other such projects, and generally engage in practical activities that would be of use to the local population. The Peace Corps was in line with Kennedy's reforming vision to call people to greater service.

DEBATE OVER THE KENNEDY ASSASSINATION

The presidency of John F. Kennedy came to an end on November 22, 1963, when he was assassinated on a campaign trip to Dallas, Texas. Much has been written about the Kennedy assassination, and while many convincing arguments have been put forward, the matter remains far from conclusive. While the Warren Commission, set up to determine the cause of the assassination, concluded that the president was killed by Lee Harvey Oswald, a lone gunman, there are many unanswered questions, contrary evidence, and lingering suspicions. Of prime importance is the film of Kennedy being shot, taken by bystander Abraham Zapruder, showing the president's head being thrown back from a bullet fired in the opposite direction from that claimed by advocates of the lone-gunman theory. While one should refrain from accepting unproven conspiracy theories, it was true that Kennedy had many enemies—both inside and outside of government—who were glad to be rid of him. Moreover, by 1963, the president had surmised that the emerging war in Vietnam was unwinnable and was prepared to withdraw American support. This would have brought Kennedy into direct conflict with the military establishment, which was urging him to expand the conflict.

PRESIDENT JOHNSON AND THE GREAT SOCIETY

Lyndon B. Johnson, who became president following Kennedy's death, was a man of a different stature. He was born in Stonewall, Texas, in 1908, and was raised in relative poverty. Johnson attended Southwest Texas State Teachers College and then entered politics, working his way up the ladder through five terms in the state legislature. He was elected to the House of Representatives in 1937 and to the Senate in 1948. Whatever his educational deficiencies, Johnson was a master politician, and the success of his domestic program was due largely to his ability to charm, cajole, threaten, bully, and sweet-talk friends and opponents alike.

Knowing poverty himself, President Johnson had an innate sympathy with the poor. He was also influenced by Michael Harrington's classic book, *The Other America*, in which Harrington chronicled the extent of poverty in the United States. With a strong economy, there were funds available for the president's administration to wage a war on poverty. The core of this "war" were the Office of Economic Opportunity (OEO), which operated a job corps program for school dropouts; a Neighborhood Youth Program for unemployed teenagers; the Head Start program, to prepare poor children for school; and a VISTA volunteer program modeled on Kennedy's Peace Corps. Perhaps the most significant contribution to the Great Society was the Medical Care Act of 1965, which provided federally funded health insurance for the elderly (Medicare), and Medicaid, which gave states financial aid to offer medical care to the poor.

THE ROOTS OF STUDENT ACTIVISM

Although the effects of student activism didn't materialize until the late 1960s, the political conformity of the 1950s was beginning to come apart during the early years of the decade. In 1960, a group called the Young Americans for Freedom, at a conference at Sharon, Connecticut, issued the Sharon Statement, which set forth a number of conservative ideas. The statement noted that "in this time of moral and political crisis, it is the responsibility of the youth of America to affirm certain eternal truths." The group's key point was "that liberty is indivisible, and that political freedom cannot long exist without economic freedom." These words mirrored President Roosevelt's speech to the Democratic National Convention in 1936, but with an obviously different meaning. By liberty, the Sharon Statement was referring to individual freedom and protection from tyranny and the power of the state. Hence, it was a reaffirmation of the definition of liberty.

Two years later, the Students for a Democratic Society (SDS), a liberal group, put forward the Port Huron Statement. The SDS message pointed to the decline of the "American Golden Age" in the face of worldwide revolutions against colonialism and the menace of war, overpopulation, international disorder, and the alienating effects of bureaucracy and super technology. Its call was for greater equality, and to replace impersonality with a system that would enable one to develop his or her full potential. Such a system would be **participatory democracy,** defined as *individual participation by citizens in political decisions and policies that affect their lives, especially directly rather than through elected representatives.* In essence, participatory democracy is true democracy as defined by James Madison (Chapter 1). Given that the right of citizens to determine their own affairs is an inalienable right, then participatory democracy could be seen as an expression of freedom. Therefore, the Sharon and Port Huron statements both promote a return to core American ideals as a basis for their ideological platforms.

BECOMING EMBROILED IN VIETNAM

There is no clear date for the United States entry into the Vietnam War as American involvement was a step-by-step process. Vietnam, as part of the Indochina region, had been a French colony, which was taken over by the Japanese during the Second World War. Following the war, when the French attempted to again assert their control, the indigenous Vietnamese, called the Viet Minh, formed a nationalist movement to win their independence. Similar to a number of other national liberation movements, the Vietnamese adopted the model of communism, which raised a red flag to Western governments, particularly the United States. After the French were defeated at the battle of Dien Bien Phu in 1954, the United States began sending advisers to Vietnam to support those supporting the former French colonial regime. As with all matters related to foreign affairs in the postwar era, Vietnam was seen as the free world vs. communism. Having just ended their involvement in the Korean War, American policy makers believed that Vietnam would be another Korea. They labored under the premise (mistakenly) that countries in Southeast Asia were like a row of dominos; if one country fell to communism, the others would follow suit. Consequently, the United States under three presidents (Eisenhower, Kennedy, and Johnson) gradually became embroiled in Vietnam.

From 1964 the Vietnam War sharply escalated. The cost of the war undermined President Johnson's Great Society programs—and ultimately his presidency. Inexperienced in foreign affairs, Johnson relied heavily on his military and civilian advisers, who urged him to expand operations and commit more personnel to the conflict. Needing an excuse to exert greater control over the war, the president and Secretary of Defense Robert McNamara used a fabricated incident of alleged attacks on U.S. destroyers in the Gulf of Tonkin to win public support, and more importantly, congressional backing for escalating their involvement in Vietnam. In April 1965, the president sent another 40,000 troops to Vietnam, bringing the total to 75,000. A month later, a coup in South Vietnam by an army officer reflected the weakness of the indigenous opposition to North Vietnam and its southern allies, the Viet Cong. Faced with a crumbling political situation, Johnson and his advisers again decided to increase the number of troops to 125,000 and to expand the monthly draft call. At the same time, the United States widened its bombing of the north and expanded its list of targets.

MAP 13.1 The Vietnam War – Major Battles, 1964–1975

FIGURE 13.1 Secretary of Defense Robert McNamara and his deputy Cyrus Vance pondering options in the Vietnam War, in May 1965.

By the mid-1960s, opposition to the war was starting to build. The Students for a Democratic Society (SDS), which spearheaded the emerging New Left movement, organized an antiwar demonstration in Washington, DC, during April 1965, drawing 25,000 people. Dr. Martin Luther King, Jr., the civil rights leader and Nobel Prize-winner, came out against the U.S. involvement in Vietnam, calling the American government "the greatest purveyor of violence in the world today." Heavyweight boxing champion Muhammad Ali also stood up against the war. By 1967, college campuses were abuzz with activism. Many students who were opposed to the draft organized teach-ins and counseling to avoid being pulled into a detested war. Those opposed to the war were further angered by revelations that the CIA was funneling money through liberal front organizations to spread pro-war and anti-communist propaganda. Moreover, J. Edgar Hoover was directing the FBI to do everything it could to disrupt the antiwar movement. In April 1967, hundreds of thousands rallied against the war in New York City, as the U.S. troop levels in Vietnam approached 525,000.

As the war intensified, the coalition of forces opposed to the United States and its allies (the National Liberation Front) launched its Tet Offensive, which caught the Americans completely off guard. Some military leaders, including Army General William Westmoreland, considered using nuclear weapons against North Vietnam. Shortly after the Tet Offensive, President Johnson, seeing his popularity sinking, announced that he would not run for reelection that year, opening the door to a field of candidates, including Eugene McCarthy, former President Kennedy's brother Robert (both McCarthy and Robert Kennedy were antiwar advocates), and Vice President Hubert Humphrey. The fatal flaw for Johnson was his unwillingness to pull out American troops from an unpopular and unwinnable war, and thus risk charges of weakness, or even treason.

THE RIGHTS REVOLUTION

Women's *Liberation*

Civil rights galvanized other marginalized groups to demand justice for themselves. In her book, *The Feminine Mystique*, Betty Friedan drew upon interviews with numerous women, who often expressed feelings of emptiness and self-unimportance, which Friedan described as "the problem that has no name." Essentially, these women wanted something more than their husbands, their children, and their home, which were considered to be the ideal goals for women in the 1950s. Due in part to the influence of Friedan's book, and the growing sense of women's dependence and invisibility, a number of feminists formed a consciousness-raising movement that triggered the call for equal rights, sexual liberation, and a demand for visibility and respect. The creation of the National Organization for Women (NOW) in 1966 was an important milestone in this process. As cited in its Statement of Purpose, NOW stated, ". . . the time has come for a new movement toward true equality for all women in America, and toward a fully equal partnership of the sexes, as part of the world-wide revolution of human rights now taking place within and beyond our national borders . . . " By the end of the decade, the movement had become more radicalized. The Redstockings Manifesto (1969) stated that women were an oppressed class, that men were the agents of their oppression, and that the movement identified with all women, especially the poorest, most brutally exploited women. To some extent the women's movement of the 1960s was a fulfillment of the hopes and demands of Elizabeth Cady Stanton and other 19th century women activists. In another sense, it was the platform for an expanded movement that has made great strides and achieved monumental successes ever since.

Other Rights Movements

There were many other rights movements. Gays, who had often been forced to live in a secret world for fear of exposure to intimidation and discrimination, began to "come out of the closet." The so-called Stonewall Rebellion in June 1969, in which gays fought against police in a weekend of disorder, proved to be a catalyst in turning the gay struggle into a political force.

Hispanics, particularly in the Southwest, who had suffered from many of the same discriminatory actions as had Blacks under segregation, developed their own Brown Power to push back against oppressive laws and behaviors. Most notable within this movement was the organization of the United Farm Workers (UFW), which was committed to nonviolent action for social justice.

A further development was Red Power, leading to the formation of the American Indian Movement (AIM), organized in 1968 to fight against injustices past and present, including the history of broken treaties, the squalor and poverty found on Indian reservations, and the overall maltreatment directed toward Native Americans. Efforts to save the environment and to bring about police and legal reforms rounded out the call for a safer, more humane and just society in the 1960s.

THE CULMINATION YEAR—1968

All the pressures that had built up during the decade came to a head in 1968. Two central figures, Martin Luther King and Robert Kennedy, were assassinated. In the case of Dr. King, there is still some question of FBI involvement. Abroad, there were uprisings, among workers and students in France that forced a change of government, and in Czechoslovakia, where the unrest was brutally put down by the Soviets. Campus revolts disrupted classes and activities at a number of colleges. The Democratic Convention in

Chicago, August 26–29, was punctuated by rioting in the streets between peace activists and the police, who had been ordered to suppress all demonstrations. While the nationally televised street rioting may have cost the Democratic presidential nominee Hubert Humphrey some votes, his fate was sealed when Republican leaders, acting with or without the consent of Republican nominee Richard Nixon, cut a deal with the South Vietnamese delegation to the Paris peace talks to pull out, thus ensuring continuation of the war. Unable to bring about a peace agreement, Humphrey lost the election to Nixon. When a peace treaty was finally agreed to seven years later, it was on similar terms that could have ended the war in 1968.

BASEBALL

BASEBALL ADDS NEW TEAMS

No sooner had the Dodgers and Giants departed for California than New York Mayor Robert Wagner set up a four-man committee to bring another National League team to town. One of the four, the lawyer William Shea, took the lead in this endeavor. He contacted a number of league owners about moving their team to New York. Some seriously considered the possibility but turned it down. Unable to attract an existing club to move, he began to push for expansion.

Shea gained the support of important allies, including Branch Rickey, to further the cause of developing a new major league to be called the Continental League. At a meeting in May 1959, all the owners put forward a list of conditions that would make the Continental League acceptable to them. These conditions included a required size for a city and stadium that would qualify them to be awarded a franchise, an agreement to accept existing regulations and contracts, and the approval of all financial arrangements by the magnates. The sticking points were how to work out a World Series arrangement with three leagues, and how new teams would get players, since all existing players were under contract to the current major league franchises.

Nevertheless, the backers of the Continental League pushed ahead and, in August 1959, announced that the league would begin play in 1961 with an eight-team circuit. Negotiations began with potential owners, and soon franchises were awarded to five cities: New York, Denver, Toronto, Houston, and Minneapolis-St. Paul. With Senate antitrust hearings in full swing, Newark applied to be the sixth Continental franchise. Simultaneously, Branch Rickey was named league president. Later, Dallas and Buffalo were added, bringing the league to eight clubs.

Fearing that Congress was poised to place limits on the number of players a team could control and thus modify the reserve clause, the American League owners got cold feet and decided to expand their own circuit. The Yankees agreed to let a National League team in New York, but only on the condition that one was added in Los Angeles. Meanwhile, Minneapolis was having doubts about joining the Continental League, and finally decided to align with the American circuit after the Washington Senators' owner, Calvin Griffith, conveniently decided to move his franchise there. Washington was then given an expansion team to replace the one that departed.

A meeting of the National League owners subsequently decided to follow the wishes of Commissioner Ford Frick and bail out as well. In agreeing to expand their own league, the Nationals were quick to approve a second New York franchise, and honoring an earlier commitment, accepted the inclusion of Houston. Thus, the Continental League was nipped in the bud by club magnates wishing to "feather their own nests" and not rock the boat more than was required.

THE ERECTION OF MULTIPURPOSE BALLPARKS

Cities now added to the major leagues through expansion required serviceable ballparks, which signaled a round of stadium building. Initially, teams used revamped minor league parks, as in the case of the Houston Colt .45s (later renamed the Astros) and the Los Angeles Angels. Metropolitan Stadium in Minneapolis was upgraded, and the New York Mets played for a couple of seasons in the Giants' old home, the Polo Grounds.

More established teams, playing in ballparks that were half a century old, pushed to have new stadiums built, largely at taxpayer expense. The growth in popularity of professional football that had similarly undergone expansion with creation of the American Football League (AFL), with teams situated in a number of major league cities, added further impetus for modern stadiums. Faced with pressure from both sports and the need to restrain costs, cities opted to construct oval multipurpose stadiums. The new home for the New York Mets was Shea Stadium (1964), built in the borough of Queens. The first indoor domed stadium, the Houston Astrodome—which was also carpeted with artificial grass—went up in 1965, followed by sports arenas in Atlanta, now home to the Braves (1966), and Oakland (1968), after the Athletics moved there from Kansas City. Construction of multipurpose parks then occurred in Cincinnati and Pittsburgh (1970) and Philadelphia (1971). The second round of expansion, which brought San Diego, Montreal, Seattle, and Kansas City into the major leagues (with three of the four also football cities), led to the erection of new stadiums. From the start, the all-purpose stadiums were roundly criticized. Decades later, when another phase of building took place, the new baseball parks were designed to capture the intimacy of those built earlier in the century.

ADVENT OF THE PLAYERS ASSOCIATION

The emphasis on civil rights, and the welfare of disadvantaged and marginalized groups that came to the fore during the 1960s, reached into baseball as well. For some time, frustration and anger had been building among the players over low pay and an inadequate pension scheme. After snubbing a number of requests to improve players' pensions, the owners in 1962 put forward a plan that seemed promising on the surface but paid little in the long run. Statistics that came to light during congressional hearings showed that the percentage of revenues that went to players' salaries had been declining over the years and was under 20% of the total intake.

In the face of the owners' arrogance and intransigence, a number of players—led by Robin Roberts, Jim Bunning, and Harvey Kuenn—thought the time had come to organize. Through various connections, Roberts, the National League players' representative, made contact with Marvin Miller, an economist who had been the chief negotiator for the United Steelworkers Union. He agreed to become the executive director of the Major League Baseball Players Association. The first thing Miller had to do was to educate the players on the benefits of unionization and awaken them to the reality that their interests were constantly undermined by their bosses. After touring spring training camps in 1966, the players elected Miller by a decisive vote to represent them. With the strong support of the players, Miller pressed for a collective bargaining agreement, which set up a mechanism for negotiating salaries, pensions, complaints, medical issues, and other such matters. Confronted with squabbles and petty differences among the owners, who were preoccupied with a multitude of distractions, which included the hiring of a new commissioner, club relocations, and a second round of expansion teams, Miller was able to manipulate the magnates into agreeing to a process that they otherwise would have rejected. On February 21, 1968, the owners' Major League Baseball Players Relations Committee and the Players Association signed the first ever basic agreement. Among its provisions were an increase of minimum salaries from $7,000 to $12,000, a formal grievance procedure, an agreement to further study possible alternatives to the reserve clause, and a substantial increase in pension plan funding.

While the election of Bowie Kuhn as commissioner in February 1969 was taking place, baseball was in the middle of a labor-management crisis. A dispute between Miller and the owners' negotiator, John Gaherin, over a new pension agreement resulted in Miller urging the players not to sign their 1969 contracts until the matter was settled. This raised serious questions regarding the reserve clause. What made it work was the one-year option clause that enabled a club unilaterally to renew a previously signed contract if the player refused to sign a current one. By not signing a contract, a team could only hold a player for an additional year, making him a free agent afterward. It was on this last point that the power of the owners to maintain unilateral control over a player would come apart over the next decade.

DEMISE OF THE YANKEE DYNASTY

By the mid-1960s, the New York Yankees, who had dominated Major League Baseball for over a decade, were showing signs of decline. This was not noticeable in 1960, when the Yankees overmatched the Pittsburgh Pirates offensively in the World Series, losing only on a dramatic home run by Pirates' second baseman Bill Mazeroski. Nor was their decline evident the following year, when sluggers Mickey Mantle and Roger Maris vied to break Babe Ruth's home run record of 60, which Maris did by smashing 61 "round-trippers" in 162 games. By 1964, however, the Yankees were a different team. Although they won the pennant that year, the players who had carried them along for many seasons were aging and/or injured. Perennial star catcher Yogi Berra was now the manager, but commanded little respect from his former teammates. The new Yankee recruits, including such players as Phil Linz and Joe Pepitone, showed indifference to the team's image and tradition. Perhaps the most important factor was the sale of the team to the Columbia Broadcasting System (CBS), which was less willing to invest money in young talent. The Yankees dropped to sixth place in a 10-team league in 1965 and ended up in last place the following year. It would be a decade before they won another pennant. In the meantime, the Baltimore Orioles, Oakland Athletics, and Minnesota Twins, whose predecessors had been bottom-feeders in the American League the previous decade, now rose to predominance.

A precursory event to the fall of the Yankees was the dramatic collapse in 1964 of the Philadelphia Phillies in the National League. Comfortably leading the league for most of the season and ahead by six games with two weeks remaining, the Phillies went into a nose dive, losing 10 games in a row, allowing the competition to catch up. When the dust settled, the Phillies wound up in second place, tied with Cincinnati, a game behind the pennant-winning Cardinals.

On the other side of the ledger, there were some dramatic surprises. The Boston Red Sox—who had degenerated from being a mediocre team in the 1950s to a bad team in the early 1960s—underwent an amazing metamorphosis. After finishing in ninth place in 1966, a half-game ahead of the last-place Yankees, they ended up on top of the American League the next year in a memorable four-team race with the White Sox, Twins, and Tigers that went down to the wire. Fortune again frowned on the Red Sox, who lost to the Cardinals in the seventh game of the 1967 World Series.

Equally spectacular was the amazing ascendency of the New York Mets, who had never risen above ninth place in the National League since their creation in 1962. Behind a dominant pitching staff led by Hall of Famer Tom Seaver and Jerry Koosman, the Mets won 100 games in 1969. Being the first year that both leagues were divided into two divisions following the addition of four new teams to the majors, the Mets defeated Atlanta to win the pennant. Then, up against the heavily favored Baltimore Orioles, the Mets dominated the World Series, winning four of the five games.

Of the many fine players to perform in the major leagues during the 1960s, the cream of the crop included Cardinals' pitcher Bob Gibson, Pirates' outfielder Roberto Clemente, Giants' pitcher Juan Marichal, and Orioles' outfielder Frank Robinson. The fact that these men were Black ballplayers indicated how far baseball had become integrated since Jackie Robinson first stepped onto a big-league diamond in 1947.

SUMMARY

The 1960s has been regarded as a decade of change when many of the conventions, norms, and traditions were questioned and overturned. It was likewise a decade of youth when the baby boomers came of age, some of whom became political activists at the forefront of a number of struggles. Civil rights and the war in Vietnam took center stage during the decade, bringing into question two of the country's vulnerabilities: race relations and proxy imperialism. These two events spawned demands by various marginalized groups, specifically the women's movement, the gay rights movement, red (indigenous American) power, and a concern for the environment.

Major League Baseball, which from the beginning of the century consisted of two leagues with eight teams, underwent a series of expansions; first to two 10-team leagues, and then at the end of the decade to two divisions in each league with the addition of four new teams. The formation of the Players Association led by labor organizer Marvin Miller served to limit the unbridled power of the club owners through the introduction of collective bargaining. This meant that issues related to salaries, pensions, and other bones of contention would be negotiated between the players' and owners' representatives, which strengthened the power of the former over the latter. Step by step the wheels were set in motion to challenge the long-standing and restrictive reserve clause once and for all.

STUDY QUESTIONS

1. Discuss the ways that America's thinking about the Cold War influenced its foreign policy in the 1960s, particularly toward Vietnam.
2. Discuss the ways that the Sharon Statement and the Port Huron Statement exemplified the definitions of liberty and freedom in America.
3. Could it be said that the structural changes to baseball (creation of the Players Association) in the 1960s were part of the rights revolution affecting other groups in society?

Credit

Fig. 13.1: "Robert McNamara and Cyrus Vance," 1965.

CHAPTER 14

Downturn and the Capitalist Revolution of the 1970s and '80s

HISTORICAL BACKGROUND

As the decade of the 1960s rolled over into the 1970s, the turbulence brought on by campus unrest, the rights revolutions, and the ongoing war in Vietnam continued. Economically, the tide was shifting, however, due in large part to a major restructuring of the economy and the underlying demographic shifts. American dominance in the industrial sphere was now challenged by resurgent economies in Europe and Asia. More fundamental was the start of a transformation from an industrial-based economy, focused on machines making things, to a service-based economy. This change would lead to a loss of jobs, stagnation in wages in relation to increased prices, and inflation. Families that had previously lived comfortably on a single income would now require more funds from an additional salary. The trend toward a two-income family would have a pronounced social effect.

The loss of industrial jobs overseas had two important consequences. The first was a shift in population from the traditional centers of population and industry in the Northeast and Great Lakes region to burgeoning cities in the South and West, where insurance, banking, retail, electronics, energy producing, and other service industries were emerging. Closely related was the steady decline in labor union membership, whose fortunes were tied to the industrial sector. When the Organization of the Petroleum Exporting Countries (OPEC) curtailed the supply of oil to the United States and other industrialized countries as a payback for supporting Israel in its war against the Arab states, the price of oil on the world market shot up 400%, contributing greatly to economic instability. The economic downturn in the United States would bring in its wake a new political climate. Consider the question: What political, economic, and social trends transitioned the United States from its progressive course in the 1960s to a more conservative society by the 1980s?

END OF THE VIETNAM WAR AND PRESIDENT NIXON'S
DOMESTIC AND FOREIGN POLICIES

In 1968, Richard Nixon was elected president. While he ran as a Republican, it would be hard to put him into any ideological category, since he was essentially a political opportunist who moved to the left or the right depending on the circumstances. Thought of as a moderate conservative, he continued federal government spending on various programs under the cloak of a new federalism, in which government funds were funneled to state and local agencies for urban renewal and other grassroots projects. He sought to reform the federal welfare system by instituting a Family Assistance Plan that would offset some New Deal programs in favor of a guaranteed minimum annual income. The Affirmative Action Program, designed to give minority groups equal access to jobs and education, was also initiated under President Nixon.

It was in the realm of foreign affairs that mostly occupied the president's attention. The war in Vietnam continued—and even escalated. In November 1970, Nixon and his secretary of state, Henry Kissinger, secretly began bombing Cambodia after authorizing the saturation bombing of North Vietnam. President Nixon even toyed with the idea of using nuclear weapons in Vietnam. At the same time, the president gradually shifted the burden of fighting from U.S. troops, whose numbers had peaked at 543,000, to the U.S.-trained and -equipped South Vietnamese. Even so, the war remained a stalemate. With no clear prospect of victory, with increased pressure from antiwar protesters (including returning soldiers from the war), and from a majority of the population at home, the administration was ready to talk peace.

The peace agreement, signed on January 27, 1973, brought an end to the war. This arrangement was similar to the one proposed at the aborted 1968 Paris conference. What the president called "peace with honor" cost the United States the lives of 58,000 troops and 3.8 million Vietnamese. In total, American bombs had destroyed well over half of the hamlets, provincial towns, and cities in North Vietnam. What the North Vietnamese understood, and the Americans didn't, was that the war was about time, not territory or body counts. Eventually, the U.S. forces would have to go home. Two years later (1975), the North Vietnamese swept into Saigon and united the country.

During the latter years of the Vietnam War, President Nixon and Henry Kissinger were looking for ways to drive a wedge between the world's two largest communist powers: the Soviet Union and China. Since the end of the Second World War, the Western nations, through the United Nations, had held to a fiction that recognized the island of Taiwan as China, while ignoring the nearly billion or so people on the mainland. In 1972, Nixon made a prearranged trip to China, where, amid much fanfare, he established diplomatic relations with the so-called People's Republic.

MAP 14.1 The United States in the Caribbean and Central America, 1954–2004

That same year, the president engaged the Soviets in a series of talks that concluded with a number of agreements, culminating in the Strategic Arms Limitation Treaty (SALT). The result of these discussions was to limit each side to two defensive ballistic missile systems, and place limits on the number of offensive Intercontinental Ballistic Missiles (ICBMs). The treaty did not slow the growth of nuclear warheads, since other categories of weapons were not included. Nevertheless, it did signal a period of peaceful coexistence.

Meanwhile, the Nixon administration continued to support right-wing dictatorships in Latin America and in other parts of the world. After Salvador Allende, the democratically elected president of Chile in 1970, called for a redistribution of the nation's wealth and the nationalization of some U.S. companies, Nixon and Kissinger took steps to covertly support the Chilean military in the overthrow of the Allende government. The result was the accession of a brutal dictatorship under General Augusto Pinochet, who murdered more than 3,200 of his political opponents, and jailed and tortured tens of thousands of others. Elsewhere, the United States continued to support dictatorships in Iran, the Philippines, Honduras, and South Africa.

Throughout his political career, President Nixon had been plagued by many inner demons. Paranoid, secretive, vindictive, and prone to depression, Nixon's craving for power matched his distrust of other people. Thus, he sought to isolate himself from others by surrounding himself with a small group of loyalists who shielded him and carried out his wishes. The Imperial Presidency, as it was called, proved to be Nixon's downfall. Fearful that the unpopularity of the Vietnam War would ruin his chances for reelection in 1972, the president authorized a series of initiatives, backed by a huge war chest of funds, to harass and destabilize his political opponents.

Beginning with the botched break-in of the Democratic Party headquarters at the Watergate building in Washington on June 17, 1972, to get compromising evidence that could be used in a political campaign, the conspiracy spread. Through courageous investigative reporting by two *Washington Post* correspondents, the trail of various incidents linked to the Watergate scandal spread. By following the flow of money and connecting the dots, investigators followed the sordid chain of events as it spread to include many of the high officials in the Nixon administration, such as Attorney General John Mitchell and close associates H. R. Haldeman and John Ehrlichman. By the summer of 1974, the scandal had reached the desk of the president. Richard Nixon, faced with certain impeachment and removal from office, became the first chief executive in American history to resign.

THE FORD AND CARTER ADMINISTRATIONS

After the fall of Richard Nixon, the presidency passed to Gerald Ford who had been appointed vice president-designate after Nixon running mate Spiro Agnew was forced to resign amid a scandal. A previously popular congressman, President Ford is probably best remembered for pardoning Nixon, who could have faced a prison term for the felonies he had committed. Ford also supported the **Helsinki Accords,** which were primarily *an effort to reduce tension between the Soviet and Western blocs by securing their common acceptance of the post-Second World War status quo in Europe.*

With the Republicans tainted with the brush of the Watergate scandal, the Democrats gained control of the White House in 1976 with the election of a former Georgia governor. Jimmy Carter came to office with a mandate to sweep aside the excesses of the Nixon administration. The reforms instituted by President Carter resembled in some ways those of presidents in the earlier progressive period. He wanted to streamline operations and make government more efficient. At the same time, he favored a policy of fiscal conservatism, the conservation of resources, and deregulation.

Inexperienced in foreign affairs, Carter sought to promote human rights as a standard for international relations. **Human rights** are defined as *a right that is believed to belong* *justifiably to every person.* The question to be asked is whose human rights? The problem was that human rights were only applied to communist countries, especially the Soviet Union, while the more flagrant abuses of right-wing dictatorships that supported U.S. interests were largely ignored. Hence, the Cold War that had thawed somewhat—thanks to détente and the arms limitation treaties of the early 1970s—was considerably undermined by the end of the decade. Urged on by his chief foreign policy adviser, Zbigniew Brzezinski, the United States refused to ratify the SALT II treaty on the pretext of Soviet aggression in the Middle East.

Two important achievements credited to Carter were, first, the return of the Panama Canal to the Panamanians, and second, a peace agreement the president brokered between the Egyptians and the Israelis at Camp David. The agreement marked the first time an Arab state had supported Israel and established preliminary conditions for a settlement of the Palestinian issue that has still not been resolved.

Support for the shah of Iran, who had ruthlessly sought to create a modern and secularized Iranian state, obscured the rising tide of Islamic fundamentalism that was emerging in the Middle East. When the tidal wave of revolt did come, in the form of the Iranian revolution that swept over the country in 1979, the United States was caught off guard. An assault on the American embassy in Tehran and the taking of a number of hostages effectively provided the death knell for the Carter presidency.

RONALD REAGAN AND THE RISE OF CONSERVATISM

The Iranian hostage crisis, the conservative drift of American society, and the perception of Jimmy Carter's weaknesses as president led to the election of Ronald Reagan in 1980. It should be noted that Reagan campaign officials met with Iranian leaders before the election and promised to allow the shipment of Israeli arms to that country if Iran would hold the hostages until the election was over.

The key point about President Reagan was that he had been a Hollywood movie actor, and some critics unkindly remarked that the presidency was his last role. Over his two terms as president during the 1980s, Reagan provided guidance on policy but exercised not much command of detail. He did have a optimistic vision for the country, however, that resonated with many of his fellow citizens. Reagan's speeches were often dominated by folksy anecdotes and Hollywood clichés.

Unlike his Republican predecessors, President Reagan was a right-wing conservative (some might call him a reactionary), and his administration was dominated by fellow travelers who formed the basis of what came to be called the neocons. Modern conservatism consists of two distinct movements. **Libertarian conservatives** *want unfettered free enterprise.* They seek to limit the power and size of the federal government, to continue the policy of deregulation, to lower taxes (especially on the wealthy), to attack trade unions, to regulate the economy through the control of the money supply, and to engage in an aggressive buildup of military weapons, and thus renew the hostilities of the Cold War.

New values conservatism *emphasized traditional moral and cultural norms within a religious context.* It was driven by the revival of Christian religious fundamentalism that had been on the rise since the 1970s. Many fundamentalists believed that the country had strayed from its religious and ethical roots caused by secularization, which included the liberal (and sometimes radical) calls for expanded rights, support for the women's movement, social justice, ethnic and religious pluralism, and modern lifestyles. They were also strong advocates of blind irrational patriotism and anticommunism. Christian conservatism included many myths, particularly that the United States was founded as a Christian nation with a divine destiny inspired by God. President Reagan embraced both of these branches of conservatism; however, his administration more effectively implemented the libertarian version, while paying lip service to the religious right.

The economic program of libertarian conservatism, known at the time as Reaganomics, proved to be a recipe for the dismantling of the country's industrial infrastructure. Many corporations—specifically the auto and steel industries—outsourced some (if not their entire) operations overseas, leaving behind a wasteland of poverty and its complementary effects, such as crime, unemployment for masses of workers, and urban blight. This was all done in the name of short-term profits, including tax breaks for corporations and the wealthy, which saw their assets and income rise dramatically. At the same time, the economic fortunes of the middle class largely stagnated, and those of the poor declined. Such was the downside of a return to a more laissez-faire free market economic system.

NEW LIFESTYLES

While the 1960s and early 1970s were characterized by the so-called **hippie movement,** defined by *young people rebelling against established cultural norms and a materialistic lifestyle,* the 1980s generation, known as **yuppies** (young urban professionals), were *seen as young people with well-paid jobs and a fashionable lifestyle.* The yuppies embraced upward social mobility and ostentatious materialism. This trend was reflected in prime-time soap operas such as *Dallas* (1978–1991), *Dynasty* (1981–1989), and *Knots Landing* (1979–1993) that portrayed the often-tortured lives of the rich and powerful. The rise of the yuppies was a market phenomenon and a social trend. Malls filled with retail stores, which had been around since the late 1950s, and by the 1980s expanded into supermalls with expensive stores such as Bloomingdale's and Neiman Marcus. The message conveyed was that greed was back in style and that there was a new individualistic ethos that overrode the communal spirit of the late 1960s and early 1970s.

IRAN-CONTRA SCANDAL

While the United States was undergoing an economic transformation at home, the country continued covert operations against countries that did not support its interests abroad or were perceived to have communist sympathies. Although the United States had a global military focus, American foreign policy chiefs directed their attention on Latin America, which had become a cauldron of ideological hostilities and civil wars. Between 1981and 1986, the United States supplied arms to the right-wing contras fighting against the Sandinista government in Nicaragua, which had pro-communist sympathies. In 1983, the United States sent troops to crush the democratically elected government on the small island of Grenada, which was seeking Cuban and Soviet military aid. Throughout the 1980s, U.S. aid poured into El Salvador, where rebel groups were struggling against an oppressive pro-American military government. In another part of the world, the United States was supplying arms to Iraq's leader, Saddam Hussein, in that country's decade-long war against Iran.

These covert operations, which were a continuation of the Cold War policies of the 1950s, set the stage for a major scandal that rocked the Reagan administration. The Democrat-controlled Congress had imposed a ban forbidding the sale of weapons to the Nicaraguan contras. To circumvent this restriction, Reagan's top aides devised an elaborate scheme, whereby the United States would sell arms to Iran with the funds diverted through Israel, and then passed along in the form of military aid to the Contras. When a cargo plane carrying weapons to the Contras crashed in 1986, this illegal scheme began to unravel. Congressional hearings brought to light details of the plot, leading to the conviction of some top administration officials. Reagan's subordinates claimed that he knew nothing of the affair. For his part, the president characteristically claimed that he could not remember the key details, which is not surprising, since by that time Reagan was in the early stages of Alzheimer's disease.

REAGAN-GORBACHEV ARMS REDUCTION TALKS

The most significant legacy of Ronald Reagan was the part he played in bringing an end to the Cold War. In fact, much of the credit belonged to his Soviet counterpart, Mikhail Gorbachev. Gorbachev had become the Russian premier in 1985. Realizing that the Soviet Union was in deep economic trouble, largely through excessive military spending, he sought to cut back on his country's commitments by engaging the United States in a program of drastic cuts in nuclear weapons. Conversely, by the mid-1980s, the United States had increased defense spending 51% over 1980 expenditures, which was paid for by massive borrowing and slashing support for discretionary domestic programs. President Reagan, who came to office as an avid Cold Warrior (he referred to

Russia as the Evil Empire), by 1987 was feeling the pinch of ballooning defense budgets. Since Reagan was most effective in relating to people on a personal level, as opposed to entertaining abstract ideas, he underwent a change of heart after meeting and talking with Gorbachev.

At the prompting of the Soviets, Gorbachev and Reagan met on several occasions to discuss arms reductions. In December 1987, they took the historic step of approving the Intermediate-Range Nuclear Forces Treaty that called for the destruction of all U.S. and Soviet intermediate-range missiles in Europe. Gorbachev wanted to push arms reductions further, on the condition that the United States would abandon its Strategic Defense Initiative (SDI), a largely unworkable plan for a nuclear umbrella that would prevent penetration by hostile long-range missiles. President Reagan, however, refused to let go of the SDI program, which ended what could have been the virtual elimination of both countries' long-range nuclear arsenals. Neither man (nor anyone else) could see the quick and peaceful end to the Cold War that lay just ahead.

BASEBALL

THE ROAD TO FREE AGENCY

The agreement between the magnates and the Players Association to bargain collectively led to the most momentous change in baseball for nearly a century. In an effort to hang onto the reserve clause, which was the basis of the owners' control over their players, the owners agreed to salary arbitration as the lesser of two evils. Rather than implementing a system whereby a neutral arbiter split the difference in salary figures between those of the club and the player, Marvin Miller opted for an either/or system that would force the arbiter to choose between one set of demands or the other. The purpose of this idea was to force both sides to be reasonable in their demands. As it turned out, arbitration greatly benefited the players. Although the club owners won 16 of the 29 cases in 1974, the year that the arbitration system went into effect, the players were offered higher salaries by owners wishing to avoid arbitration hearings. In effect, players could no longer be "low-balled" without recourse.

A far more important consequence of the collective bargaining agreement was the integrity of the reserve clause. It had generally been assumed that the reserve clause enabled a club to renew the contract of a player indefinitely, whether he signed or not. When Marvin Miller carefully read the contract, he was struck by the explicit language that allowed a player, who remained unsigned for a full year after it expired to become a free agent. Hence, Miller began looking for a test case. He did not have to wait long. When Bobby Tolan, an outfielder with the San Diego Padres, refused to sign his 1974 contract, the Players Association filed a grievance, claiming that he was now a free agent. Tolan, however, retired at the end of the season.

The matter was put on hold because of a further development that opened another door to free agency. James (Catfish) Hunter, the Oakland Athletics' star pitcher, signed a two-year contract in 1974 calling for a yearly salary of $100,000. For tax purposes, Hunter stipulated that $50,000 be deferred to a third party that would pay him an annuity. Owner Charlie Finley never paid that amount as requested. Hunter then filed a grievance with the Players Association. The standard player contract allowed for two possibilities. Hunter could accept a belated payment of the funds owed to him, or he could claim that the contract had been violated and become a free agent. On Miller's advice, he selected the second option.

As a free agent, Hunter could now negotiate with any club for his services. Being a top-of-the-line player, he could command top dollar. The Yankees, now owned by George Steinbrenner, who was willing to spend money for good talent, obliged Hunter with a five-year, $3.2 million contract. The Hunter deal was a game changer insofar as clubs would now be forced to compete for star players, forcing salaries upward to record levels.

Miller's final test case emerged in 1975, when pitchers Andy Messersmith of the Los Angeles Dodgers and Dave McNally of the Baltimore Orioles agreed to go through the season without signing a new contract. At the end of the season, the Players Association filed a grievance, stating that both men were now free agents. The owners countered by filing a civil suit restraining the Association from proceeding with its grievance. The case then went to an arbitrator, Peter Seitz, who agreed that the reserve clause only allowed a team to renew a player's contract for one year. From there, the matter then went before a judge at the district court who concurred with the arbitrator's opinion. Thus, any player, with the exception of those with multiyear contracts, would be a free agent a year after their previous contracts expired. Consequently, the reserve clause that had been in existence since 1879 was now dead.

EMERGENCE OF THE NEW RESERVE SYSTEM

The "New Reserve System," as it was called, was hatched in a climate of bitterness and distrust. The owners contended that free agency would force teams into bankruptcy. "Baseball cannot function under the Messersmith decision," so said Commissioner Bowie Kuhn in 1976. The players, according to the owners, were being duped by Miller, who they said was out to feather his own nest. On the other hand, the players asserted that the owners were lying about their finances and the effect it would have on the game. This was borne out by the growth in revenues as major league attendance, which had been on the increase since 1975, broke all previous records in 1979. The clubs continued to reap millions of dollars from television revenues.

Inevitably, an impasse occurred. A major sticking point was compensation to be given a team that lost a player through free agency. Whereas agreements were reached as to increases in the minimum player salary and allotments to the pension fund, the question of compensation was deferred. Intractably, both sides were now on the slippery slope toward a strike, made all the more plausible since owners and the Players Association had ample resources to cover a prolonged work stoppage.

After a series of futile negotiations before and after the start of the 1981 season, play stopped on June 11 and remained so until July 31. The owners finally gave in on the compensation issue—not out of conviction, but because their strike-insurance money had run out. Having lost a third of the season, the teams decided to divide the season into half, determined by the games played before the strike and those afterward. They decided that the division winners of each half would play for the league championship. In the end, two familiar foes, the Yankees and the Dodgers, met in the World Series, which the Dodgers won.

EXPANSION AND MODIFICATIONS TO THE GAME

Major League Baseball during the 1970s witnessed a number of modifications. One such change was another round of expansion, following on from the previous enlargements in 1962 and 1969. Commissioner Kuhn put forward the idea of having a National League team in Washington and an American League team in Toronto, which would force clubs to engage in interleague play. The National League, however, didn't buy it. Consequently, two new teams were added to the American League in Seattle and Toronto, bringing the total number of clubs in both divisions to 14. No new additions were made to the National League, which continued to have 12 teams.

As far back as 1969, minor league clubs had experimented with the idea of having a designated hitter (DH), meaning a position player who would bat in place of the pitcher, but not play in the field. Hoping to enhance the offensive side of the game, the American League voted at the end of the 1972 season to adopt the DH, which was also supported by the commissioner. The National League chose to forego this adaptation. One of the consequences of this modification (which was added to the *Official Baseball Rules* in 1976) was that a team would require fewer players, since there was less of a need for pinch-hitters and defensive replacements. Also, the DH would allow older players, and those considered a defensive liability, to remain in the game as hitters. While the DH modified the style of play by increasing batting averages and limiting the number of innings for pitchers, the overall effect has been modest. Nevertheless, the DH rule rapidly caught on, with the exception of the National League, throughout the baseball world, as it allows for more players to get involved in the game.

THE MERRY-GO-ROUND OF COMMISSIONERS

Since Ford Frick resigned in 1965, Major League Baseball was governed by a series of less-than-effective commissioners, beginning with William D. Eckert, a three-star general who was hampered by being ignorant of baseball. He was replaced in 1968 by Bowie Kuhn, a Wall Street lawyer who had worked on cases for the National League. He loved the game so much so that he tried to micromanage the actions of the magnates, which brought him into conflict with a number of them, particularly Oakland Athletics' owner Charlie Finley. The extent of Kuhn's unpopularity was evident in 1982, when a move to extend his contract was rejected. Kuhn's replacement was Peter Ueberroth, who, as head of the Olympic Organizing Committee, showed that he could turn a profit. Rigid and focused on his public image, Ueberroth alienated many of those around him. Sensing that his chances to be rehired were slim, he announced that he would be leaving when his contract expired.

BART GIAMATTI AND THE PETE ROSE SCANDAL

Ueberroth's replacement was A. Bartlett Giamatti. A classics scholar and former president of Yale University, Giamatti seemed an unlikely person to become commissioner, save for the fact he had served a term as National League president and was an avid baseball fan. His favorite team was the Boston Red Sox.

Giamatti was a baseball purist who thought that the game stood on its own. He was rightly fearful of the power of television to turn baseball into a major entertainment industry. Philosophically, Giamatti did not think much of the DH rule or of domed stadiums, and was not in favor of major league expansion, though he did nothing to oppose it. Essentially, he wanted to bring law and order to the game and was quick to levy fines for brawling on the field, cheating (such as the practice by pitchers of doctoring their pitches), and other kinds of misbehavior.

During his short term as commissioner (he died in 1989), Giamatti is best remembered for the Pete Rose affair. Rose was an outstanding player, whose feats included collecting more hits (4,256) than anyone else in the history of the game. On the other hand, there was a darker side to Rose that included an addiction to gambling. News that he bet on his own team surfaced during the 1989 season, which led to an investigation. On August 24, he signed an agreement, drawn up by the commissioner, permanently banning him from baseball, yet allowing Rose to deny any allegation that he bet on major league games. Debate still continues as to whether Rose should be admitted to the Hall of Fame, for which he would certainly qualify on the basis of his statistics, but questionably on the basis of his character.

MEMORABLE SERIES

The decade of the 1980s had its share of highlights, broken records, and personal achievements. The World Series provided a number of memorable moments. In 1985, the Kansas City Royals became only the second expansion team (after the New York Mets) to win the World Series, defeating the St. Louis Cardinals in seven games.

The Boston Red Sox, which had been denied a World Series championship since 1918, looked poised to win it all against the New York Mets in 1986. Ahead 5–3 in the ninth inning of what would have been the final game, the usually reliable Red Sox first baseman Bill Buckner let a groundball pass through his legs, opening the door for the Mets to score three runs. The Mets won the final game and the Series the next day.

In 1989, Oakland and San Francisco squared off in the first all-metropolitan World Series since the Yankees played the Brooklyn Dodgers in 1956. Just minutes before the start of the third game of the Series, a catastrophic earthquake hit the Bay Area. Although no one at the ballpark was hurt, the earthquake caused considerable damage and some loss of life in the surrounding region. Symbolically, it was a metaphor for the difficulties that would confront baseball in the next decade.

SUMMARY

After nearly three decades of postwar prosperity, the American economy entered a period of instability and decline. This was due in part to the high cost of the Vietnam War and the resurgence of industrialized countries in Europe and Asia. At a deeper level, the United States was shifting from an industrial economy, predicated on manufacturing, to a service-based economy. This led to an acceleration of population movement away from the industrial Northeast to the Sunbelt states, which also had political ramifications. The Watergate scandal, coupled with the divisions within the country after the Vietnam War, effectively brought an end to the reforming spirit of the 1960s.

By the late 1960s and early 1980s, the United States was becoming more conservative. With the election of Ronald Reagan in 1980, two brands of conservatism rose to predominance: libertarian conservatism, which was a restatement of traditional conservative policies, and new values conservatism predicated on Christian fundamentalist cultural beliefs. The 1980s also witnessed rampant materialism, an increase in Wall Street profits, and continued deindustrialization. The Iran-Contra scandal and the Reagan-Gorbachev arms reduction talks rounded out the decade.

The 1970s finally brought an end to the reserve clause by enabling players to become free agents at the end of their contracts. Rather than have loads of players on the free agent market at any one time, Marvin Miller devised a scheme, accepted by the owners, that would allow a player to become a free agent after six years. This worked to the advantage of the players, who, because of limited supply, found themselves in greater demand. The "New Reserve System" did not go smoothly, and forced a strike that shortened the 1981 season.

STUDY QUESTIONS

1. In what ways did President Carter's human rights policy conflict with American foreign policy objectives?
2. To what extent was the conservative revival of the 1980s an expression of American exceptionalism?
3. Discuss some of the implications of the post–reserve clause system. How did it affect Major League Baseball and which group, owners or players, benefitted the most?

CHAPTER 15

The New Millennium

HISTORICAL BACKGROUND

The years 1989 to 1991 marked a period of global transition that came about quickly and unexpectedly. The reforms instituted by Soviet Premier Gorbachev opened a Pandora's Box of pent-up anxiety and frustration that had been repressed for a long period. The closed system of Soviet state communism, both in Russia and eastern Europe, proved to be untenable, and essentially fostered economies of inefficiency and corruption. The refusal of Gorbachev to use force to back up Russia's puppet governments in eastern Europe, along with incipient pro-democracy movements in those countries, brought an end to the Cold War virtually without bloodshed. Simultaneously in China, student riots in Beijing's Tiananmen Square calling for greater democracy were answered by military repression, in which hundreds were killed and thousands arrested. Conversely, South Africa, which had harbored racial segregation for decades, dissolved without significant bloodshed following the release of African leader Nelson Mandela from prison. This led to a new constitution and the ending of apartheid. After supplying arms to Iraq during its decade-long war against Iran, the United States—with the sanctity of a United Nations resolution—declared war on Iraq and its leader, Saddam Hussein. The justification for the war was that Iraq invaded neighboring Kuwait. While the Cold War had ended, the American involvement in Middle East affairs was beginning. We are left with the question as to what would the new world order be like after the end of the Cold War?

MILITARY ACTION IN PANAMA AND THE PERSIAN GULF WAR

With the close of the Cold War, there was hope that an era of peace and stability would be achieved. This did not happen for several reasons. For one thing, the Cold War had spawned a national security establishment that had a vested interest in finding new conflicts so as to justify high rates of defense spending and maintain a global military presence. Also, the collapse of the hegemonic Soviet system and the emergence of regional nationalism led to an upsurge of local ethnic and tribal disputes that threatened regional stability. Conflicts erupted, particularly in the Middle East and the Balkans.

While many people hoped that the election of George H. W. Bush in 1988 (Reagan's vice president, 1980–1988) would inaugurate a period of domestic tranquility, the United States continued the practice of supporting regimes (authoritarian or democratic) that furthered American global interests. The Reagan administration had backed the government of Manuel Noriega in Panama, overlooking—and sometimes abetting—his drug dealing, as long as he toed the line. When the Panamanian president decided to pursue an independent policy, the United States turned against him. Acting unilaterally and without the consent of Congress, President Bush ignored the **War Powers Act of 1973**, *a federal law intended to check the president's power to commit the United States to an armed conflict without the consent of the U.S. Congress,* and sent 15,000 troops to assist the 12,000 already in Panama. In a classic case of overkill (called "Operation Just Cause"), American forces destroyed civilian neighborhoods and military targets alike, causing much loss of life. The mission accomplished the twin objectives of capturing Noriega and ending, for a time, Panamanian independence by placing the country under U.S. military control.

The use of military power also proved effective against Iraq. Having received support from the United States in the past, Saddam Hussein, the Iraqi leader, felt he had a green light to invade neighboring Kuwait, which was rich in oil and had been part of Iraq until 1961. Despite assurances that the United States had "no opinion" on Iraq's border dispute with Kuwait, President Bush reversed course and pushed for war, on the dubious claim that Iraq posed a threat to nearby Saudi Arabia. The United States then put pressure on the United Nations, thereby securing a series of tough resolutions, culminating in Security Council Resolution 678 authorizing "all necessary means" to liberate Kuwait. What followed was Operation Desert Storm, in which the United States utilized massive air attacks, destroying nearly half the Iraqi tanks before launching a heavy ground operation that proved effective within weeks. The war cost the lives of only 240 allies, but many more Iraqi troops and civilians.

The Persian Gulf War was limited only to protecting Kuwait. Saddam Hussein remained in power and extracted reprisals against his internal enemies, particularly the Kurds. Since the Iraqi leader had proven to be unreliable with respect to American interests, the United States imposed a policy of forcing regime change through a variety of economic sanctions and the implementation of no-fly zones. Demands that inspectors be allowed to search Iraq for weapons of mass destruction proved to be futile since such weapons, if they existed, had been destroyed during the war. Nevertheless, the stage was set for later catastrophic events.

THE CLINTON PRESIDENCY

With the economy coming out of a mild recession, William Jefferson Clinton (a Democrat) became president following 12 years of Republican control of the White House. Clinton was a moderate but had big plans to bring about change. One proposed change was a reform of the health care system. With insurance, pharmaceutical, and business interests (among others) against him, this needed overhaul of the health care establishment failed. It would take nearly two decades for the Affordable Health Care Act to be passed.

After the Republicans gained control of Congress in 1994, Clinton was forced to shift his priorities. With pressure from conservatives, the president abandoned the Aid to Dependent Children program, which had supported poor families since the Great Depression, and replaced it with temporary assistance, known as workfare, requiring those on welfare to actively seek work or enroll in school. Congress through legislative action sought to more actively pursue both the **war on drugs,** which was *a series of actions tending toward a prohibition of illegal drug trade,* and also tough crime measures. The U.S. prison population, largely the result of drug convictions, mushroomed from half a million in 1980 to two million by the end of the century.

Clinton had more success in foreign policy. He helped broker peace in Northern Ireland, which had undergone decades of internal terrorism perpetuated by the Irish Republican Army (IRA) and pro-British militias. Clinton also contributed to the 1993 **Oslo Agreement**, in which *Israel, for the first time, recognized the Palestine Liberation Organization, leading to the creation of a road map designed to bring about a two-state settlement. While* the United States faced no clear threat from hostile nations, the Clinton administration started a new wave of military spending, adding $115 billion to the Pentagon's Five-Year Defense Plan.

THE WAR IN THE BALKANS

In the early 1990s, the independent communist state of Yugoslavia disintegrated into five distinct nations: Slovenia, Macedonia, Croatia, Bosnia, and the remnants of the former Yugoslav state, dominated by Serbia. These nations were also divided along religious lines between Orthodox Christians, Roman Catholics, and Muslims. In an attempt to assert their dominance and hold together what was left of Yugoslavia, the Orthodox Christian Serbs engendered a bitter civil war in neighboring Bosnia and engaged in ethnic cleansing against the predominantly Muslim population. So defined, **ethnic cleansing** is *the expulsion, imprisonment, or killing of an ethnic minority by a dominant majority in order to achieve ethnic homogeneity.* While unable to stop the atrocities that were being committed by other means, U.S. and European (NATO) troops intervened in 1995 to enforce a fragile peace accord that divided the region into Bosnian and Serb sectors.

These outside forces returned in 1999 to stop the repression of Muslim Albanians by Serbs in the province of Kosovo. NATO forces began a bombing campaign against Serbian military bases and forces. Targets in the capital city of Belgrade were also hit. In June 1999, Serbia agreed to withdraw its troops, to be replaced by a peacekeeping force of 50,000 from five European countries and the United States. NATO, created 50 years earlier as the North Atlantic Treaty Organization to prevent the perceived threat from the Soviet Union in Europe, did not die with the end of the Cold War, but expanded and redefined itself.

THE COMPUTER REVOLUTION AND ECONOMIC CHANGES

It was during the 1990s that the computer revolution hit its stride. Businesses and private individuals were learning to communicate through the Internet and were sending messages through e-mail. Information, previously kept in paper files, was transferred to massive databases for quick and easy access. The ease by which information could be sent and received hastened the process of globalization. This gave rise to a demand for expanded free trade. Organizations such as the North American Free Trade Agreement (NAFTA), formed in 1993, helped to expand the global reach of the American economy by opening new markets to U.S. corporations. While free trade facilitated the flow of goods, it did little to help the millions in poorer countries who labored in sweatshops at starvation wages so that affluent consumers could enjoy cheap products.

The upsurge in computer technology spawned a plethora of new start-up companies, which in turn rolled over vast sums of money into the stock market. Investor greed opened a large derivatives market of unregulated trading. A **derivative** *is a contract that derives its value from the performance of an underlying entity. This underlying entity can be an asset, index, or interest rate, and is often simply called the "underlying."* This led to a further call for more deregulation. In 1999, Congress repealed the Glass-Steagall Act, passed in the early years of the Great Depression, which prevented commercial banks from speculating on Wall Street. Increases in unearned wealth, brought about by the deregulation of the stock market, reflected the capitalist paradox of heightened creativity and innovation and massive corruption. The prime example of corporate greed and corruption was the Enron scandal. Enron was the world's largest energy company, and over a number of years it engaged in elaborate and fraudulent accounting practices to make the company appear that it was turning a profit, while money was being siphoned off into the pockets of company directors.

CULTURAL WARS

The cultural wars may be defined as battles over interpretations of rights, freedom, liberty, identity, and values. In part, the cultural wars were fueled by the largest influx of immigrants to enter the United States since the progressive era of the early 20th century. Whereas earlier in the century immigrants came primarily from Europe, the new wave of newcomers came mostly from Asia and Latin America, and to a lesser extent from Africa, bringing with them a multicultural mixture of religions and ethnicities. For the most part, the new immigrants settled in California, Florida, the border states of Texas, New Mexico, and Arizona, and in large metropolitan centers. As immigrants went looking for work, they moved into the hinterland, challenging the ethnocentric attitudes of resident populations. Conflicts developed over questions of bilingual education, racial profiling, and the allotment of equal rights and benefits to resident aliens. These matters have been magnified by the number of undocumented workers in the United States. While they are a vital part of the economy, some see the presence of undocumented people as a security threat and a challenge to their traditional way of life.

As religious conservatives became more politicized, they began to become a dominant force in the Republican Party and helped shape the GOP's agenda and policies. As such, domestic politics became increasingly dominated by conservative social issues. Abortion remained at the top of the list, and with the backing of religious groups, a number of states passed laws restricting a woman's right to have an abortion. Attacks have been made against worthy organizations, such as Planned Parenthood, which provides women with many useful health services along with abortion counseling. The funding of "faith-based" social services raised critical questions as to the constitutional separation of church and state under the first amendment. Federal funding of the arts also came under attack by those who found certain forms of artistic expression to be objectionable. Opposition to homosexuality, based on cherry-picked biblical scriptures, led to the passage of the Defense of Marriage Act in 1996, barring gay couples from spousal benefits.

The politicization of religion also has its drawbacks, insofar as it has forced those religious groups to support policies and programs that are sometimes incompatible to their stated values. When a religion ties itself to a political party, it inherits the baggage of that party. This scenario continues to be played out.

THE ELECTION OF 2000

The election of 2000 matched Democrat Albert Gore, Jr. and Republican George W. Bush. Gore had served as vice president under Bill Clinton. Bush was the son of President George H. W. Bush, and aside from a brief tenure as governor of Texas, he had little political experience. It was a close election that resulted in one of those rare instances in American history (three previous times) in which the candidate with the largest overall plurality of votes (544,000) lost. The outcome centered on the vote in Florida. With the state controlled by Republican officials, tens of thousands of pro-Gore African Americans were purged from the voting lists on the often-incorrect pretext that they were convicted felons. After much delay and the constant recounting of ballots, the outcome of the election was decided in the U.S. Supreme Court. The Court upheld Bush's narrow lead in what can only be described as a questionable election. While similar questions would be raised about the 2004 election, the evidence of wrongdoing appears to have been less blatant.

SEPTEMBER 11, 2001

When George W. Bush assumed office, he brought with him, as did Ronald Reagan, a number of advisers (neocons) committed to the myth of American exceptionalism who had a preconceived idea of remaking the rest of the world in the image of the United States. The drastic policy changes that Bush and the neocons had in mind could not have been achieved without a major crisis. The events of September 11, 2001 (9/11), provided that crisis.

According to the official version, two planes flown by Islamic terrorists crashed into the twin towers of the World Trade Center (WTC) in New York, causing the towers to collapse within an hour. Another hijacked plane smashed into the Pentagon. About the same time, a fourth plane mysteriously crashed in Pennsylvania, killing all aboard.

The evidence, however, shows that the official story has severe problems. Without specifying all the numerous irregularities, it is clear that the World Trade Center (WTC) buildings could not have collapsed at free-fall speed (about 10 seconds) through fires caused by the crashes. Nor does the official story account for the sudden and unexplained collapse of Building 7 of the WTC later that evening. Scientists, who have studied the evidence, along with a number of eye-witnesses, concluded that the demise of all three structures was due to a controlled demolition. With respect to the Pentagon and the crash in Pennsylvania, there was a surprising lack of airplane wreckage.

The improbability of the official story is all the more serious, insofar as it became the excuse for the United States to attack two Middle Eastern countries and impose greater (and permanent) security restrictions at home. While the causes of what happened on 9/11 beyond the physical evidence is a matter of conjecture and speculation, its disastrous consequences are all too clear.

WAR AGAINST AFGHANISTAN AND IRAQ

Months after 9/11, the United States went to war unilaterally (with only a few allies, including Britain) against Afghanistan. The stated motive for the invasion was that the ruling Taliban regime was harboring Osama bin Laden, the assumed mastermind behind the 9/11 attacks. The United States had at one time supported the Taliban during the Afghan civil war when Islamic forces were fighting against a puppet government backed by the Soviet Union. Two decades later, after Islamacism replaced communism as the designated enemy, American policy shifted focus. **Islamacism** refers to *diverse forms of social and political activism advocating that public and political life should be guided by Islamic principles, or more specifically to movements that call for full implementation of sharia law.* Since the Taliban were now the alleged supporters of terrorism, the United States backed the anti-Taliban tribes in Afghanistan. American bombing essentially brought an end to that regime in three months.

The Bush administration then turned its attention to Iraq. Despite the fact that Iraq had nothing to do with the events of 9/11, the neocons saw it as a golden opportunity to get rid of Saddam Hussein and exert American influence over the region. On May 1, 2003, President Bush declared war on Iraq. The "shock and awe" of heavy air attacks, characteristic of the Panamanian and Persian Gulf wars, quickly brought about regime change and the instillation of a caretaker government under Paul Bremer, head of the Coalition Provisional Authority (CPA), who rewrote the Iraqi constitution to suit American interests. The attack on Iraq, and the chaos that followed, unleashed tribal hatreds between the majority Shi'ite and minority Sunni factions. These factions entered into a quasi-civil war that spread throughout the country. Al Qaeda and extreme militant militias that had not been present before the war now entered the fray and complicated the problem. By December 2005, more than 2,100 American soldiers had died in Iraq. Only after the Sunni insurgents turned against Al Qaeda and began cooperating with American forces did the violence subside. Fighting continued after Bush left office.

EMBELLISHING THE SECURITY STATE

The statement made by journalist Ralph Bourne during the First World War that "war is the health [power] of the state" certainly applied to the years of the Bush presidency. Putting forth the doctrine that the United States would "oppose any nation that harbored terrorists," the president used the war as an excuse to round up suspected terrorists, some of whom were clearly innocent. Many were sent to the military base at Guantanamo Bay, Cuba, where torture was used to extract information. Detainees were defined as alien combatants and thus denied constitutional protections. Other suspects were sent to countries for interrogation, which were known to practice torture. American citizens, so classified, were not exempt.

The Bush administration also took aim at constitutional protections within the United States. Shortly after 9/11 the president rushed through Congress the USA Patriot Act, which expanded the government's surveillance and investigative powers. In addition, the administration created the Department of Homeland Security, which had a broad agenda that included everything from protecting the country's borders to airport security, among other duties. Meanwhile, the government violated federal wiretapping laws by giving the officials access to personal information without protection from the courts.

THE SECOND 'GREAT DEPRESSION'

The Wall Street boom of the 1990s and expanding financial markets put more money into circulation, encouraging banks and other lending agencies to become increasingly reckless. Since banks found it more profitable to loan money to high-risk clients with no down payment and at steep interest rates, the financial system was headed for trouble. As increasingly more homeowners defaulted on their mortgages, commercial banks and other lending institutions found themselves in possession of low-value properties, coupled with a radical drop in their assets. Since lending agencies lacked sufficient capital to back up their losses, this led to dramatic stock market declines and the ruin of some of the largest brokerage firms. By the same token, since commercial institutions possessed a global reach, the panic spread around the world. With banks unwilling or unable to make loans, businesses were unable to get credit, and were forced to close shop or lay off workers, causing unemployment to rise above 10%.

After Barack Obama assumed the presidency, the government pumped billions of dollars to prop up collapsing banks and industries (such as the auto industry) that were considered "too large to fail." While much of this money has been paid back to the government, it has left many people wondering why financial help was so readily available to the rich, while much of the rest of the population struggled financially with little help. The occupy Wall Street movement that began in New York on September 11, 2011, and spread across the country sought to highlight the plight of the poor and the growing disparity between the very wealthy 1% and the masses of American citizens.

THE OBAMA YEARS

The election of Barack Obama as the 43rd president of the United States was a landmark event since, as an African American, he symbolized the significance of the changes in racial attitudes over the previous half century. Over the past 60 years, Black culture moved into the mainstream. Likewise, Blacks, as with many previously marginalized minorities, had fought their way into the middle class. On the other hand, latent racism still existed. Racial profiling contributed to the disproportionate number of Blacks who continue to be incarcerated in prison. Statistics reveal that Blacks (and other minorities) are given longer prison sentences than Whites, often for the same crimes.

Before becoming president, Obama worked as a community organizer and distinguished himself as a legal scholar in the sphere of constitutional law. His instincts and motivation while in office were to achieve compromise and bring people together. This approach was constantly thwarted by a deeply divided Congress and public opinion that has taken irreconcilable positions on many issues. On the one hand, progressive forces have pushed for greater equality in all spheres of life, which is akin to greater freedom. Conversely, those possessing a settler society mentality have held fast to the notion that liberty is based on personal freedom and property rights. This latter group coalesced around the tea party movement, a coalition of groups that was suspicious of government and stood for a libertarian program that included lower taxes and personal liberty. Wealthy financial backers of this movement have interjected their own agendas.

Overshadowing these matters have been the so-called "wars" on drugs and on terror. What the war on drugs accomplished was to put thousands of people in jail for substance abuse violations, while doing little to curtail the use of drugs. The war on terror has been used to justify vast expenditures for going after alleged foreign terrorists, in the meantime paying lip service to the real problem of domestic terrorism, which has occurred in a number of venues. Mass killings that have taken place in Newtown, Connecticut, at Virginia Tech, in Colorado, Arizona, Parkland, Florida, and elsewhere on a regular basis have spawned a national debate over gun control. While the majority of Americans favor some sort of restriction on guns, powerful lobbying groups such as the American Rifle Association are staunchly opposed to any limitation on gun ownership, citing the right to bear arms embedded in the second amendment to the U.S. Constitution. The lack of compromise and reasonable debate on gun control among other things has, for the time being, become a stumbling block to public safety and national unity.

TRUMPISM

The election of 2016 led, surprisingly, to the ascent of Donald J. Trump to the presidency. He ran for president on the slogan "Make America Great Again," which has been translated into a program of extreme nationalism, the roll-back of the federal government bureaucracy, a unilateral foreign policy, coupled with racism and ethnocentrism. Some would argue that the irony of the above slogan has resulted in political, economic, and social crises.

Unlike all former presidents, Trump had no political experience, having worked as a real estate developer and television personality. After coming to office, President Trump set about rolling back many of the Obama policies and achievements including the **Paris Agreement on Climate Change**, signed in 2016, *dealing with combatting greenhouse gas emissions,* the **Iran nuclear deal,** which *sought to limit Iran's capacity to make nuclear weapons in exchange for relief on sanctions,* and provisions of the Affordable Care Act. The president has also warmed up to some of America's historic enemies, such as Russia and North Korea, at the expense of the country's traditional allies.

Central to President Trump's plan for America has been to limit immigration and stem the tide of illegal immigration into the United States. With many undocumented workers pouring into the country, immigration has proven to be contentious and has divided Americans between those concerned with border security and opposed to benefits for undocumented aliens, and those who favor a way for resident undocumented aliens, and children of those aliens born in the United States called "dreamers," to achieve citizenship. This matter has raised important humanitarian and security issues.

In many respects, the Trump presidency has resembled the urban boss politics of the late 19th and early 20th centuries with its emphasis on nepotism, corruption, patronage, bonds of loyalty, maintenance of the status quo, and catering to a particular base of voters. The most significant difference is that while the urban political machines catered largely to the immigrant population, Trump and his supporters have eschewed this group in favor of support for White nativist Americans.

BASEBALL

FURTHER LABOR TROUBLES AND THE PROBLEM OF COLLUSION

When Deputy Commissioner Fay Vincent was elected to complete the late Bart Giamatti's term in office, he inherited the ongoing disputes between the Players Association and the owners that had grown even more toxic since the 1981 strike. In 1984, negotiations began over a new collective bargaining agreement (CBA). The sticking points were a salary cap—which the owners wanted, and the players didn't—and the demand by the players for an increase in funding for their pension plans, proportionate to the increase in national television revenues. As salaries continued to rise, the owners cried poverty, though when challenged, the amount of club debt declined significantly. When the owners put forward a proposal that included a salary cap, the players threatened to go on strike. The walkout by players was averted when the commissioner intervened, and the threat of a salary cap was removed.

The new CBA, covering the period 1985 to 1989, contained a provision preventing players from acting collectively in salary negotiations and, by the same token, refraining owners from agreeing among themselves on what players to sign and for how much. At the end of the 1985 season, it became obvious that players with at least six years of service were not getting offers from clubs other than their own team. The Players Association cited collusion and filed a grievance. When the case was heard in September 1987, the arbitrator found for the players. The judge who ruled over the case declared seven players to be free agents and indicated that 132 others were entitled to damages. In the years after the ruling was handed down, in 1990, collusion ended, and players' salaries shot up again.

The year 1990 was the start of a new CBA. The owners again raised the salary cap matter, but this time the issue was over salary arbitration. The deadlock led the magnates to lock the players out of spring training, as had previously been done in 1973 and 1976. On March 18, 1990, owners and players announced a settlement that forced the opening of the season to be delayed a week, with the outstanding games to be made up through double-headers and play on open dates. The salary cap issue remained on the owners' agenda.

With the next CBA on the horizon, the owners wanted to amend the agreement by drawing up new rules affecting the powers of the commissioner, which the players opposed. With the addition of two new teams in Miami and Denver (Colorado), there was an asymmetrical alignment of clubs, forcing each league to be divided into three divisions. The owners and the Players Association could not agree on how the divisions should be organized or on a playoff schedule. Unable to find common ground on any of the core issues, the likelihood of another strike appeared inevitable. On August 12, 1994, the players walked out, marking the third work stoppage since 1971. With no resolution in sight, the strike continued for the remainder of the season. For the first time since 1903, there was no World Series.

DRUGS AND STEROIDS

Since the 1960s, the use of recreational drugs has pervaded American society. Not surprisingly, drugs have become an integral part of the baseball culture. In his best-selling book, *Ball Four*, based on observations made as a player with the Seattle Pilots in 1969, Jim Bouton quoted sources who believed that perhaps half the players in the American League used pep pills known as "greenies," and that they were readily available.

Over time, the problem became more serious. Twenty players in 1983 on the Kansas City Royals were named in a drug case, resulting in four of them going to jail. When Peter Ueberroth became commissioner in 1984, he tried to enforce regular drug testing, which was opposed by the Players Association as an invasion of privacy. Throughout the 1970s and 1980s, cases of addiction among players became more widespread, as seen in subpar performances and drug recidivism. A particularly egregious example was Dodgers' pitcher Steve Howe, who failed numerous drug tests and was in and out of rehab centers. Nevertheless, little action was taken by the owners, who were bankrolling large profits, or from the Players Association. By 1986, Ueberroth was calling for mandatory testing.

The drug issue took a new turn in the 1990s with the widespread use of steroids and other body-building and performance-enhancing drugs. Players with an average physique one season would reappear the next year resembling the Incredible Hulk. Highlight films showing spectacular home runs on ESPN and other sports shows encouraged a frenzy of long-ball hitting that fostered muscle building and steroid use. It was also thought that the use of drugs gave athletes a competitive edge. Three players—Mark McGwire, Sammy Sosa

(1998), and Barry Bonds (2001)—hit more home runs in a single season than did Babe Ruth or Roger Maris, and all three were linked to the use of steroids.

Public revelations of drug use by ballplayers led to a congressional investigation in 2005. After a day of incriminating testimony, members of Congress threatened to impose an anti-steroid law for the entire industry if baseball didn't get its act together. This was the wake-up call that management and the Players Association needed. Shortly thereafter, both sides agreed to a tough policy of 50- and 100-day suspensions for first- and second-time offenders, respectively, and a lifetime suspension for the third offense. After this policy was put in place, the number of home runs decreased dramatically.

BASEBALL AND 9/11

As it was in the past, baseball was utilized to serve the real and manufactured patriotism that burst forth after the September 11 incidents. Every major ballpark was filled with patriotic symbols and activities. Moments of silence for those who had died were observed. Patriotic music was played, and "God Bless America" replaced the traditional "Take Me Out to the Ballgame" during the seventh-inning stretch. Players wore caps honoring New York's police, firefighters, and emergency crews, and the American flag retrieved from Ground Zero flew over Yankee Stadium.

Politicians were quick to use baseball to further patriotic and military objectives. New York Mayor Rudy Giuliani spent more time at Yankee Stadium than at Ground Zero. For a nation at war, he said, there's a "functional bonding of sport and violence." President Bush used baseball to make a political statement at the World Series and elsewhere. The ease by which baseball is co-opted to serve patriotic ends is the result of reducing the game to the level of myth and symbols, and then marrying it to national myths and symbols to serve some predetermined purpose.

THE MEGA-BASEBALL CORPORATION

Over a period of several decades, the ownership of major league teams changed hands. Gone were the Wrigleys (Chicago Cubs), the Yawkeys (Boston Red Sox), the Fetzers (Detroit Tigers), and the Galbreaths (Pittsburgh Pirates), long-time baseball people whose ownership of teams reflected a primary interest in baseball. The new owners were investors and syndicates whose interest in baseball was often subsidiary to other corporate goals. Ted Turner in 1976 bought the Atlanta Braves for $12 million, but when he unleashed his vast cable network empire, which carried Braves' games across the country, the team's value climbed dramatically. In 1989, Texas Rangers' owner Eddie Chiles sold the club, along with Arlington Stadium and additional real estate, to a syndicate that included future President George W. Bush, for $70 million. Thirteen years later, the Yawkey Trust sold the Boston Red Sox to commodities broker and billionaire John Henry, along with Tom Werner, head of a syndicate that had owned the San Diego Padres and a group of partners, for $700 million. In addition to the Red Sox and Fenway Park, Henry owned 80% of the New England Sports Network (NESN), the Liverpool FC soccer team, and a 50% interest in a stock car racing team. The Red Sox employed a staff of more than 225 full-time employees, exclusive of coaches and players, as part of its overall operations.

In a world driven by marketing and multimedia exposure, baseball has become an important component of a massive entertainment industry that is said to have grown by 66% between 1998 and 2010. Moreover, at no previous time has the corporate intrusion into baseball been so extensive and blatant. Luxury boxes at ballparks, the widespread use of corporate logos, and the trend of naming ballparks—for example, AT&T Park in San Francisco, Coors Field in Denver, the Rogers Center in Toronto, and Citizens Bank Park in Philadelphia—are evidence of the extent to which the game is affected (and influenced) by big-time money. This is not to mention excessive media attention that has thrust baseball into popular culture.

BASEBALL: THE GLOBAL GAME

The increasing number of foreign-born players in organized baseball is indicative of the predominance of baseball outside of the United States. The game is played throughout the Caribbean, inclusive of leagues in Brazil, Colombia, and Venezuela. Japan has a long-standing history of baseball that is now widely played in China, Korea, Taiwan, Malaysia, and the Philippines. The sport has become popular in Australia and to a lesser extent, New Zealand. European baseball has taken off in recent years, and there are active leagues in a dozen countries, from Austria to Ukraine.

The globalization of baseball has moved forward with creation of the World Baseball Classic (WBC). The WBC brings together 16 teams from assorted countries that play an elimination tournament during the time when major league clubs hold spring training. The first WBC took place in 2006, when Japan defeated Cuba for the title. Three years later (2009), Japan again won the tournament, this time against Korea. The Dominican Republic and other Caribbean nations have also played well. The enthusiasm and the peculiarities of style that each national team brings to the tournament give baseball a further dimension of color and inclusiveness.

With globalization, baseball is moving into a wider sphere that will continue to expand and develop. What does this say about baseball as an American game? An answer might be provided by soccer. The game was started in England during the 19th century where it provided recreation for students at Oxford and Cambridge. From there, it spread out, and was adopted by other countries. Today, soccer is played by approximately 250 million people in more than 200 countries around the globe. Soccer is still very popular in England, with many leagues and teams at all levels, but it has long since ceased to be the English game. What baseball will be like in 25 or 50 years remains to be seen. If baseball follows in the footsteps of soccer, it could well be America's gift to the world.

SUMMARY

The end of the Cold War has been accompanied by continued globalization that has affected countries around the world. As life for many people has become more impersonal and bureaucratic, there has been a counterreaction from those groups seeking to hold on to the past and resist the forces of change. This is nothing new, but it has become more accelerated. Within the United States, massive migration and the influx of peoples from other lands, mostly from Central America, has challenged the cultural norms of American society. Cultural diversity vs. ethnocentrism, coupled with heightened racial, ethnic, and gender identities, has further exacerbated the massive political, social, and economic divide that threatens the stability of the nation. The tragedy of September 11, 2001, marked by deceptions, embroiled the United States in a series of wars in the Middle East that have lasted for well over a decade. What the future holds for the United States is difficult to say as it seeks to make sense and adapt to a changing world.

Two major themes have guided baseball over the past few decades: one is the continued globalization of baseball, and the other is its transformation into a corporate entertainment enterprise. Whereas for decades, baseball was the national pastime, it has been somewhat overtaken by other sports that vie for public support and media exposure. At the same time, baseball is very popular and remains an integral part of American culture.

STUDY QUESTIONS

1. Could it be said that the United States today functions more as a democracy, a republic, a plutocracy, or a proxy imperialist power? Give specifics in support of your answer.
2. Discuss the effect that 9/11 has had on the balance between security and freedom in the United States.
3. In what ways have the labor troubles experienced by professional baseball since the 1960s been a reflection of America's labor history?

Closure

TRENDING TOWARD THE FUTURE

There is no simple answer to the question, "What is America?" Essentially, the United States is a number of things. In the tradition of the town meeting the country functions as a democracy, through local government, school boards, and other agencies in which people have a direct and personal voice. Constitutionally, it is a republic, or a representative form of government that serves various interests and protects property. It is also an empire with a penchant for expansion, exploitation, and interference (for better or worse) in the affairs of other countries, often through proxy governments and organizations. Finally, the United States can be seen—primarily at the national level—as a plutocracy, in which money and powerful interest groups direct and control policy. These functions are often in conflict.

Can it furthermore be said that there is such a thing as the American nation? One might argue that the country is a myriad of subcultures bound together by a common set of values and rules. "A nation of inconsistencies," so said the American Populist Party leader, Mary Elizabeth Lease. Thus, the history of America is one of diversity, discontinuities, and conflicts, as opposed to myth, which sees institutions, events, and trends in singular terms.

From whatever perspective one chooses to take, there are three inescapable tendencies. While the benefits of technology are self-evident, the ability to manage huge quantities of data and establish systems of control is leading toward a surveillance society, in which the activities and movements of just about anyone can be closely watched and monitored. The balance between maintaining security and protecting personal liberties is tipping more toward the former than the latter. Such eavesdropping capabilities point toward a totalitarian society, which is at odds with America's core values of liberty and freedom. What does the future hold for those values? Can such a bleak picture be avoided?

The second tendency has to do with the nature of capitalism itself, which has spawned huge multinational corporations that control an increasing amount of the world's resources and force poorer people and nations into a condition of dependency. Inequality at home and abroad, which has to do with a lack of sharing, is one issue, and another is the environment. Since it is the nature of capitalism, and hence corporations, to expand and utilize natural resources, often at an exponential rate, and since the availability of resources can only expand arithmetically, or are finite, the depletion of the environment, unless checked, would appear to be inevitable. This is not to mention the effect that industrialization and overproduction have on the overall quality of the environment, contributing to global warming, species depletion, along with erratic and dangerous weather patterns. Again, is there a solution to this conundrum?

The last tendency involves the nature of a global society, which poses a number of challenges. Writing on the anniversary of her brother's death in the 9/11 disaster, Rita Lasar noted that the tragedy served to invite Americans to join the world. "The question is whether we will accept that invitation." By this, she means world citizenship, through which global unity, the welfare of humanity, and right human relations trump national self-interest. America, born in independence, is now confronted with the challenges of interdependence, and beyond that, whose interdependence?

These questions cannot easily be answered, but the starting point is right thinking. By refusing to be swayed by superficial myths, to look beyond surface explanations to deeper causes, and to confront the world with a sense of humility, knowing that there is much we do not know (or can know) can reveal the path ahead.

REFLECTING BACK TO THE PAST

The reference to baseball as the national pastime might seem perplexing to those of the millennial generation who live in a world of seemingly endless diversions and athletic opportunities. Soccer (and in certain places, lacrosse) has replaced baseball in schools as the predominant sport during the warm spring months. Participation in girls' sports is at an all-time high, but softball, not baseball, has always been the game of choice for women. While professional baseball continues to enjoy considerable popularity, other professional sports are equally—if not more—popular.

What makes baseball the national pastime is its link to the past. After the Civil War, the game grew up with the country and reflected its glories and failings. A. Bartlett Giamatti observed, "To know baseball is to continue to aspire to the condition of freedom, individually and as a people, for baseball is grounded in America in a way unique to our games." He goes on to say that baseball is within the outline of America's national story, and therein lies its importance.

Moreover, the historical value of baseball is its ability to establish connections. Wrote poet Donald Hall: "Baseball connects American males with each other, not only through bleacher friendships and neighbor loyalties, not only through barroom fights but, most importantly, through generations." Historically, baseball has passed from father to son, not mythically, but in fact. In no other sport have sons followed in the footsteps of their fathers. In organized baseball, there have been 200 instances in which a son(s) has followed his father to the major leagues. In several cases, the line of big-league players goes back three generations.

There are also generations of memory. Gone is the time when every town, village, and hamlet boasted its own baseball team that played out the summer in city leagues, industrial leagues, country leagues, etc. Often forgotten is the time when every Memorial Day, Fourth of July, and Labor Day would be celebrated with great fanfare, most always featuring baseball matches. An urban game framed in a rural setting. We live at a time when Americans (particularly the young) are disassociated from their past. To lose the past is to lose one's identity, which is the context for our lives. This is a serious matter. If knowledge of baseball can be the thread that binds the past to the future, it will have served a noble purpose.

Bibliography

Alexander, Charles C. (2002). *Breaking the slump*. New York, NY: Columbia University Press.

Badger, Anthony J. (1989). *The New Deal: The Depression years, 1933-1940*. Chicago, IL: Ivan R. Dee.

Block, David. (2005). *Baseball before we knew it*. Lincoln, NE, and London, UK: University of Nebraska Press.

Bouton, Jim. (1990). *Ball four*. New York, NY: Macmillan.

DeMotte, Charles. (2013). *Bat, ball & bible*. Washington, DC: Potomac Books.

_____. (2019) *James T. Farrell and baseball: dreams and realism on Chicago's southside*. Lincoln, NE and London, UK: University of Nebraska Press.

_____. Baseball's winter of discontent, 1926-1927. In *The Cooperstown symposium on baseball and American culture, 2011-2012*, edited by William M. Simons. Jefferson, NC, & London, UK: McFarland & Company.

_____. How World War I nearly brought down professional baseball. In *The Cooperstown symposium on baseball and American culture, 2009-2010*, edited by William M. Simons. Jefferson, NC, & London, UK: McFarland & Company.

Elias, Robert (Ed). (2001). *Baseball and the American dream*. Armonk, NY, and London, UK: M. E. Sharpe.

Elias, Robert. (2010). *The empire strikes out*. New York, NY, and London, UK: The New Press.

Fischer, David Hackett. (1989). *Albion's seed: Four British folkways in America*. New York, NY, & London, UK: Oxford University Press.

_____. (2012). *Fairness and freedom*. Oxford: Oxford University Press.

_____. (2005). *Liberty and freedom*. New York, NY, & London, UK: Oxford University Press.

Foner, Eric. (2008). *Give me liberty: An American history* (2nd ed.) (Vol. 2). New York, NY: W. W. Norton & Co.

_____. (2005). *Forever free*. New York, NY: Alfred A. Knopf.

_____. (1998). *The story of American freedom*. New York, NY: W. W. Norton & Co.

_____. (2008). *Voice of a free people: A documentary history* (2nd ed.) (Vol. 2). New York, NY: W. W. Norton & Co.

Giamatti, A. Bartlett. (1989). *Take time for paradise*. New York, NY, et al.: Summit Books.

Goldfield, David, et al. (2007). *The American journey: A history of the United States* (4th ed.). Upper Saddle River, NJ: Pearson Education.

Goldstein, Warren. (1989). *Playing for keeps: A history of early baseball*. Ithaca, NY, and London, UK: Cornell University Press.

Griffin, David Ray, & Scott, Peter Dale (Eds.). (2007). *9/11 and the American empire*. Northampton, MA: Olive Branch Press.

Hall, Donald. (1985). *Fathers playing catch with sons*. New York, NY: Dell Publishing Company.

Hall, Kermit L., Finkelman, Paul, & Ely, James W. Jr. (2005). *American legal history* (3rd ed.). New York, NY, and Oxford, UK: Oxford University Press.

Hamilton, Nigel. (2014) *The mantle of command: FDR at war 1941-1942*. Boston: Houghton Mifflin Harcourt.

Hensler, Paul. (2013). *The American League in transition, 1965-1975*. Jefferson, NC: McFarland & Co.

Helyar, John. (1994). *Lords of the realm*. New York, NY: Ballantine Books.

Hofstader, Richard, & Hofstadter, Beatrice K. (1982). *Great issues in American history*. New York, NY: Vintage Books.

Hofstader, Richard, (1965). *The paranoid style in American politics and other essays.* New York, NY: Vintage Books.

Keene, Jennifer D., Cornell, Saul, & O'Donnell, Edward T. (2013). *Visions of America* (2nd ed.). Upper Saddle River, NJ: Pearson Education.

Kirsch, George B. (2003). *Baseball in blue & gray.* Princeton, NJ: Princeton University Press.

Klein, Naomi. (2007). *The shock doctrine: The rise of disaster capitalism.* New York, NY: Henry Holt and Company.

Koppett, Leonard. (1998). *Koppett's concise history of major league baseball.* New York, NY: Carroll & Graf Publishers.

Lamster, Mark. (2006). *Spalding's world tour.* New York, NY: Public Affairs.

Lerner, Michael A. (2007). *Dry Manhattan: Prohibition in New York.* Cambridge, MA, and London, UK: Harvard University Press.

McGerr, Michael (2003). *A fierce discontent: rise and fall of the Progressive movement, 1870–1920.* New York et al: Free Press.

Oakes, James, et al. (2010). *Of the people: A history of the United States.* New York, NY, & Oxford, UK: Oxford University Press.

Perrett, Geoffrey. (1982). *America in the twenties.* New York, NY: Simon & Schuster.

Rana, Aziz. (2010). *The two faces of American freedom.* Cambridge, MA, & London, UK: Harvard University Press.

Riess, Steven A. (1999). *Touching base.* Urbana and Chicago, IL: University of Illinois Press.

Ritter, Lawrence S. (2002). *The glory of their times.* New York, NY: HarperCollins.

Seymour, Harold. (1960). *Baseball: The early years.* New York, NY, and Oxford, UK: Oxford University Press.

_____. (1971). *Baseball: The golden age.* New York, NY, and Oxford, UK: Oxford University Press.

Solomon, Bert. (1997). *The baseball timeline.* New York, NY: Avon Books.

Stone, Oliver, & Kuznick, Peter. (2012), *The untold history of the United States.* New York, NY, et al: Gallery Books.

Thorn, John. (2011). *Baseball in the garden of eden.* New York, NY: Simon & Schuster.

Tygiel, Jules. (2002). *Extra bases.* Lincoln, NE, and London, UK: University of Nebraska Press.

_____. (2000). *Past time: Baseball as history.* New York, NY: Oxford University Press.

Vecsey, George. (2006). *Baseball: A history of America's favorite game.* New York, NY: The Modern Library.

White, Sol. (1995). *History of colored baseball.* Lincoln, NE, and London, UK: University of Nebraska Press.

Zimbalist, Andrew. (1992). *Baseball and billions.* New York, NY: Basic Books.

Zinn, Howard. (2003). *A people's history of the United States.* New York, NY: HarperCollins Publishers.

_____. (2004). *Voices of a people's history of the United States.* New York, NY, et al.: Seven Stories Press.

CPSIA information can be obtained
at www.ICGtesting.com
Printed in the USA
LVHW100839180821
695519LV00004B/23

9 781516 588435